John .... us
caree .... d
the S .... r
years .... Japanese POW camp during the
Second World War and then worked in
American intelligence. He subsequently became
a journalist, travelling to China and Europe. He
was the top selling author of murder stories for
True Detective magazines and wrote over a
thousand accounts of true crime.

He lived in Luxembourg as a full-time
writer, until his death in 1990.

MURDEROUS WOMEN

This book is due for return on or before the last date shown below.

swell Ltd., London, N.21   Cat. No. 1207   DG 02242/71

MURDEROUS WOMEN

Shocking true stories of modern lady killers

JOHN DUNNING

ARROW

Arrow Books Limited
20 Vauxhall Bridge Road, London SW1V 2SA

An imprint of Random House UK Ltd

London Melbourne Sydney Auckland
Johannesburg and agencies throughout
the world

First published in Great Britain
by Hamlyn Paperbacks 1983
Reprinted 1983 (twice) and 1985
Arrow edition 1986

7 9 11 12 10 8

Printed and bound in Great Britain by
Cox & Wyman Ltd, Reading, Berkshire

ISBN 0 09 943710 4

CONTENTS

FOREWORD

Rather incredibly, the book you are now holding is no less than the third in a series of improbable true-crime collections and, as for the first two volumes, I have been besieged with requests not to write a foreword.

I did not comply with these requests in the first two books and I shall not comply now. There is little point in going to all the trouble of writing a book if you are not going to take the opportunity of inflicting your opinions on your readers. After all, people who write relatively short articles for the newspapers do, and it is seen as modern and progressive, and known as interpretive journalism. The writer not only tells you the story; he tells you what conclusions you are to draw from it.

I seldom go quite as far as this, not because I am any less opinionated or arrogant than my fellow journalists, but because I am not infrequently unable to draw any conclusion myself, other than the most banal ones, e.g. if you take a large number of mentally deficient persons and encourage them to breed freely, you will, in the next generation, have a still larger number of mentally deficient persons who may well display a tendency to kill each other or anyone else who happens to be available.

This is what many western countries have been doing for some little time now and the results are becoming rather noticeable. Although all of the crimes recounted in this book involve women, this preponderance of a single sex is, to my mind, less significant than the fact that many were committed for reasons which I find incomprehensible. Indeed, in several cases, the criminals themselves are at a loss to explain their motives.

Generally, today, the explanation of motives is left to the professional psychologists who, having read a good deal on the subject, have at hand a large selection of suitable motives for nearly any deed.

Curiously, these motives almost invariably place the responsibility for the act on some other person or thing. The man who rapes and murders a half-dozen little girls does so because his mother discouraged his attempts at bestiality with the family dachshund at the age of four. The idealistic young woman who tortures to death elderly persons in order to relieve them of their savings has been warped by the failure of the rotten, capitalist society to provide for her to be born rich.

Interestingly, this relief from responsibility has now gone so far that a not uncommon defence in European courts today is based on the assertion that the crime was so terrible that no sane person could have committed it. The defendant, therefore, must not be condemned, but given sympathy, a short period of psychiatric treatment at taxpayers' expense and be released to take up his place as a useful member of society.

Alas! It appears that the science of psychology still lacks a certain precision and many of these reborn useful members of society become mainly useful to me and my colleagues. I write approximately one hundred true crime stories a year and they supply quite a large percentage of them.

In the relatively short period of time that I have been involved with the true-crime field, I have had some regular customers returning for the third time, having been twice cured of their unfortunate tendencies and released.

I confidently look forward to writing about them again in the future, perhaps many times until age and disability on their part or mine dissolves our association.

Callous as it may seem, I do not really feel too bad when one of these homicidal maniacs, to use a term now regarded as shamefully old-fashioned and probably as over-pejorative, dismembers a voter. After all, the voter brings it on himself. It is ultimately his responsibility that the minority group dedicated to the rights of the accused is allowed to gain ascendency within the political and legal system, and whether a psychologist would ascribe this irrational behaviour to youthful frustrations with Fido matters little when the killer's knife is slicing through your entrails.

Let persons of voting age, therefore, look to themselves. They shall receive no sympathy from me. It is those who have no vote and not even the physical strength to defend themselves whom I would like to see defended and whom I would defend if I could see any practical way of doing so. I refer not to the mentally handicapped nor to the socially and financially disadvantaged, but to the children.

It is, perhaps, true that the word 'child' today conjures up a terrifying vision of something unwashed, hairy, regarding rape as a parlour game, puffing on a joint and sharpening a switch-blade in preparation for the financing of something stronger through the disembowelment of the first elderly passer-by, but these are the older children, some of whom have learned to read and are subject to the influence of the press and all of whom have been studying their methods on television for years.

It is the others of whom I speak, the ones under the age of, say, ten. It is they, I feel, who should be given the protection of our liberal, enlightened society.

No doubt they will eventually grow up to be as vicious as the rest, but, for the moment, they are as helpless as kittens, as innocent as mice and naïvely devoted to the simple pursuit of happiness.

Year after year, thousands upon untold thousands of these harmless little creatures are raped, mangled, tortured, beaten and killed, not infrequently by their own parents.

The punishment for these acts is, in many western countries, derisory, a year or two in a prison often more comfortable than home and much of that suspended.

As women now have equal rights and may no longer be regarded as weaker members of society, they, I am afraid, must share the responsibility and the risks of the male voters and look to their own skins, but, at the risk of prejudice to the professional well-being of myself and my colleagues in the true-crime field, I sincerely feel that there is only one way to deal with persons who intentionally murder or attempt to murder or even seriously harm small children.

Kill them.

John Dunning

1

GIANTKILLER

At thirty-four minutes past ten in the evening, the alarm bell in the emergency room of the hospital in Cherbourg, France, began to ring.

'Twenty-six, Cité Fougère,' called the ambulanceman, running out of the ready room and climbing into the ambulance. 'Ground-floor apartment.'

The ambulance slid smoothly out of the bay and headed east in light traffic. It was Monday, June 23, 1980, and there was not much going on in Cherbourg which, although an important port and shipbuilding centre, has only a little over thirty-five thousand inhabitants, then mostly glued to their television sets.

The Cité Fougère was a new development on the outskirts of the city, but, because of the small size of the community, most of the occupants of the apartment building at number twenty-six knew each other. When the ambulance arrived, they were all gathered in the entrance hall or on the front steps. Some of the women were crying.

When the ambulanceman saw the task that awaited him, he felt like crying too.

Lying in the tiny entrance hall of one of the ground-floor apartments was the body of a huge man, well over six feet four inches tall and so sturdily built that his weight exceeded two hundred and fifty pounds although there was not an ounce of fat on him.

He had apparently suffered some sort of head wound, for the blood had rushed and was still rushing from his scalp and the entire hall was drenched with it.

The ambulanceman ran forward and dropped to his knees beside the giant and immediately saw two things.

The man was still alive and there was what looked like the handle of a screwdriver sticking stiffly out of the side of his head!

Although a faint moaning sound was coming from the injured man's parted lips, he appeared to be unconscious and the ambulanceman quickly slapped compresses over the top of his

11

head with a view to slowing the bleeding. It was vital that he be brought to the hospital as quickly as possible, but, considering his size and weight and the narrow confines of the hall, it was not going to be an easy task even to get him to the ambulance.

It turned out to be easier than the ambulanceman had expected, for as many of the tenants of the building as could find room lent a hand and minutes later the ambulance was racing for the hospital, its blue warning lights flashing and its siren howling like a tortured tomcat.

The trip did not take long and the patient was still alive on arrival, but the duty doctor took one look at him and directed the ambulance to continue on to the hospital in Caen. Caen is seventy-five miles from Cherbourg, but it is bigger and has better medical facilities. In the doctor's opinion, the man was going to need the best he could get and, although he knew that persons had lived and had even suffered no ill effects after having something rammed through their brains, he had grave doubts that the best would be adequate.

As the ambulance moved out into the highway and began to accelerate to its top speed of over a hundred miles an hour while the ambulanceman in the back struggled to keep his patient alive and as comfortable as possible, at the apartment building in the Cité Fougère, the police were arriving. The ambulance crew had not had the time to summon them, but someone from the apartment house had.

This first unit consisted of nothing more than the first patrol car to answer the switchboard's call to investigate a report of an injury at number twenty-six Cité Fougère, but it was soon followed by the evening duty team from the Department of Criminal Investigations, the officers from the patrol car having reported that the victim was gone, but that from the amount of blood it seemed unlikely he would survive his injuries. At the moment, no one knew what these injuries were or how he had sustained them.

This was, of course, important and, having arrived and viewed the blood-soaked hall, Inspector Jules Maréchal, the senior officer on the team from the Department of Criminal Investigations, immediately called the Louis Pasteur Hospital where the man had been taken.

There, he was told that the patient was on his way to Caen, that he had a screwdriver sticking out of the side of his head and other head injuries and that it was unlikely that he would survive.

'Could the injuries be accidental?' said the inspector. He found it hard to accept that someone had deliberately attempted to murder the man. Cherbourg is as tough as most ports and people do get murdered there, but usually during a fight in some waterfront bar and not in an apartment house in the suburbs.

'I don't see how,' said the doctor. 'How do you think a man could ram a screwdriver into the side of his own head?'

The inspector saw no reason to answer this question and, having obtained the name and telephone number of the hospital at Caen to which the man was being taken, hung up. A man without any particular distinguishing characteristics, brown haired, brown eyed, of average height and weight, with a clean-shaven neither handsome nor ugly face, he was, like so many of his colleagues throughout Europe, basically a civil servant, businesslike, matter-of-fact and not to be hurried. His system for investigating criminal cases was patient hard work, attention to detail and the elimination of potential suspects until only one remained. As he had had a good deal of experience, he frequently solved his cases.

His assistant, Detective-Sergeant Anatole Bertrand, was much younger, much less patient and, technically, better trained, as he had attended a police school which did not exist at the time that the inspector was beginning his career. He was dark, sleekly handsome and looked faintly sinister, although he was actually very good natured, extremely fond of children and the father of four of them. He was inclined to mistake the inspector's experience for brilliance.

'Should I go through the apartment and see if I can find his papers?' he asked when the inspector had finished briefing him concerning the comments made by the doctor at the hospital. 'If it's murder, you'll want to move on it immediately, won't you?'

'Even if it's no more than attempted murder,' said the inspector. 'You were talking with the other tenants? What do they say?'

'The ones I talked to say that the man's name is François Jeanne,' said the sergeant. 'He's a carpenter at the shipyards. Middle or late thirties. Not married apparently. Everybody here seems to have a high regard for him.'

'Somebody didn't,' said the inspector. 'Well, all right. Call the shop and tell them to send us out a couple of men to take statements and the duty squad from the lab. Don't know what to tell you to look for. The murder weapon, if it is one, seems to still be sticking in his head. If the neighbours know him so well, they may be able to suggest a suspect.'

13

The neighbours were not. François Jeanne, they said, had been universally loved by everyone who knew him. A giant of enormous physical strength, he had been as gentle as a day-old lamb and, despite great provocation, had never got into so much as a scuffle.

The provocation had, indeed, at times been great. Considering Jeanne's size and strength, provoking him would seem an act motivated by severe mental disorder or tendencies to suicide, but small men, rendered aggressive by their complexes over their size, often challenge the largest men they can find. For the big man, this is a no-win situation. If he fights and the little man wins, he appears a feeble Goliath, deservedly slain by plucky David. If the big man wins, he is a bully beating up a man half his size. Jeanne, it seemed, had never fought and, even if the little men had physically assaulted him, had merely let them pound him until they got tired of it. On one or two occasions, he had lifted some particularly persistent or irritating specimen a foot off the floor and held him until his belligerence had subsided.

'And that,' said the inspector, 'may be the motive for this attack. There could hardly be anything more humiliating for a small man than to be picked up and held like a child until he promised to be good.'

'There wouldn't seem to be any other motive,' said the sergeant. 'It surely wasn't robbery. A shipyard carpenter makes a good living, but not the kind of money for anyone to murder him for. Of course, he may have had an inheritance or something. The lab people may be able to determine that when they get here.'

'You wait here for them,' said the inspector. 'I'm going back to the office to call Caen. I want a report on Jeanne's condition as soon as he gets there so we'll know whether we're investigating a homicide or not and also whether he'll be able to tell us who did it. Until we know for certain, we'll treat it as homicide. Have the lab people go over the apartment carefully and then seal it. Tell our men when they get here to take statements from everybody in the building and get them all on tape. See if there are any reports of his receiving female visitors. This could be nothing but a jealous husband or boyfriend.'

The inspector went back to his office and telephoned the hospital in Caen where he was told that the ambulance was already there, but that Jeanne had been dead on arrival.

'Send the body back with the ambulance,' said the inspector. 'We'll need to autopsy it here.'

The autopsy was carried out by the Cherbourg coroner, Dr

Claude Terrance who reported that Jeanne had died as the result of the screwdriver, a large tool with a thick six-inch-long shaft, being literally hammered into his head. He had also suffered a large number of blows to the head with some heavy, relatively smooth object, but, although these had split the scalp and had caused profuse bleeding, they had not had sufficient force to fracture the skull and would not, therefore, have been fatal.

The investigators already knew what this heavy, relatively smooth object with which Jeanne's scalp had been split and which had, presumably, been used to hammer the screwdriver into his head was, for the laboratory technicians had found it lying in the blood on the floor of the hall. It was a twenty-four-inch crescent wrench and, like the screwdriver, it came from Jeanne's own tool kit which he had kept stored in a closet off the kitchen.

'That's as strange a development as I could imagine,' said the inspector when the sergeant told him about it.

'How so?' asked the sergeant. 'It was simply what happened to be to hand. Or do you mean that there would be other, better murder weapons in the tool kit such as hatchets and hammers and and . . .?'

'I mean how did the murderer get his hands on the tool kit in the first place?' asked the inspector. 'You tell me the lab people say there's no indication that the murderer ever penetrated further into the apartment than the front hall and that the murder definitely took place there. Jeanne's tool kit was in a closet off the kitchen. What did he do? Bring out a selection of tools for his caller to murder him with?'

'Hmmm, I see what you mean,' said the sergeant. 'It makes our theory that somebody rang the doorbell, he came to the door and was hit over the head, impossible. Well, maybe it was another ship's carpenter.'

'How do you reach that conclusion?' asked the inspector.

'Because the murderer must have brought Jeanne's tools with him so it could be that he had borrowed them and was returning them,' said the sergeant.

'Very sound deduction,' said the inspector approvingly. 'But it wouldn't have had to be a ship's carpenter. A crescent wrench and a heavy screwdriver are common enough tools for anybody doing some home repairs to have need of.'

'And it would be more likely that someone who wasn't a ship's carpenter or a carpenter of any kind would have to borrow them,' said the sergeant, a little crestfallen. 'A professional would already have them.'

The group of potential suspects which had contracted down to the relatively small number of shipyard carpenters had abruptly expanded again to take in most of the male population of Cherbourg. Curiously, however, one of the few men against whom Jeanne had had a real grievance was a ship's carpenter and lived at 56 Avenue de Paris, less than two hundred yards from where the murder had taken place.

Emile Montigny, thirty-four years of age and, therefore, three years younger than François Jeanne at the time of his death, had been a colleague at the shipyard, but had been fired the preceding year for a marked lack of energy in his work. A short, scrawny man with an unorthodox approach to the problems of personal hygiene, he had been living on unemployment benefit ever since.

Having a great deal of free time, he had taken to dropping around to visit his old colleague, François Jeanne, but, invariably, when Jeanne was at work and not at home.

At home was thirty-one-year-old Hugette Pivain, a divorced former waitress, with whom Jeanne had been living since 1973. They were not married because Miss Pivain, a woman so small that she barely escaped classification as a midget, had stoutly resisted all of Jeanne's efforts in that direction. They were, however, on close terms for she had borne him a daughter, Katia, who was now four years old.

Despite the lack of conventional legal and religious sanctions of the union, Jeanne had promptly claimed paternity of the child and had had her registered legally as his daughter at a time when she was only slightly larger than his fist.

By all accounts, Jeanne had loved his little daughter to distraction and had been only slightly less attached to her mother.

Hugette had been less attached to him for, although he had dutifully turned over his entire pay packet to her and had humbly accepted whatever allowance she saw fit to grant him, she had moved out of the apartment and had set up housekeeping with Emile Montigny in May of that same year. She took Katia with her.

'If only Pivain or Montigny or, preferably, both had been murdered, we'd have an open-and-shut case,' said the sergeant. 'I never saw anybody with a better motive for murder than the one Jeanne had against those two. The woman bragged all over the neighbourhood that she didn't actually care anything about the child. She just wanted to keep Jeanne from having her.'

The sergeant had called on the Pivain-Montigny ménage the evening of the murder and had not been favourably impressed.

He had been met at the door by Hugette and Emile, both stark naked and both smelling strongly, but not pleasantly, as their ideas on personal hygiene were very similar.

They had ushered the somewhat embarrassed sergeant in without bothering to put on any clothes and had informed him that he had interrupted them at a rather delicate moment in their sexual relations. They would appreciate it if he would be brief so that they could return to the bedroom and get on with it.

The sergeant had been brief. What did they know about an attack on François Jeanne?

Nothing, said Emile Montigny. They had been in bed since shortly after eight.

Nothing, said Hugette Pivain, and added that she hoped that the attack had been painful. She appeared to be a savage, malicious little woman.

The sergeant had thanked them for their co-operation and had hurriedly left. The apartment was so dirty that he had been afraid of brushing the furniture with his clothes. He had not seen the little girl and did not know of her existence, as the neighbours at number twenty-six had only said that Hugette had been Jeanne's mistress and was now living with Montigny.

Later, he got to thinking about the condition of the apartment and took a walk over to the Juvenile Welfare Department where he suggested that it might not be a bad idea for one of the social workers to drop in and see that the child did not actually drown in the filth.

He was informed that the suggestion had already been made by François Jeanne soon after Hugette had moved in with Montigny and that they had made periodic checks ever since then. The child was not overly clean and the apartment was filthy beyond belief, but she appeared to be well fed and there were no signs that she had been mistreated in any way. There were no grounds to justify taking the child away from her mother.

'All of these people seem a little crazy to me,' said the sergeant when he and the inspector were discussing the progress or, rather, lack of progress in the case. 'Jeanne was patient and long-suffering beyond what anyone could expect of a normal human being and Pivain is plain malevolent. Jeanne never showed her anything but kindness and she apparently never overlooked an opportunity to injure him. The woman must be a sadist.'

'About the same impression I got talking to her,' said the inspector. 'What do you think of Montigny?'

'All the strength of character of a boiled noodle,' said the

17

sergeant. 'His ambitions extend to food, sex and shelter. Nothing more.'

'He could have all that in jail,' remarked the inspector. 'With the exception of the sex, of course. Could he and the woman have done it?'

The question was actually directed to himself, but the sergeant answered.

'I don't see how,' he said. 'If they stood on each other's shoulders, they'd be just about tall enough, but I doubt either one of them has the strength.'

'Never underestimate women,' said the inspector. 'The female is deadlier . . . Well, anyway, it doesn't matter because, without material evidence or a confession, we'd never be able to get an indictment against either one of them. The examinations judge doesn't believe in giantkillers.'

Hugette Pivain and Emile Montigny were thus eliminated from the list of potential suspects and the investigators continued their search for better and more probable ones. Unfortunately, almost every lead they attempted to follow brought them straight back to the unsavoury and redolent couple.

Although Hugette had moved out of the apartment in the Cité Fougère, she had kept the key and had returned almost daily to do her laundry in Jeanne's washing machine and empty the refrigerator and, indeed, the entire apartment of everything edible or portable. This had represented such a saving that she and Montigny had scarcely had to buy groceries at all.

The important aspect of this discovery was that it meant that Hugette had had access to the apartment and to Jeanne's tool kit in the closet off the kitchen. She could have been waiting for him in the entrance hall, standing on a chair or something so as to be able to hit him on the head.

The trouble with this theory was that she had no reason to hit him on the head and she had good reasons for not wanting to murder him, as his death had, of course, terminated her use of the free laundry facilities as well as the supply of food and drink.

'It can't be her,' said the inspector a little desperately. 'She had a motive for wanting him alive, not dead. Anyway, she would have been physically incapable.'

'The motive doesn't matter,' said the sergeant gloomily. 'She's vicious enough to have killed him even if it wasn't in her interests. What's worse is that I can't find the slightest evidence that Jeanne left the apartment at any time after he came home from work that evening. If he was there all the time, how could she come in, get

18

the wrench and screwdriver from the closet off the kitchen, climb on a chair in the hall and wait for him? Besides, where was the chair then? It wasn't in the hall.'

'There wasn't any chair,' said the inspector. 'It would have had blood on it even if she'd put it back, and the lab people didn't find a trace of blood anywhere else in the apartment. It wasn't her. It's a physical impossibility for a woman of that size to beat to death a man as big as he was.'

Or was it? The investigations continued and, once again, came back to Hugette Pivain.

'This is ridiculous!' said the sergeant, bursting into the office with a sheet of form paper in his hand. 'I've just come from the hospital and they confirm it. He's been in there a couple of dozen times. Once it took seventeen stitches to close the gash in his throat. Done with a bread knife apparently.'

The sergeant had been following up a lead which indicated that during the past few years François Jeanne had been a frequent visitor at the hospital and, indeed, he had. From mid-1977 up to a few weeks before his death, he had appeared on average twice a week to be treated for cuts, severe bruises and smaller broken bones. In every case, he had said that the injuries were accidental and self-inflicted. The doctors had noted in the record that, in many instances, this could not be the case. Somebody had been cutting Jeanne and beating him.

Obviously, there was only one person who could have done the beating and cutting and it did not take the sergeant long to determine that mid-1977 had been when Hugette, presumably wearied of domesticity, had started to go out to bars and taverns and make contact with men who believed in free love in the sense that they did not have to pay for it. Cherbourg being an exceedingly small place, Jeanne had, undoubtedly, heard of it and objected. Hugette had, it seemed, objected to his objections. There was no record of her having received any treatment at the hospital for cuts, bruises or broken bones.

'It can't be her,' said the inspector weakly. 'She's too small! There was no opportunity, no motive, no . . . If it is her, we can't solve the case. We've no real evidence.'

'No, I guess not,' said the sergeant regretfully. 'But I think it must have been her. We've talked to every soul in Cherbourg who knew Jeanne and they all say the same thing; nobody in the world had any reason to murder him. Pivain's the only one who really seems to have hated him and for no reason at all.'

'All right,' said the inspector. 'I'm forced to agree. It was the woman. She had no motive. She barely came up to his belt buckle. She'd lived with him for nearly seven years. She'd borne his daughter. He'd never shown her anything but kindness and affection. And his death represents a financial loss to her. But you're right. From the time that the neighbours heard him groaning in the hall and called us, up to this moment, we've never found anyone who even looked like a suspect other than Pivain. Now, go away and let me think how we are going to bring her to justice.'

'You'll never do it,' said the sergeant with conviction. 'There's no material evidence and she and Montigny have a mutually supporting alibi. In addition, you've just outlined all of the reasons why the examinations judge will never hand down an indictment. The case cannot be solved.'

'Perhaps not,' said the inspector, 'but I have exactly eleven years, four months and two days to retirement. If I have not thought of anything by then, you can send it to the Unsolved file.'

The case of the murder of François Jeanne would not have been alone in the Unsolved file. There were other cases and the inspector had sent them there. No police department has a perfect record.

On the case of François Jeanne, however, the inspector was not prepared to give up until every possibility and most of the impossibilities had been exhausted. It had not been possible to investigate the case without forming a very favourable picture of François Jeanne, the gentle giant who had wanted nothing but a home, a wife and children. And it had not been possible to investigate the background of Hugette Pivain without arriving at a diametrically opposite conclusion. One of the most puzzling questions in the case was why Jeanne had been attracted to her when he could easily have found much more attractive and affectionate partners.

There was little doubt as to why Emile Montigny persisted in his relationship with his sharp-tempered and unwashed mistress. He was terrified of her.

'But what,' said the inspector, fixing his assistant with a sombre and somewhat expressionless gaze, 'if he were confronted with someone even more terrifying? Would he continue to cling to her? To support her statements? To provide her with an alibi for the time of the murder?'

'He would abandon her instantly,' said the sergeant without hesitation. 'He has a character to make Judas look like a collie dog.'

'Good,' said the inspector. 'You are a man with a terrifying appearance. At least, I have heard suspects say so. Arrest Montigny. Bring him here to police headquarters and interrogate him personally. There is no need to be particularly gentle or considerate. He seems masochistically inclined so he will appreciate a firm hand.'

Whether Emile Montigny appreciated the sergeant's firm hand or not, the latter's estimation of his character proved to be accurate for he resisted the interrogation for less than two hours.

At the end of that time, he confessed to the murder of François Jeanne – by Hugette Pivain.

He himself, he said, had taken no part in the murder and had, indeed, not even known that a murder was going to take place when Hugette asked or, rather, ordered him to accompany her to Jeanne's apartment on the evening of June 23.

She had said that she had been in the apartment that afternoon and had borrowed some tools which François had not taken to work with him. She intended to return them.

'I knew she was annoyed with him,' snivelled Montigny, 'but I swear I had no idea she was going to hurt him. She had the wrench in her hand and the minute he opened the door, she jumped as high as she could and hit him over the head with it. She used both hands. François went down on his knees and she kept on pounding him on the head with the wrench. She couldn't break his head or even knock him out completely, but he fell over on the floor and then she just put the screwdriver on the side of his head and hammered it in with the flat side of the wrench. Even then he didn't stop groaning, but she said it didn't matter, he would die after a while and so we left and went home and had sex. Hugette said if we were having sex when the police came, they'd think we didn't do it.'

'Not a certain way of drawing off suspicion,' remarked the inspector who had been called in to listen to Montigny's statement, 'but, at least, pleasant and inexpensive. Bring in Pivain. We'll charge her immediately.'

He was in a relieved and expansive mood. Hugette Pivain's confession was not yet on tape, but he was confident that it soon would be. Couples who engage in murder nearly always end up incriminating each other and, eventually, themselves when it comes down to who will draw the longest sentence.

Actually, Hugette Pivain's confession did not come quite so quickly or so easily as he had anticipated. Hugette had, perhaps, some undesirable aspects to her character, but weakness was not one of them.

Even though formally charged with the murder and confronted with her lover's incriminating statement, she refused to accept any responsibility and suggested that Montigny had committed the crime alone and without her knowledge because he feared that she might leave him and return to François Jeanne. It took a great deal of patient interrogation before she finally came to the conclusion that the inspector was not going to give up and admitted that Montigny's version of the events was essentially the right one.

With one exception, however. Montigny, said Hugette, was as responsible for the murder as she was. Although she had struck the first blow which had brought the giant to his knees, once he was down where Montigny could reach him and was incapable of defending himself, the little man had pounded his head with the wrench as enthusiastically as she. He had, however, been no more successful in his efforts to crush Jeanne's skull and they had driven in the screwdriver together.

Montigny denied this almost hysterically and became so agitated that, at one point, he refuted his previous statement and said that he had not even been present when the murder took place, that Hugette had only told him about it afterwards.

More patient interrogation straightened out this point as well and, in the end, both Hugette Pivain and Emile Montigny were charged with first-degree homicide, formally indicted and bound over for trial.

The investigation was completed and the case was officially closed, but with one important element missing. Why did Hugette Pivain and Emile Montigny wilfully, feloniously and with malice aforethought murder François Jeanne?

It was not for money. Hugette had already taken everything of value in the apartment and Jeanne was still turning over his pay packet to her after she had left him to live with another man. Quite the contrary to a financial advantage, Jeanne's death represented a severe financial loss to his murderess.

Was the motive sex? Hardly. Emile Montigny was apparently taking care of Hugette's sexual needs such as they were and none of the parties concerned seemed to have suffered the pangs of sexual jealousy.

Or was it Katia? Did Hugette fear that the father of her child would succeed in taking her away from her? If she did, she certainly concealed it well, for she told a number of persons including the social worker from the Juvenile Welfare Office that she had no interest in the child, but intended to keep her because in made her father suffer. Even after she had confessed to the murder, it did not occur to her to cite the child as a possible motive for the crime.

As a matter of fact, she was completely unable to offer a motive of any kind for her act. She admitted that she had gone to the apartment on that evening with the intention of murdering Jeanne, but she was unable to say why.

Montigny was of no help in the matter. He insisted that he had not known when he accompanied Hugette to the apartment that she had murder in mind and she had never mentioned anything about it to him before.

The case, therefore, came to trial with no motive at all suggested by either prosecution or defence for the crime. The defence attempted to make something of this, but quickly became confused, gave up and, on behalf of his clients, sought the mercy of the court.

Whatever the inclination of the court, the jurors were not inclined to mercy. On June 5, 1981, they found both defendants guilty as charged and without extenuating circumstances. They were sentenced to life imprisonment and, as one juror later said, had the new socialist government not abolished the death penalty, they would have got the guillotine.

2

WITCHES

Not far to the west of the city of Cork, Ireland, the number twelve trunk route, running along the eastern coast to end eventually in Dublin, is joined by the number six route which, passing further inland, arrives at the same city.

This is wild moor country, rocky, desolate, treeless.

In winter, the black, savage storms rage in from off the Atlantic and sweep, screaming, across the southern tip of the island into St George's Channel to fall upon England and, subsequently, the Continent.

The night of December 22, 1979, was the winter solstice, the shortest day of the year when the sun is at its furthest point south and the heart of darkest winter in Ireland.

Far out over the Atlantic, a storm was building but, by eleven ten in the evening, the precise moment of the winter solstice, only the outriders of the gale had reached the barren lands to the north of Cork.

As the rising wind ripped to shreds the clouds covering the face of the half-moon, by its light, a strange knot of flesh like some clumsy, prehistoric monster could be seen shuffling over the moor. Tall figures in long, black gowns marked with strange devices, stood silently waiting as the monster paused before them, divided into two and revealed itself as a man bent double beneath another man carried on his back.

The man carried was bound and gagged and he who carried him dropped his burden heavily and carelessly on to the rocky ground.

The body made a dull thud as it struck the earth and the man gave a pained grunt through his gag. Porter and robed figures engaged in a brief transaction and the former turned and made off in the direction of Cork as fast as his legs could carry him. Behind him, there arose a series of long, wailing cries which cut through the sound of the wind like a knife.

To the running man, they sounded far too much like the banshee, the Irish spirit which heralds death or worse.

During the night, the storm veered south to hammer one of its favourite victims, the Bay of Biscay, and, by nine o'clock the following morning, it had become relatively clear and the wind had died to no more than a stiff breeze.

It was at nine o'clock that forty-two-year-old Thomas Gilligan set out in his truck from the city of Cork for the long drive up to Dublin. It was a Sunday. He was happy to be going home in time for Christmas and he whistled as he drove. He had, however, only just turned into the number six road and gone less than half a mile when something caught his attention on the perfectly bare ground fifty or sixty feet from the road.

'Well now,' said Thomas Gilligan, stopping the truck and climbing down from the cab, 'that looks like a shoe sticking out of the ground.'

He walked over to the shoe, took hold of it and pulled. A strip of the freshly turned earth beyond the shoe lifted slightly. Gilligan stopped pulling.

'Just as I thought,' he said. 'There's a foot in it.'

He went back to the truck, turned it around and drove into Cork where, after asking directions, he located the central police station, parked the truck and entered the charge room.

A sergeant doing the Sunday-morning duty at the charge desk looked up, said, 'Yes?' and waited patiently.

'There's a man lying buried just to the north of the route six turn-off,' said Gilligan without preamble.

'You mean he's dead?' said the sergeant uncertainly. Cork only has a population of around 125,000. Reports of bodies lying buried beside the public roads are not that common.

'That, I can't say,' said Gilligan. 'I didn't stop to speak with him. Not that I've had much experience in the matter, but as a rule when they're buried, they're dead.'

'Sit down there and wait,' said the sergeant. 'We'll soon have this straightened out.'

He pressed the button of the intercom to connect him with the switchboard in the communication centre and requested that a patrol car come to the station and pick up Mr Gilligan so that he could lead the way to the scene of his discovery.

Approximately half an hour later, the patrol car arrived at the scene and one of the patrolmen in it reported over the radio telephone that Mr Gilligan's report was essentially correct. There was a man buried in the open moor to the north of the city and all that was sticking out was one of his shoes. As it seemed unlikely that this was an authorized burial, the patrolmen had neither

25

disturbed the corpse nor even attempted to uncover it.

The sergeant told the patrolman to remain where he was and to allow no one to approach the body until the arrival of the detachment from the Department of Criminal Investigations. Mr Gilligan, whose name and address he already had, could proceed on his way.

Following which, he again called the switchboard and asked them to alert the inspector in charge of the Homicide Squad, his assistant and someone from the Cork Coroner's Office.

Not much more than an hour later, these three men were standing looking down at the shallow grave from which only the tell-tale shoe protruded. They were all lean, muscular men with black hair and pink complexions so that they looked almost like triplets with only a difference in size, the doctor being the largest and the sergeant the smallest. In addition, the inspector had a moustache and was going a little grey over the ears.

At the moment, all that they could do was to look because the inspector did not want to disturb the grave until the experts from the police laboratory had arrived to photograph the scene and secure any clues that might be present. He was assuming that this was murder and had called for nearly the entire staff of the police laboratory who, not being on call, were not so easily located.

Two more patrol cars had arrived in the meantime and patrolmen, under the direction of the sergeant, were staking off an area some five hundred yards square with the grave containing the corpse in the centre.

Shortly before noon, the laboratory technicians arrived, made their pictures and, having examined the ground around and over the grave, reported that the only clues present were a great many splashes of blood, presumably from the victim, and a confused tangle of footprints. It looked, they said, as if someone had either been dancing or had had a fit there, around and over the grave.

Pictures and, where possible, casts of the footprints were made and the earth was carefully removed from the corpse.

This was not a difficult task as the body had been buried a scant six inches beneath the surface.

'Lazy beggars,' remarked the inspector. 'If they had given him another six inches, we might never have found him. What seems to have been his trouble?'

The doctor had got down on his knees and was examining the corpse.

'I cannot say,' he said. 'It looks as if he's been beaten with a club, but he's bound and gagged and, until we get the things off him, I'll not be able to tell anything. For certain, it didn't happen long ago. He's still as stiff as a board.'

'Well, let's get him back to the morgue then,' said the inspector. 'We'd best let the laboratory people take the ropes and the gag off. They may find a clue to who did this.'

'Maybe there's something in his clothing that tells who he is,' suggested the sergeant. 'Not counting the face, he looks like a gypsy to me.'

The face of the corpse did not look like a gypsy or anything else human. It was a mass of raw, swollen, burst flesh from which bits of broken bone and teeth protruded. It had probably looked worse when it was fresh. By now, the blood which covered it had dried to a relatively smooth, dark brown mask.

The search of the man's pockets produced nothing.

'Let us hope that we have his fingerprints on file,' said the inspector. 'For no reason, I've a feeling that he'll not be reported missing.'

The autopsy determined nothing other than that the victim was in his middle thirties and in good health and that he had been subjected to a fair number of beatings in the past, prior to the final one which had ended his life.

'He's been beaten over the bare back and buttocks with a dog whip or the like,' said the doctor. 'The fatal beating was, however, with something hard, heavy and angular. Iron bars, I should say, and there seems to have been more than one of them. The marks of the blows on the flesh are not quite the same.'

'And which killed him?' asked the inspector. 'The beating on the chest or the head?'

'Either or both,' said the doctor. 'His skull was fractured and his entire face was smashed, which caused massive haemorrhaging. However, his rib cage was smashed, too, and the ends of the broken ribs penetrated several of the vital organs. The blows to the testicles were not so hard. Perhaps they didn't want him to lose consciousness.'

'I'm wondering what a man could do to bring him enemies like that,' said the inspector. 'Well, we still don't know who he was. The laboratory's trying to trace the rope and the gag, but they're not optimistic. The gag is just a rag that could have been fished out of any dustbin and the rope is old and has been used for years for tying up everything from horses to pigs. Pat's trotting a squad through the bars. From the way he was dressed, he looks like a man who would spend a good bit of time in bars, but, as all we have to describe is his clothing, I'm not expecting much in the way of results there either.'

The inspector was, however, unnecessarily pessimistic. The sergeant did succeed in finding several persons who recognized the clothing that had been worn by the victim.

He had not, however, spent so very much time in bars as he had seldom had the money to buy anything in them. If the identification was correct, he was thirty-six-year-old Eric Willmot, a man who made his living going around to the fairs and markets where he sold pots and pans and sharpened knives.

'Well, you were close,' said the inspector. 'Not a gypsy, but a tinker. It may be one of those things where only a gypsy can understand the motive at all. I suppose you've had no luck tracing him?'

'None at all,' said the sergeant. 'There was a man named Eric Willmot, thirty-six years old, living here in Cork or, at least, he was here some of the time. I've not found anyone who's seen him since the twentieth of December.'

'If this is Willmot, he was formerly married and I've located the ex-wife. She's coming down to take a look at the body. She says that, if it's him, she can identify it without the face.'

'It sounds like it could be Willmot,' said the inspector. 'When did he and the wife break up? Could it have anything to do with the murder?'

'I doubt it,' said the sergeant. 'They were divorced in 1972 and by mutual agreement. It's said Willmot's been living with another woman since about 1973 and I'm trying to find out who she was and what she knows about this now.'

'Report as soon as you get something,' said the inspector. 'I have a few other things that I have to attend to right now, but it strikes me that there's something strange about this case. It must be an unusual motive for somebody to murder a man who goes around sharpening knives and selling pots and pans and didn't have enough money to go into a bar. Did the witnesses say he was particularly handsome?'

'Nothing extra,' said the sergeant.

A day later, he returned with the information that he had located the woman with whom Eric Willmot had been living since late 1973. She was forty-three-year-old Phoebe Brady and she had expressed great astonishment to learn that Eric Willmot was dead. She had thought, she said, that he had gone to Canada.

'And that corresponds exactly to what everyone who knew him has been telling me,' said the sergeant. 'For months, he's been talking about nothing but emigrating to Canada. He's been saving his money and he told somebody that if he sold his wedding ring, he would have enough to pay for the ticket. They all thought that he had gone to Canada.'

'Mrs Brady is more than a common-law wife then?' asked the inspector.

'Sure and their marriage wasn't officially registered anywhere,' said the sergeant. 'Mrs Brady says she performed the ceremony herself.'

'Performed it herself?' said the inspector. 'And has the church now started ordaining women priests?'

'It's not the Catholic church,' said the sergeant. 'She's the head of some kind of a sect. Devil worshippers, so they say. There's not above twenty or thirty members to the whole church and they all travel around the country together in caravans and old buses. She makes her living telling fortunes, but how the others do, God knows.'

'They sound like gypsies to me, the lot of them,' said the inspector.

'They're not,' said the sergeant. 'They're ordinary Irish, but they're not good Catholics.'

'I can believe it,' said the inspector. 'Does Mrs Brady have any idea as to who beat her husband to death? Or was it the devil? What about the ex-wife? Did she come down to identify the body?'

'Indeed, she did,' said the sergeant. 'He had a few moles and things and she told us in advance where they would be before she looked. The doctor has declared it officially identified. Mrs Brady says that Willmot was killed by the satanists in order to harm her.'

'I thought she was the head of the satanists?' said the inspector.

'No, she's the High Priestess of the devil worshippers,' said the sergeant. 'The satanists are another group who call themselves the Third Coven. The devil worshippers haven't a name for themselves. They just call themselves the devil worshippers.'

'Things are changing here in Ireland,' said the inspector, shaking his head. 'It's not the same place anymore. All right. Who's in charge of the satanists and do you have him in custody?'

'It's a woman,' said the sergeant. 'Most of these sects seem to have women in charge. The satanists are better looking. Maureen Donahue, the high priestess, is twenty-nine and a fine figure of a woman. She's got a bigger congregation too and some of them are even employed. They wash themselves more than the devil worshippers. I've not taken her into custody because we've not a scrap of evidence that she had anything to do with Willmot's murder. There's a good bit of rivalry between the devil worshippers and the satanists and it could be that Mrs Brady is simply taking a crack at the competition. I've talked to Miss Donahue and she says that she wouldn't go close enough to the devil worshippers to beat one to death.'

'What about the devil worshippers themselves then?' asked the inspector. 'Maybe Mrs Brady thought that she needed a new husband and wanted to get rid of the old one.'

The sergeant shrugged. 'She's changed often enough before,' he said, 'but she's never needed to kill one. There's a good bit of background material available on her and on the sect too because the police all over the country have been keeping an eye on them for years. They seem to be too prosperous to be permanently unemployed and they look like the sort that would steal things. If they do, they're good at it. Not one of them has ever been charged.'

'Let's hear the background report,' said the inspector.

The sergeant delivered it. Phoebe Brady, it seemed, was a second-generation devil worshipper, who had taken over the sect following her mother's death in 1973. Although born and raised in Dublin where her mother had founded the sect three years prior to her birth, she had spent much of her life travelling around the country with her followers who displayed all the attributes of a gypsy tribe, if not the customs.

The sect's primary sources of income lay in telling fortunes, dealing in secondhand goods and junk and peddling household wares at fairs and market places. The devil worship was largely confined to the odd ritual and a little dancing on the moor by the light of the full moon, followed by sex orgies, weather permitting.

Mrs Brady's love life had, inevitably, been complicated and had begun at an early age. At the age of sixteen she had given birth to a daughter named Verren who was now Assistant High Priestess and heiress to the leadership of the sect.

Verren's father had not been inclined to enter into matrimony and the members of the sect had beaten him to within an inch of his life, following which the marriage had been performed by Phoebe's mother in her capacity as High Priestess. The bride, however, retained her maiden name, possibly because she did not believe that the marriage would last long enough to make it worthwhile changing it.

She was quite right, as the reluctant spouse took to his heels at the first opportunity that presented itself.

Phoebe was not overly stricken. She was already pregnant by another man.

This was a pattern which would be followed throughout the rest of her life. Whether a devil worshipper with strict Catholic principles or a woman with a profound ignorance of birth-control techniques, Phoebe seldom came into contact with a male whom she found attractive without progressing to motherhood.

Generally, she came into contact with these attractive males in the course of her profession of fortune teller. Romance was clearly foreseen in the cards or the crystal ball. It was near, very, very near . . . near enough to touch . . . Followed by a mutual laying on of hands and Phoebe was on her way to a new pregnancy.

Up to this point, the males rarely displayed any signs of resistance. Even at the age of forty-three, Phoebe Brady was a remarkably attractive woman with a stunning figure and long, jet-black hair. It was only when she sought to regularize the union that the male tended to take flight.

The flight was usually of short duration. Accustomed to the fickle ways of men, Phoebe was prepared, the strong-arm division of the sect was summoned and the prospective bridegroom was offered the choice of being married conscious or unconscious.

These marriages were invariably performed by Phoebe herself, as, in her religion, she was the only High Priestess and the only person authorized to perform them. They were followed by a period which might be described as a honeymoon, during which the happy couple spent most of their time in bed, appearing only for meals with Phoebe radiant and the spouse pale and inclined to buckle at the knees. Phoebe Brady was a very healthy woman with remarkably strong appetites.

Later on, once the magic had gone out of the marriage, the husbands usually tried to escape, some successfully and others less so, in which case they were returned by the faithful members of the sect so roundly beaten that they not infrequently required medical attention for their injuries.

This, it seemed, had been the case with Eric Willmot, a classic example of the High Priestess' consorts. He had come to have his fortune told, had learned that romance with a handsome, dark woman was in the immediate offing, had ended up in the fortune teller's bed and had unwillingly become her husband with the sanction of the Devil and beneath an arch of crossed clubs held by his worshippers. He had since made a number of unsuccessful escape attempts, the last a scant six months before his murder. This had resulted in a broken arm and three cracked ribs.

'It's possible that they killed him more or less accidentally,' said the inspector. 'Got carried away and pounded him a bit too hard or something. Have you had any luck tracing his whereabouts on the evening before he was killed?'

The sergeant had not, but a few days later a lead turned up which indicated that Willmot had been seen nursing a beer in one of the local bars up until ten o'clock on the evening of December 22. He had left the bar alone and no one could be found who admitted to having seen him after that time.

From the conversation that he had had with other patrons of the bar, it was obvious that Eric Willmot had been planning yet another escape attempt from the exhausting embraces of the High Priestess of the devil worshippers. He had told people that he was anxious to go to Canada, that he had been saving up small sums for a long time and that, if he could sell the wedding ring which Phoebe had given him, it would be enough to make up the fare. The indications were that he had succeeded in making the sale.

Granted that this was a lead as to a possible motive for the crime, it still did not explain how Willmot came to be out on the moor bound and gagged. The members of the devil worshippers' sect had not bound and gagged him, for the investigations had shown that they were all rather conspicuously present elsewhere on the evening in question.

Nor could Phoebe and Verren have done it. Their whereabouts on the night of the murder could not be determined, but Willmot had been a large, heavy and muscular man. It would have been a physical impossibility for the two women, strong as they were, to have overpowered him, bound and gagged him and carried him all the way out on to the moor where he had been killed, and it was not at all likely that Willmot would have accompanied them voluntarily. Someone else had been involved.

A possible candidate for this role had turned up in the canvassing of the bars where Willmot had been drinking, but he was so improbable in appearance that he was at first dismissed by the inspector and only returned to the suspect list when his police record became known.

This suspect, thirty-five-year-old Michael Harmsworth, was skinny, largely bald, wore glasses and had the timid manners of an incompetent bookkeeper. He also had a long record of convictions for theft, robbery and simple assault and, when he was drunk, which, since the time of Willmot's murder, had been often, he was less timid, describing himself to anyone who would listen as a desperate criminal who had only recently participated in a murder and who had been well paid for it.

As the inspector was extremely anxious to meet any desperate criminals who had recently participated in a murder whether they had been well paid for it or not, he was arrested, brought to police headquarters and interrogated.

Not surprisingly, he denied all connection with the crime, said he had never met Willmot in his life, a statement which appeared to be true, although the two men had frequented some of the same bars, and insisted that he had known neither Phoebe Brady nor her daughter nor had he ever encountered the names.

As for his boasting of desperate crimes in the bars, that, he said, had been the alcohol talking. He was a man who normally drank but little and alcohol went quickly to his head.

This last statement was a flat lie. Harmsworth was so steeped in alcohol that he had to be careful about approaching an open fire. The remainder seemed to be true. There was no evidence of any contact between him and the Bradys.

This did not mean that there had not been any and while the sergeant continued his efforts to trace a possible connection between Harmsworth and either the Bradys or Eric Willmot, the inspector kept his suspect in the detention cells and subjected him to a physical examination. The results were startling and, for the inspector, gratifying.

'The man's as strong as a bull,' he told his assistant. 'He may not look it, but he could have carried Willmot and the women too out to the moor and brought along a case of beer for refreshments. Have you found out that he knows Brady?'

'I have not,' said the sergeant. 'There's no evidence that he knew either Brady or Willmot. He knows Donahue, the queen of the satanists.'

'That's no help at all,' said the inspector. 'Donahue didn't murder Willmot. She didn't even know him. Or did she?'

'Not to my knowledge,' said the sergeant, 'but, with people like this, she wouldn't need to know him to have him killed. She could have done it just to get the devil worshippers into trouble. They're full of diabolic schemes, the lot of them.'

'Well, whoever paid for it, I'm thinking it was Harmsworth did the killing,' said the inspector. 'He had the strength. He's come into some money lately and I'll take my oath he didn't work for it. I expect he killed him while the Brady women jumped about and sang songs at the devil.'

'Then, why not charge him?' said the sergeant. 'He's a weak enough character for it to shake the truth out of him.'

'And I might just do that,' said the inspector. 'As a matter of fact, I think I will.'

And he did.

The sergeant, it turned out, had been remarkably accurate in his prediction. The formal charge of homicide shook Michael Harmsworth up uncommonly.

'Now, wait a minute!' he protested. 'I didn't kill that fellow. He was alive when I left. I'd nothing to do with the killing.'

There was so much implication of guilt in this statement that it took the inspector and the sergeant no time at all to extract the remaining details of the crime from the now highly nervous Harmsworth.

Like so many before him, he had met Phoebe Brady when he went to have his fortune told, but the pattern of events which followed had been different. Harmsworth was no movie star and Phoebe had not found him sexually interesting. She had, however, had other uses to which he could be put.

Being a good fortune teller, she had been able to inform him that he had been in jail more than once and that he was now largely without means or income. Things were, however, she said, going to improve. He was going to make a lot of money. Soon. Very soon.

Harmsworth, who was quick at catching the drift of such conversations, asked how and what he had to do.

Mrs Brady had told him that there was a very bad person named Eric Willmot who was trying to harm her and her daughter. She wanted him brought at a certain time to a certain place on the moor where she planned to teach him a lesson. She mentioned the sum of eight hundred pounds, half now and the other half when he delivered the goods.

According to Harmsworth, he had virtuously replied that he would not be a party to anything illegal, but that, if it was only a sort of joke . . . a little lesson to a friend . . .?

Phoebe had replied that that was exactly what it was, had paid over four hundred pounds and had told him what Willmot looked like, where he could often be found, where he was to be delivered and when.

'It's to be well before eleven of the evening,' she said, 'or you'll not see the other four hundred.'

Harmsworth had told her to have the other four hundred ready and, on the evening of the twenty-second, had begun following Willmot whom he located nursing his beer in the bar. At a little before ten o'clock, Willmot had left the bar and had gone into an alley, apparently to relieve himself.

Harmsworth had walked up behind him and had struck him a violent blow with his clenched fists on the back of the neck. He had then picked up the unconscious man and had walked blandly through the streets of Cork and out to the moor, assuming very rightly that anyone who saw him would take him for a good Samaritan carrying home a drunken friend.

Phoebe and Verren had been waiting for him dressed in their ritual robes and armed with long iron bars. He had dumped Willmot, whom he had stopped to bind and gag once he had left the city, on the ground, taken the four hundred pounds and run for his life. As a professional criminal, it had occurred to him that the ladies could, if they so wished, save four hundred pounds and eliminate a witness at the same time by making an unpleasant use of those long iron bars. It was obvious that, if what they had in mind was 'only a sort of joke', it was going to be a rough one.

Taken into custody and confronted with the confession of their accomplice, Phoebe and Verren Brady at first maintained their innocence and described Harmsworth's statement as a pack of lies. Finding, however, that this did not procure their release, they eventually admitted that what he had told the police was true, but that he had known very well that Willmot was to be executed.

After all, the execution was completely legal, said Phoebe Brady. Willmot had stolen a valuable ring which she had given him on the occasion of their marriage and was planning to flee the country.

He had been tried in absentia by a court of the sect and had been condemned to death. She, as High Priestess, and her daughter, the Assistant High Priestess, had merely been carrying out the functions of their respective offices. If they had not executed Willmot in accordance with the doctrines of their religion at the precise moment of the winter solstice, who then was supposed to do it?

Both women expressed regret that they had not buried the body deeper, but offered as an excuse that the ground was hard and it was difficult to see what they were doing in the darkness.

Michael Harmsworth expressed regret that he had ever got mixed up in the business at all.

This sincere repentance did not influence the jury and on July 25, 1980, all three defendants were sentenced to life imprisonment.

3

GENERATION GAP

Since the somewhat confused termination of the Second World War, Berlin, the once proud capital of Germany, has remained in a sort of purgatory to which it was condemned by the division of the Third Reich between those convinced that the world would soon be uniformly communist and those who believed that it would not.

Split in two by the Berlin Wall and embedded deep inside hostile, communist territory, the moribund city survives on hope, propaganda and massive West German subsidies.

Although the propaganda and the subsidies continue unabated, hope has tended to wear a trifle thin and not many young working families come to the conclusion that Berlin is the ideal place to seek their future.

As a result, the population of the city displays a disproportionately large number of elderly, retired persons, attached to the former capital for emotional or patriotic reasons, and an equally large number of students, attracted by the generous financial incentives offered at the expense of the West German tax-payers.

This demographic mixture enjoys the distinction of being one of the least compatible in the world. The elderly retired are generally as conservative as clams. The students are normally radical to the point of frenzy. In Berlin, there is no generation gap; there is a generation chasm.

It being well known that the future belongs to youth and also that, while the voting patterns of the elderly are difficult to change, devil-may-care, young revolutionaries sometimes grow up to become middle-aged stockbrokers, the students have rather the better of it.

To begin with, the qualifications are not demanding. Registration at one of the universities suffices. No actual studying or attending of dull lectures is required. With a bit of finagling, it is possible for dedicated, idealistic young persons to spend ten and more years at a Berlin university at tax-payers' expense without learning anything at all.

Nothing academic that is. Socially and in the field of meaningful human relationships a great deal is learned. It is possible to plot the destruction of the current social and economic systems sitting alone in a room, but it is not much fun. Students, therefore, tend to gather in large, hairy, unwashed, panting heaps, something like a basketful of sexually precocious puppies.

This phenomenon is rarely encountered among the older members of Berlin society as, like everyone else, the elderly dislike mixing with old people. Although some have friends or relatives not yet estranged or dead, the majority sit alone and isolated, embedded like molluscs in some less than beautiful coral reef in the grimy stone of the aging apartment houses, watching television and waiting to die.

As a rule, this vigil is kept with the dignified apathy expected of worn-out members of society, but occasionally there is some individual who still dares to dream of adventure beyond the television screen and who longs to be not a spectator but a participant.

In modern, liberal Germany, this usually means some form of sexual activity and, should such an adventure beckon, there are those who will take risks that make the blood run cold.

In the summer of 1971, such an adventure did beckon to sixty-eight year old Otto Moerre who was not particularly handsome, was largely bald, had poorly fitting false teeth and only one leg, the other having been lost in an accident a good many years earlier.

The risk he took made the blood run cold. His blood. Literally.

The adventure began with a visit from a remarkably attractive young person which was amazingly different from the visits which he frequently had from another, somewhat less attractive young person named Willi Kastner, who was but fourteen years old and lived in the same building.

Willi, being too young to be a student, did not despise old people or anyone else, and he regularly supplemented his modest allowance by running errands for them and buying their groceries. Otto Moerre, having only one leg and being consequently loath to leave his apartment, was one of his better customers and it was, therefore, with dismay that Willi reported to his mother on the afternoon of August 6, 1971, that Mr Moerre was no longer answering his doorbell.'

'I've gone up every day for three days now,' he said. 'He doesn't answer and his mailbox is stuffed full of advertising. He always takes it out and reads it.'

Mrs Kastner looked throughtful, but not surprised. Like many another apartment house in the city, more than half the tenants at number twelve Floriangasse were old. An ambulance or a hearse parked in front of the building was not unusual.

'Well, I suppose we'd better call the police,' she said. 'Or does he have any relatives you know of?'

Willi did not know of any and Mrs Kastner called the police who arrived shortly in the form of a patrol car manned by a team of officers who had answered a good many such calls before.

Their handling of the call was, therefore, largely routine and, having knocked and rung the doorbell with no more results than those obtained by Willi Kastner, they inquired as to whether the building superintendent had pass keys to the apartments, and learning that he did not, they prepared to enter by the simple expedient of breaking the door down.

As the door was rather flimsy and as one of the patrolmen weighed well over two hundred pounds, this was quickly and easily accomplished and the patrolmen entered to find precisely what they had expected, i.e. Mr Otto Moerre dead in his own living room.

This too fell within the area of routine. The older people frequently died in their apartments and it was sometimes a good deal longer than three days before their bodies were discovered.

Where routine ended was the manner in which Otto Moerre had died, although this was not immediately apparent.

As a matter of fact, Otto was seated in what appeared to be a comparatively comfortable position on the sofa with his leg sprawled out in front of him and his head tipped back against the back. As his trousers were unzipped and his genitals exposed, the patrolmen both thought that he had been masturbating and had suffered a heart attack.

'Hard to think of a better way to go,' said the smaller of the two patrolmen, going forward to make the check for signs of life required by regulations. 'Oops! What's this? His hair's full of dried blood! This is homicide!'

And so it was, although Otto Moerre did not really have very much hair and the dried blood was mainly covering his bald spot.

This was not, however, an important detail and, while one officer remained with the corpse, the other hurried down to the patrol car and notified the station. Twenty minutes later, the Homicide Squad arrived.

As the main task of this squad was to determine whether the officers from the patrol car were right and that a homicide had, indeed, taken place, it was not very large, consisting only of an Inspector Hermann Fritsch, a somewhat red-faced man with a pleasingly egg-shaped figure, he being larger in the middle than at either end, his assistant, Detective-Sergeant Max Krause, who was dark, glum and pessimistic-looking, and a young, blond, round-faced expert in forensic medicine named Dr Ulrich Staufe.

While the sergeant remained downstairs to take formal statements from Mrs Kastner and Willi, the inspector and the doctor proceeded to the second floor where the doctor began an examination of the body and the inspector began nosing about the apartment looking at everything but touching nothing.

After a short time, the sergeant came up to report that the Kastners knew nothing of the matter and believed that Moerre had died a natural death.

'He didn't,' said the doctor without turning around or stopping what he was doing. 'Somebody smashed his head in.'

'With the Coco-Cola bottle on the floor there?' asked the inspector.

'That or one just like it,' said the doctor, which was, of course, no more than a witty remark, as he would actually have no very accurate idea of what had been used to crush Otto Moerre's skull until he had completed the autopsy and had consulted with the other experts from the police laboratory.

'Humph,' said the inspector. He did not care much for witty remarks nor for medical experts either.

'Robbery, I suppose,' said the sergeant morosely. Robberies of the elderly were common and difficult to solve as the city was full of youthful drug addicts with expensive habits to finance and a good many of them had addled their brains to the point where they did not know whether they had committed some specific offence or not.

'Doesn't look like it to me,' said the inspector. 'There's a coin collection here that's worth money and a stamp collection that is too, unless I'm mistaken. Easy things to dispose of.'

'Then, why has the place been ransacked?' asked the sergeant. 'Everything's been turned upside down.'

'Ask the experts,' said the inspector. 'They're paid to know the answer to things like that.'

'You mean I should call for the lab crew?' asked the sergeant.

'Yes,' said the inspector. 'Why are his trousers open if he was murdered?'

'Maybe because he was having an orgasm at just about the same time,' said the doctor, rightly judging that the question was addressed to him. 'Manual manipulation, I would say.'

'What in the devil do you mean by "manual manipulation"?' growled the inspector. 'Was he masturbating or wasn't he?'

'I cannot say whose hand did the deed,' said the doctor. 'Cause of death, skull fracture. Time, two or three days ago. Indications of motive, sexual activity resulting in orgasm shortly prior to death. If you want any more, you'll have to wait until after the autopsy. I'll be waiting for the body at the morgue.'

And, having thus made his formal report as required by regulations, he packed up his instruments and left, meeting the sergeant, who was returning from telephoning for the squad of detection specialists from the police laboratory, on the stairs.

'Looks as if we'll be hunting for female suspects,' said the inspector as the sergeant entered the room. 'It begins to look as if he had a prostitute in for a house call and he may have been careless about showing what he had in his wallet.'

'Then, why did she ransack the apartment and leave the stamp and coin collections?' asked the sergeant. 'I think it was somebody looking for something specific.'

To the inspector's irritation, the detection specialists from the police laboratory were inclined to agree with the sergeant. Although it was true that no cash was found on the body or any-where in the apartment, the stamp collection was worth over five thousand marks and the coin collection more than double that. Either could have easily been sold with no questions asked, but even more significant, a bank pass book which could have been used by anyone and which showed a balance of nearly twelve thousand marks had been found lying in open view on the night table in the bedroom. The drawer of the table had been pulled out and the contents thrown on the floor.

'The only logical assumption is that the person or persons who ransacked the apartment were not interested in money,' read the report. 'Even the most brain-damaged addict could not have overlooked such obvious objects of value. The indications are that Otto Moerre was murdered by someone who knew or believed that he had in his possession and in his apartment something which they desired.

'There are no indications as to what this object was, whether it was actually in the apartment or, if so, whether it was found.'

'Blast!' said the inspector. 'Don't tell me this is another case of some old Nazi blackmailing his former friends. What have you turned up on his background?'

'Nothing, except that he's the right age,' said the sergeant.

'Served in the Volkssturm at the end of the war, but he's not listed anywhere as a party member. Worked for the railway most of his life. Had a pretty good pension and didn't spend much. If he was blackmailing somebody, he wasn't getting much out of it. The people in the neighbourhood say he liked young girls.'

'A man with many hobbies,' said the inspector. 'Stamps, coins, young girls. Anything else?'

'A little pornography,' said the sergeant. 'There were a few magazines in the apartment. Not a lot. About normal for the older generation trying to catch up with the new morality.'

'A problem for all of us,' said the inspector. 'This attachment to young girls. What do you mean by that? Did he distribute gum-drops to female infants? Or did he offer female adolescents the price of a fix in return for a little sex?'

'More likely the latter,' said the sergeant, 'although I don't have anything definite. Young girls were seen going up to his room. The statements say "student types", but that could mean anybody who didn't wash.'

'I don't think you appreciate the importance of the youth movement,' said the inspector. 'All right. Let us say that Mr Moerre's interest in young girls was not entirely platonic. And let us further say that he invited some young girls to his room for a little close contact between the generations . . .'

'The boy who ran his errands in the apartment house said the old man was afraid of young people,' interrupted the sergeant. 'He said he would never have let a young person other than himself into the room. He was afraid of being robbed. He was afraid of going out for much the same reason. Told the boy that the young idealists kept kicking him into the gutter when they saw he had only one leg.'

'Do you have witnesses who saw girls going up there or not?' asked the inspector. 'The point I'm trying to make is that there are girls in this town, and not little bitty ones, who might not realize that coin and stamp collections are worth money and that you can draw cash out of the bank with a pass book.'

'That there undoubtedly are,' said the sergeant. 'I see what you're getting at. It was robbery after all, but the robbers were too dumb to identify the loot.'

'Something like that,' said the inspector. 'Remember the condition of the corpse. Trousers open and the autopsy report stated that he'd had an orgasm minutes before he died. It's close to a hundred per cent certain that he didn't have it all by himself.

'Okay. He had his orgasm and he pulled his wallet to pay for it.

The young lady got a look at the banknotes and tried to get them away from him. The autopsy report states that he was strangled by someone who lacked the strength to finish him.

'Coming to the realization that Moerre's neck was too tough for her dainty fingers, the young lady picked up the Coke bottle and slugged her host over the head with it, but his head proved to be as hard as his neck.

'She then took his crutch and beat his brains out. Smart remarks by Staufe notwithstanding, the autopsy report states that the primary murder weapon was his crutch.

'The lady having quieted Moerre's objections, she went through the apartment in search of cash and I have no doubt she took any she found. The other things she left because she didn't know they were worth anything.'

'And how old do you suggest this young lady is?' asked the sergeant. 'Are you saying that Moerre was killed by a child?'

'A mental one in any case,' said the inspector. 'What else could it be? He wasn't blackmailing anybody or he'd have had more money. He was afraid of full-grown females, so he wouldn't have let a young woman into his apartment. Also the autopsy report say there were no traces of saliva or female secretions on his sex organs so it was assumed that the orgasm was produced manually. What does that make you think of?'

'The babyfingers,' said the sergeant promptly. 'All those poor little kids, girls and boys too, who are on heroin and who hang around the Underground stations offering sexual services to all-comers so they can get another fix. They don't like actual intercourse because they're so small. Poor little devils! To that extent, the students are right. The society is rotten.'

'But liberal and progressive,' said the inspector, 'and that's what counts. Anyway, do you agree? I say what we're looking for is a female pre-adolescent on hard drugs.'

'Of which there are not more than a few thousand in Berlin.' said the sergeant. 'How are we supposed to know when we have the right one?'

'There are fingerprints on the Coke bottle and the same ones on the crutch,' said the inspector.

'And the Identification section reports "no record",' said the sergeant.

'Ah! But there will be,' said the inspector. 'If a child thinks she's got away with something like that once, she'll try it again.'

'If she doesn't die of an overdose first,' said the sergeant. He was a man with a pessimistic turn of mind and his profession had done little to alter his way of thinking.

In this particular instance, optimism would have been of little help in any case. The investigation was at a standstill. There were no new leads to be followed up. And neither the circumstances nor the motive of the crime were as yet clear. Whether the inspector's theory was correct or not, it was as good as any for the moment.

Even so, the case was not entirely abandoned and the sergeant continued to collect what information he could from the police informers, of which there were a great many on drugs, who might hear of someone who had pulled off what they believed to be a successful robbery and murder. Strangely enough, persons who do such things not infrequently talk about it.

And, rather to the sergeant's surprise, for, being a pessimist, he did not really expect any results, word did begin to filter in of two young ladies who, it was said, had been boasting of a heroic feat in which they had allegedly robbed and beat up an old man.

'I think it may be something,' said the sergeant, reporting to the inspector, 'because the accounts say that the old man had only one leg. Otherwise, everything is different from what we thought.'

What he actually meant was, 'different from what the inspector had thought,' but, not being new to his job, he chose to express himself more discreetly.

'How different?' asked the inspector, who was not deceived. 'She's not on drugs?'

'They,' said the sergeant. 'There's two of them and I don't know whether they're on drugs or not. All I have are the first names, Sylvia and Heidemarie, and a description that would make them out to be around twenty years old. They're definitely not pre-adolescents.'

'If they're around twenty, they're students,' said the inspector. 'Why don't you check with the university? Maybe they have their fingerprints.'

'I doubt that the universities fingerprint the students,' said the sergeant, uncertain as to whether the inspector was being completely serious or not, 'but I'll try.'

The universities did not, of course, fingerprint the students, and the registration records showed a larger number of Sylvias and Heidemaries than it was practical to check out individually.

'Anyway, most of the addresses are wrong,' said the sergeant. 'They admitted to me that they had students registered who haven't even been in Berlin for the past five years. They get one of their friends to register for them so they can stay on the subsidy trough.'

'Never mind,' said the inspector. 'We've got another point of reference. Any more on the descriptions?'

'Sylvia is supposed to be the voluptuous type,' said the sergeant. 'They say you couldn't actually call her fat, but she's generously built, very generously.'

'An old man's dream,' said the inspector. 'Moerre may have thought it was worth it.'

Whether the inspector was inclined to agree was not brought out in the conversation, but on the afternoon of August 13 a gentleman who was anxious to remain anonymous apparently did, for he took nearly as great a risk as had Otto Moerre and for precisely the same reason. Although more than ten years younger than Moerre and far less lonely, as he was still living with his wife of thirty years, he too apparently found the voluptuous type irresistible and, when he saw this one dressed in an exceedingly short and semi-transparent mini-skirt standing beside the road and looking approachable, he promptly stopped and offered her a ride regardless of the direction in which she might be going.

The young lady accepted the offer promptly and, seating herself rather carelessly next to the driver, gave him to understand that she was open to other offers as well. As for her destination, she was not particular. She had no engagements. She was, so to speak, at liberty.

Which was not, of course, quite the same thing as free. She was not, however, unreasonably expensive, and after being shown a sample of the merchandise, the gentleman decided that the price was right and drove happily off to a secluded spot in the woods near the Brandenburger Tor.

There, he parked the car and he and the young lady, whose name he had not learned, entered, as the rather formal language of the police report would put it, into contacts of a sexual nature.

Although not specifically stated in the report, these contacts apparently arrived at a satisfactory biological conclusion, but not inside the car.

The reasons for this were mechanical. The car was not large. Both driver and passenger were. The weather was warm. Fresh air is beneficial when taking exercise and Germans are very health conscious. In any case, the important point is that both parties left the vehicle and, a relatively short time later, re-entered it. What then took place is best described in the official police report.

'I was preparing to start the car,' reads the statement of the anonymous gentleman, 'when she said, "Wait! I have left my purse outside.'' She then opened the door and got out and began looking around in the grass and saying, ''I cannot find it. I cannot find it.''

'I said that I would help her look and I got out of the car as well. I left the key in the ignition although I had not yet started the motor.

'As soon as I had got a little distance from the car, she suddenly jumped in behind the wheel, started the motor and tried to drive away.

'I saw immediately that this was some kind of trick and I ran after the car shouting, ''Stop thief!''

'She then tried to turn the car around and go back down the road we had come, but she did not have enough room to turn and the front of the car came up against a tree so that she could not go any further without backing up.

'When she saw that she would not have time enough to do this before I got up to her, she jumped out of the car and ran off into the woods. The car was only a little damaged from hitting the tree.''

Although the gentleman was of the opinion that the lady was an accomplished car thief who had performed her trick more than once before, he did not come to the police to bring charges. He was, he said, satisfied with the young lady's services and felt that he had received his money's worth. The damage to the car was negligible. Moreover, he was aware that, were he to press charges, it would be difficult to remain anonymous. The actual purpose of his call was to return the young lady's purse. In her haste, she had left it in his car.

Of course she had. Her claim of having lost it in the grass had been no more than a trick to lure the driver out of the car so that she could make off with it. The purse had been in the car all the time.

This rather enjoyable system of stealing cars did not surprise the police officers, as they had already heard of it. It was, in fact, neither new nor original. What interested the police was the student identity card found in the handbag. It was in the name of Sylvia Dartsch whose age was listed as twenty and whose local address was given.

There were, by this time, few police officers in Berlin who did not know that the Homicide Squad was looking for a young and voluptuous female whose name was Sylvia and, in less than an hour, the report was on Inspector Fritsch's desk.

Thirty seconds later, the sergeant was on his way to the address given in the identity card, but this very prompt reaction proved to be in vain for he returned with the information that Miss Dartsch, believed by the landlady to be engaged in the fur trade, had not lived there for over a year.

The sergeant's time was not, however, entirely wasted for, although the landlady did not know her former tenant's present address, she did know the names of some of her friends, a supposedly engaged couple named Heidemarie Sabeikov and Dieter Jagdmann.

'She doesn't know their ages, but says that they're young, wear their hair long and smell rather strongly,' said the sergeant. 'Looks like we're on the right scent. Sylvia and Heidemarie are the names we're looking for.'

'Not for long, I hope,' said the inspector. 'Alert all the check points into East Berlin, the airfields, the railway station and the autoroutes to West Germany so they can't get out, and then start looking. Use as many men as you need. I want to get this case sewn up, so we can get on with other things.'

Although somewhat larger, Berlin is something like a mouse-trap. If you are inside, it is not so easy to get out, and all that the police needed to do was to determine exactly where in the mousetrap the mice were. The inspector did not have to wait long.

Sylvia Dartsch, the actual murderess, was taken first and promptly betrayed her companions, informing the police where they could be found and accusing them of the murder.

Twenty-five-year-old Heidemarie Sabeikov and twenty-four-year-old Dieter Jagdmann were arrested a few hours later and returned the compliment by accusing Sylvia of the murder and, eventually, each other, a breach of faith which effectively terminated their engagement.

None of the three were, however, particularly quick-witted and it did not take the interrogators very long to extract the true details of the case which were, as might be expected, sordid.

The whole affair had begun early in July with what was described as an idealistic effort to bridge the generation gap and, at the same time, turn a small profit.

Sylvia, who was of an inventive turn of mind, had come to the conclusion that there were undoubtedly many older residents of the city who would like to take part in the sexual revolution, were still physically capable of it and had the money to defray any expenses incurred, but were prevented by lack of suitable partners.

She proposed that this obvious need be filled by herself and

Heidemarie. Charges were to be maintained at a level to fit the budget of the average senior citizen and services, with a view to avoiding over-exertion and possible heart attacks, were to be limited to what might be termed the helping hand.

Superficially, the scheme was sound, even if somewhat unconventional, and there were beyond doubt many lonely, elderly men whose physical and financial conditions were such that they would have participated with enthusiasm. As a matter of fact, there were others in addition to Otto Moerre, but how many and who they were remains a secret of the police. Even almost hysterically liberated West Germany was at that time not yet ready for the senile sex scene.

Whatever the case, Otto Moerre and his fellow clients must have thought that they were dreaming. Lonely, old men, no longer physically attractive and not rich enough to buy even a simulation of love, they would be sitting in their cheerless, little apartments when there came a knock on the door.

Cautiously opening the door on the chain lock because no old person in his or her right mind would let a stranger into the apartment in such a big city, the old man finds two young, pretty, voluptuous maidens standing on the doorstep with a proposition. They want to bridge the generation gap and they explain in unmistakable terms how they plan to go about it.

Otto Moerre was close to seventy. He had lived through a couple of world wars, at the end of both of which Germany had got the short end of the stick. He was not naïve and he undoubtedly knew the risk of allowing young people of any sex to enter his apartment, but, according to his murderess, he threw open the door wide.

'Welcome!' cried Otto Moerre.

The inspector was right. Otto Moerre had thought that it was worth it.

Whether the scheme had started out as benevolent and then degenerated into robbery and murder or whether the robbery had been planned from the start was something that the police were unable to determine. All three of the accused swore that they had had no intention of harming their elderly victim, but Sylvia and Heidemarie eventually admitted that they had been planning to rob him from the beginning of August.

According to the original scheme, the robbery was to have been carried out by Dieter Jagdmann who was to be let into the apartment by the girls. Dieter, who was anything other than a forceful type, had, however, declined and had then been demoted to acting as a look-out outside the apartment. The two fearless girls would do it alone.

They had, subsequently, entered the apartment on one of their regular appointments and while Sylvia set about bridging the generation gap with Otto on the sofa, Heidemarie had begun going through the apartment looking for money.

Occupied as he was, Otto had noticed this and had called upon her to cease and desist. Sylvia had, however, removed his crutch and had her free hand and arm wrapped tightly about his neck so that he could not get up to protect his property.

When even these measures proved inadequate and he began to call for help, Sylvia had picked up the empty Coke bottle from the table and hit him over the head with it.

The result had been unsatisfactory. Otto had too hard a head for a simple Coke bottle and, presumably now realizing that he was about to pay the price of his imprudence, he began to roar for help at the top of his lungs.

Heidemarie had shouted to Sylvia to shut him up and Sylvia had seized the crutch and complied.

Asked why they had not taken the stamp and coin collections or the bank pass book, all three of the accused expressed utter astonishment over the fact that these things could be turned into money. Technically university students all, they had not been sufficiently well informed to operate as competent burglars.

Their professional problems were solved on January 7 of the following year when a court found all three guilty of murder and conspiracy to commit murder and sentenced them to life imprisonment.

In Germany, this normally means six or seven years.

4

FINGERED

Forty miles to the west of the Austrian capital of Vienna and a mile to the north of the E-5 autoroute running west to the German border lies the ancient city of St Pölten, the core of which dates back to the thirteenth century.

Although moderately industrialized, St Pölten suffers little from air pollution, for beginning at the edge of the city limits a great forest stretches away to the Danube river twenty miles to the north.

This forest is known locally as Lovers' Wood and, like lovers' woods elsewhere in the world, it is a fairly promising place for homicide.

The sad fact is that where lovers congregate to perform those acts which make being a lover such a pleasant avocation, there too congregate voyeurs, rapists and other representatives of those mentally or emotionally unbalanced persons who make our bright, modern, world so interesting, even though, perhaps, a trifle dangerous.

The autumn and winter of 1973 were a dangerous time for the users of the St Pölten Lovers' Wood. Maintaining an ecological balance like hares and foxes in the Arctic, the large numbers of lovers in the preceding years had, in turn, attracted large numbers of sex nuts. This distressed the lovers, but it did not trouble in the least a Mr Franz-Josef Faust, an elderly, retired widower, who lived on the edge of the Dunkelstein Forest, the official name of Lovers' Wood, and who went for walks in it every day, weather permitting or not.

It was, however, more pleasant if the weather cooperated and, upon rising on the morning of May 2, 1974, he was gratified to see that the day had dawned warm and sunny. Making himself a hurried breakfast and packing a generous lunch to take along, he set off into the forest.

As he had wasted no time and had left early, it was exactly twenty-six minutes past seven when he came upon the corpse. He would be able to confirm the time later with confidence for, immediately that he saw the body, he looked at his watch.

This was a rather amazing demonstration of phlegm for the body was a far from pleasant sight.

Judging by the size of it, the corpse was that of a man, although it now looked more like a gigantic, overcooked sausage. The skin was covered with huge blisters, the flesh had split open in places, the face was burned black, no vestige of hair or clothing remained and the rotting entrails protruded through the ruptured walls of the stomach. It was covered with flies and it stank beyond belief.

Franz-Josef Faust understandably did not approach it, but, holding his breath, made a check of the landmarks so that he could find it again and set off at a deliberate pace in the direction of the nearest place which would have a telephone. There was little point in hurrying. The man had obviously been dead for some time.

This opinion was confirmed not long thereafter by Dr Julius Stengler, the young, plump and horn-rimmed-spectacled Assistant Coroner from the St Pölten Coroner's Office, who arrived at shortly after eight-thirty with the advance party from the Department of Criminal Investigations.

'He's been dead for several weeks,' said the doctor. 'And he was already dead when somebody burned him up here.'

'And when did the burning take place?' asked the inspector in charge of the detail, a huge man with ox-like shoulders, a drooping, blond moustache and a completely bald head.

The doctor shrugged. 'Recently,' he said. 'Within the past forty-eight hours, I suspect. I may be able to determine something more precise when we get him down to the morgue.'

'Here's a set of car tracks,' called Detective-Sergeant Max Friedmann, the inspector's assistant and the third member of the advance party. 'They look clear enough for the lab people to take casts.'

Inspector Anton Hochbauer walked over to where the slight, sandy-haired sergeant was squatting beside a pair of tyre tracks in the soft mould of the forest floor.

'They didn't carry him far,' he remarked.

The body lay a scant two yards from one of the logging roads used by the state forestry workers, although it was not the same road by which the police party had arrived at the scene.

'They?' said the sergeant. 'More than one person?'

The inspector nodded. 'I think it was professional. It's got all the earmarks. I suspect we'll find that every scrap of identification has been destroyed. We'll be lucky if we ever even find out who he was.'

The inspector's pessimistic prediction unfortunately turned out to be accurate. Although some burned clothing was found near the body and although some of the fingers were still sufficiently intact to permit the taking of an identifiable set of prints, no clue to the identity of the corpse could be found. The face was too badly burned and rotted to permit a picture or even a very accurate police drawing, the clothing was of Austrian origin, but with no indication of where it had been purchased and the car-tyre tracks were in earth too soft to take a very satisfactory cast.

'According to Stengler, he was killed about the middle of April by two very violent blows on the left temple with a sledge hammer or something like that,' said the inspector, looking glumly at the pile of reports on his desk. 'He was a man in his late thirties or early forties and in good health except for a broken left index finger.'

'Broken at the time he was murdered?' asked the sergeant.

The inspector shook his head. 'Earlier,' he said. 'It was almost healed. He was wearing this splint on it.'

He picked up a long, slender splint made of bent wire from the desk.

The sergeant took it in his hand, looked at it and laid it back down on the desk.

'Do you still think it was a professional job?' he asked.

'What else?' said the inspector. 'There isn't a missing-person report in all Austria that corresponds to this body. Either it was a person who hasn't been missed or it's somebody from out of the country altogether.'

'It could be a foreigner of course,' said the sergeant thoughtfully, 'but why bring him all the way up here to St Pölten? I'd think that professional gangsters who wanted to dispose of a body outside the country would do it as close to the border as possible. The nearest border here is Czechoslovakia and that's communist. I've never heard anything about there being gangs or professional killings over there and, if there were, how'd they get over the border? It would be easier to break out of jail than to get out of Czechoslovakia with a two-weeks-old corpse!'

'A little less than two weeks probably,' said the inspector. 'Stengler says he was set on fire on May 1. They used a mixture of gasoline and oil. They didn't use enough of it or they would have reduced the corpse to ashes.'

'Well, why didn't they?' said the sergeant. 'These people don't sound like professionals to me or foreigners either.'

The inspector did not reply immediately, but sat silently sunk in thought. After some little time, he pushed back his chair, dug into the lap drawer of his desk, extracted a somewhat battered, short, black cigar which he looked at dubiously and having bit off the end, lodged it in the corner of his mouth.

The sergeant leaned over the desk and held out his lighter. Inspector Hochbauer only smoked when he was confronted with a problem which bothered him a great deal and to which he could see no reasonable solution.

'You're right,' he said finally. 'It couldn't be a professional job. Nobody carries decomposing corpses over the Czech border nor any other border for that matter. Professionals wouldn't wait for two weeks to dispose of the body. Professionals wouldn't run out of petrol for burning it. This is a local murder.'

'But he's been dead for over two weeks now and nobody's reported him missing,' said the sergeant. 'Would that be possible?'

'Oh yes,' said the inspector, making a wry face and snubbing out the cigar in the ashtray. He did not really like cigars, but he believed that they helped him to think. 'People can be missing for very considerable periods of time without anyone noticing it. Salesmen on the road, people, who have gone off to look for work or to pay visits in other cities, single persons living alone. Sometimes there isn't anyone to report them missing. Sometimes there's nobody who gives a damn.'

'Somebody knew him well enough to kill him,' said the sergeant.

'Not necessarily,' said the inspector. 'Take a hypothetical case. A salesman is driving along the highway and he stops and picks up one or more hitchhikers. They rob him, bash in his head and drive around with his body in the trunk of the car for a couple of weeks until the smell gets too bad. Then they take him to the nearest woods, pour the reserve can of petrol over him, set him on fire and beat it. The car they sell to a shady dealer no questions asked or they simply junk it. I don't say that this is what happened here, but it's something that has happened often enough in other places.'

The sergeant picked up the file from the desk.

'Off to the Unsolved Section?' he asked, gesturing with it in the direction of the filing cabinet against the office wall.

The inspector hestiated. He did not like sending an investigations file to the Unsolveds if he could possibly help it.

However, what else was there to do? Everything that could be checked had been checked and it had all led nowhere. If it had only been possible to identify the body . . .

He picked up the wire finger splint from the desk and began twirling it in his finger.

'I wonder how many men break their left index finger here in Austria on any given day?' he muttered thoughtfully.

Abruptly, he straightened up, laid the splint down on the desk and reached for the telephone. 'Let's see if Stengler can tell us when this fellow broke his finger.'

Dr Stengler could. 'It was approximately three weeks before he was killed,' he said. 'Say the last week in March. Why? Have you got a lead?'

'Not yet,' said the inspector. 'But maybe this is one.'

He hung up the telephone and held out the splint to the sergeant.

'We should have done this before,' he said. 'It's my fault we didn't. I was so convinced that it was a professional killing and that the victim wasn't from this area that I let it slip. Take this splint and check out all of the hospitals around here. See if they recognize it and find out if there's any difference in finger splints. Maybe they all come from one central factory, but it looks to me like this was a hand-made sort of job. Maybe the hospitals make them thesmelves. Anyway, get the information on it and report back. If there is a difference we'll start checking hospital records to see who broke his left index finger the last week in March. We'll make up a list of broken left index fingers and run the people down one by one. If there's one we can't find, that could be our boy in the morgue.'

'A broken finger could have been splinted in a doctor's surgery too,' said the sergeant, taking the splint. 'It wouldn't have to be a hospital. This is going to take a lot of checking. I'll need men.'

'Then, take them!' said the inspector. 'Take what you need. I've got a feeling that this may be the opening we need to crack this case.'

The inspector's cigar had apparently been more efficacious than the sergeant or, for that matter, he himself would have believed. A scant four hours later, and with far less effort than the sergeant had feared, the origin of the finger splint was known. The hospitals all made their own splints and this one had come from St Pölten's general hospital.

'I can recognize any splint from this hospital,' said hospital technician Peter Boost. 'This is one of ours.'

'And who received it?' asked Sergeant Friedmann.

'Ah!' said the hospital technician. 'That I can't say. I know that this is one of our splints, but I have no way of knowing which one or when it was issued. Our splints are different from those of the other hospitals but not from each other.'

'So,' said the sergeant, reporting back to Inspector Hochbauer, 'all we can do is check the individual records for broken left index fingers. However, we do know that it was at the general hospital.'

'Shouldn't take much checking then,' said the inspector. 'We know the hospital. We know the type of injury and we know the approximate date. You should be able to pull the card right out of the file.'

One week later, the sergeant and a detail of four men completed the sorting of five thousand, three hundred and eighty-two card files from the hospital records and presented the inspector with a list of three names of males who had suffered broken left index fingers during the period from the middle of February to the middle of April and who had been treated at the general hospital.

'The hospital is like everybody else nowadays,' said the sergeant. 'They're so understaffed that the records are a mess. Even now I'm not completely sure that this represents all the people who got left-index-finger splints during that period, but it's all that we can locate.'

'Fine,' said the inspector. 'Now, the next step. Find these people.'

The sergeant quickly found two of the three. They were both alive and well. The third seemed to be missing.

'He isn't missing,' said Mrs Anneliese Madler. 'He's in Vienna looking for work. He called me on the telephone only two weeks ago.'

'Something's wrong,' said the inspector. 'This fellow Friedrich Madler is just about the right size, he's thirty-nine years old and he broke his left index finger on March 24. It was splinted at the general hospital with a splint similar to that which we found on the body. Yet Mrs Madler talked to him on the telephone nearly a week after the time when he is supposed to have been murdered. She has to be mistaken.'

'After twenty years of marriage and four children, she doesn't know her own husband's voice?' said the sergeant. 'And what about the boy, Johann? I understand he spoke to him too. They couldn't both be mistaken. But even if they were, who was it and why would he do it? Madler wasn't rich. He was a casual labourer

54

and out of work more often than in. If Mrs Madler didn't have a good job, the family could hardly live.'

This was quite true. With four teenage children, Johann, seventeen, Hubert, sixteen, Lotte, fourteen and Josef, thirteen, the family was almost entirely dependent upon thirty-five-year-old Anneliese Madler's salary which she earned as a top secretary in a St Pölten insurance company office. Madler, it seemed, did not work often and then, reluctantly.

'Which may account for the fact that he didn't register with the employment office in Vienna,' said the sergeant. 'He may have gone there more to get away from his responsibilities than to find work.'

'They say he's not registered, do they?' said the inspector. 'What about the police? Have they been able to find any trace of him?'

The sergeant shook his head. 'They've checked out the cheap hotels and boarding houses, but so far, nothing. Actually, there's no indication that Madler ever was in Vienna at all.'

'Could be right here in St Pölten,' said the inspector. 'He told his son and Mrs Madler that he was calling from Vienna, but there's no way they could be certain that he really was.'

'So what do we do now?' asked the sergeant. 'Drop the Madler lead?'

'Can't,' said the inspector. 'Until we're certain that that body in the morgue isn't Friedrich Madler's, we've got to keep hunting for him. Contact the newspapers and the radio station and have them put out an appeal for Madler to report in to us. Maybe that will produce something.'

The only thing that the appeal produced was two calls from practical jokers and one from a mentally deranged person who said he had murdered and eaten Madler because he was the anti-Christ. In the meantime, however, the investigations which had been continuing without interruption had produced a fact which made the appeal pointless.

The burned body in Lovers' Wood was that of Friedrich Madler. Comparison of fingerprints taken from the Madler house had made the identification positive.

'Confusing, confusing,' sighed the inspector. 'We have the body identified, but we're no further along than we were before as to who killed him. In fact, the identification makes the murder harder than ever to understand.'

'If we're to assume that someone called Mrs Madler and her son and pretended to be Madler after he was already dead, I find it impossible to understand,' said the sergeant.

'Obviously, the person who called must have been the murderer, but how could he deceive a woman and her son into believing that they were talking with their husband and father when they weren't?'

'Well, the failure of the relatives to note the deception could be explained by the fact that it was a telephone,' said the inspector. 'People expect others to sound different over the telephone and, if he said the right things, it would probably pass off. After all, they had no reason to doubt that it was Madler. What I still find more puzzling is why he did it. What advantage did he gain from it? It wasn't to gain time. Mrs Madler said she wouldn't have reported her husband missing even if he hadn't called. As a matter of fact, they were all surprised that he did call.'

'Maybe the murderer didn't know that though,' said the sergeant.

'Maybe,' said the inspector, 'but he must have known the family circumstances well to have passed himself off as Madler and he must have known that Madler had gone to Vienna to look for work.'

'It's more than we know,' said the sergeant. 'All we really know is that he's supposed to have told his family that.'

'Well, whatever the case,' said the inspector, 'the obvious fact that he did know so much about Madler shows that the murderer was either a relative or a very close friend. That's where we have to look.'

'That's where we have already looked,' said the sergeant, 'and it's where we're still looking, but we haven't found a thing. Madler didn't have any close friends and he didn't have many relatives either. He didn't even have any serious enemies.'

'I wouldn't think a common labourer would have any enemies at all,' said the inspector.

'He didn't really,' said the sergeant. 'A lot of people didn't care for him much, thought he was shiftless and lived off his wife, but you don't murder people for such reasons.'

'Unless you happen to be the wife,' said the inspector.

'Yes, that occurred to me too,' said the sergeant, 'but there are a number of things that make it impossible. For one, the telephone call. Mrs Madler could be lying, but what about Johann? He also spoke with the man who had presumably killed his father and the other children were present when the call came. Secondly, Mrs Madler is too small to have lugged her husband out to the woods by herself even if she'd had the strength to murder him. She couldn't have done it without help.'

'Perhaps she had help,' said the inspector. 'Her husband doesn't seem to have been much of a bargain. She may have had a friend and she may have wanted to get rid of Madler so she could marry him.'

'The checking of Mrs Madler that we've done so far hasn't produced any trace of a lover,' said the sergeant, 'but maybe we haven't checked hard enough. God knows, it's about the only theory that makes any sense.'

After another week of intensive investigations, the theory was still the only one that made sense, but there was not a scrap of evidence to support it.

'If Mrs Madler has or had a lover, she's done the best job of concealing it that I've ever seen,' said the sergeant. 'It's true that some of her time can't be accounted for. She drives a silver-grey Sunbeam saloon so she doesn't depend on public transport. But we've found no one who ever saw her with another man. We've checked all the discreet bars and the hot-bed hotels and nobody there could recognize her picture. If she had a lover, I don't know where she was meeting him.'

'Simple,' said the inspector. 'She picked him up in her car and they drove out to Lovers' Wood. That's where they had their meetings and that's where they got rid of the body of her husband.'

'All right,' said the sergeant. 'But, where did they kill him then? And where was the body all the time from between when he was killed until he was taken out to the forest to be burned up? Stengler thinks it was brought out there just before it was set on fire.'

'Ah! That's not so simple,' said the inspector. 'By the time that the body was brought out to the forest it was in an advanced state of decomposition. It must have stunk unbearably for days. God knows where they could have kept it without anyone noticing. The basement of the house maybe?'

'It would have been taking an awful chance,' said the sergeant. 'If one of the children happened to go down . . .'

His remark was interrupted by the ringing of the telephone. The inspector reached over and picked it up. 'Hochbauer,' he said.

For a second or two he listened silently and then began to signal frantically to the sergeant to pick up the extension. The sergeant caught it up and was just in time to hear a man's voice say, '. . . got what was coming to him, but you'll never get me!', followed by a sharp click as the connection was broken.

'Who was that?' exclaimed the sergeant.

'Friedrich Madler's murderer,' said the inspector. 'Nip down the hall and see if the switchboard got a tape on that, will you?'

The switchboard had made a tape, standard procedure in the case of anonymous telephone calls, and it was played over and over again in the inspector's office. It was not very long.

'This is the executioner of Friedrich Madler speaking,' the voice had said the moment that Inspector Hochbauer had answered. 'You're wasting your time going around asking questions. No one who knew Madler knows me or my name. He played a rotten trick on me seventeen years ago and now he's got what was coming to him, but you'll never get me!'

'Speaking with a folded handkerchief over his mouth,' remarked the chief technician from the police laboratory who had been called over to listen to the recording. 'That's what makes it sound fuzzy like that. I have the impression that this is not a very old man.'

'He'd have to be close to forty if Madler did him an injustice seventeen years ago,' said Sergeant Friedmann. 'Could it be some kind of a nut?'

'It's always possible,' said the inspector. 'You get all kinds of crackpots calling in whenever there's an unsolved murder case, but what impresses me is the number seventeen. Why just that number? I don't think that a joker would have picked an exact time like that. He'd have said, 'a long time ago' or 'once', but not 'seventeen years ago'. That number means something.'

'Johann Madler is seventeen years old,' said the sergeant.

There was a short silence.

'Would a boy consider being fathered by a man he hated a rotten trick?' said the inspector finally.

'Possible,' said the technician. 'It's the sort of dramatic statement that a very young man might make. But what would be the point of it?'

'The call or the murder?' said the inspector. 'The call may have been intended to lead us away from the direction the investigation has taken lately and that, of course, is Mrs Madler.'

'The boy is big enough,' said the sergeant. 'He could have bashed in his father's head while he was sleeping or drunk and then his mother could have helped him hide the body and later bring it out to the woods in her car.'

'Which would also explain the telephone call Madler was supposed to have made from Vienna,' said the inspector. 'They could have faked it for the benefit of the other children.'

'Or maybe the other children are in on it too,' said the sergeant. 'Madler wasn't much of a husband or a father. The whole family may have plotted to get rid of him. The question is, if that's the case, how are we ever going to prove it? Mrs Madler and the older boys obviously aren't going to talk and we can hardly grill the younger ones. The Juvenile Office would crucify us.'

'The only possibility is physical evidence, even after all this time,' said the inspector. 'If what we're thinking is true, then Madler was probably killed right in his own home and his body may have been kept there too, until it began to rot so badly that they had to dispose of it. There could still be some trace of that. Get a court order and go over the house by the square centimetre. If we don't find anything, we can give up. It'll be a perfect murder.'

It was not, however, a perfect murder although it was close. Beneath the big double bed in the master bedroom of the Madler home, the bed which Anneliese Madler had shared with her husband and the one in which she had slept alone ever since his disappearance, the detectives discovered an enormous pool of dried human blood. Friedrich Madler, it seemed, had been murdered in his own bed.

Under the shock of the disclosure of this great pool of her husband's blood, the presence of which she had not even suspected, Anneliese Madler broke down completely and made a full confession to the murder.

'I intended to come to the police the day after it happened,' she said, 'but Johann said, "Why should you have to go to jail for that rotten bastard? You've suffered enough from him already!" and so I didn't. I'm sorry I've caused so much trouble.'

According to Mrs Madler's confession, her marriage had been twenty years of uninterrupted martyrdom, during which she had had to support the entire family and had received in return nothing but beatings, torture and sexual abuse.

Friedrich Madler had been, as some of his acquaintances had reported, obsessed with sex and he had subjected his wife to every form of perversion known to man. A refined sadist, he had stimulated his own appetites through the torture of his helpless wife and a subsequent medical examination showed the woman's breasts and sex organs to be covered with the scars of old burns, cuts and whip marks. Her statements were supported by those of the children who said that they had often been kept awake by the sound of their mother's moans and screams.

On the night of April 18, Friedrich Madler had come home more than half drunk and had subjected his wife to a bout of sexual perversions and beatings which only came to an end at three in the morning when he fell asleep.

The exhausted, tortured woman had crept out of the bed and had gone to the bathroom to bathe her wounds. There had been repairs carried out in the bathroom the day before and she saw that a heavy mason's hammer was still lying there.

To the nearly hysterical woman the hammer had seemed a sort of an omen.

'All I could think of was that I couldn't stand any more,' she said. 'It kept going through my head over and over again, "You've got to kill him now! You've got to kill him now!" I picked up the hammer and walked back to the bedroom.'

Anneliese Madler had raised the heavy hammer in both hands and had brought it down with all her strength against the left temple of her sleeping husband. He had jerked once and had then lain still.

Mrs Madler raised the hammer and struck again. Then she went to the living room and had spent the rest of the night sitting huddled in a chair where Johann found her the following morning.

Johann had persuaded her not to go to the police and for three days the body lay in the bedroom, unbeknown to the other children. It had, apparently, been during this time that the pool of blood had collected beneath the bed.

At a loss as to what to do with the body, Mrs Madler and Johann had carried it out during the night and put it in the trunk of the car, and for nearly two weeks she had driven to work, to church and to do her shopping with the body accompanying her, trying to cover the odour of the steadily decomposing flesh with disinfectants and deodorants.

At the end of that time, the stench had become impossible to conceal and on the night of May 1 she and Johann had driven to Lovers' Wood where they had dragged the body out of the trunk and had attempted to burn it with a mixture of petrol and oil.

Under the heat of the burning petrol, the rotting body had begun to twitch and writhe in a horrifyingly lifelike manner and mother and son had fled in panic.

The only question which remained unexplained was the identity of the person who had placed the call to Inspector Hochbauer. Johann Madler denied it and had apparently been in the presence of other persons at the time the call was received.

Anneliese Madler was tried in the spring of 1975 on a charge of unpremeditated homicide and sentenced to four years' imprisonment.

Her son was brought before the juvenile court and convicted of acting as an accessory after the fact to murder and aiding and abetting in the concealment of a felony. He received a sentence of five years' confinement in an institution for juvenile offenders.

Both sentences were suspended by the court.

5

INDESTRUCTIBLE

It was the day before Christmas and all over the city of Bielefeld people were running about buying last-minute presents and sending off Christmas cards to those from whom they had not expected to receive one but had.

The atmosphere was reasonably festive. Bielefeld, lying well to the north in West Germany on the edge of the low mountains of the historic Teutoburger Wald where the early Germans staged some of their more significant battles, it was crisply cold and it was snowing. The country was at its peak of post-war affluence and the jingling of the cash registers in the downtown shopping district nearly drowned the sound of the Christmas bells.

In the suburbs, however, thirty-one-year-old Karl-Wilhelm Lange, a former plumber who now worked in an aluminium factory in the nearby town of Borgholzhausen, was preparing to go to work. Climbing into his aged car, a model in which the petrol tank was suspended over the motor in front, he was agreeably surprised to find that it started with amazing ease.

This was something which did not happen often in winter and Lange, a handsome man with a black moustache and sideburns who stood six feet two inches tall and weighed close to two hundred pounds, drove gratefully off.

He had gone less than a half block when the car blew up.

Before his astonished eyes, the bonnet rose perpendicularly into the air followed by a spray of metal fragments formed from what had been the engine.

The spectacle was succeeded instantly by the deafening sound of the explosion and by flames.

Inexplicably, the windscreen did not break and not a single metal fragment penetrated inside the car. The vehicle did, however, come to an abrupt halt.

Startled nearly out of his wits, Karl-Wilhelm tumbled out of the briskly burning car and began to run around it in a state of considerable excitement. It was only later when someone had called the fire department and the fireman asked him if he needed medical attention that he realized what a narrow escape he had had. The car was, of course, a total loss, but Karl-Wilhelm had not so much as a scratch.

A poor way to start off the Christmas holidays, but there was no help for it. Returning home only long enough to swallow several shots of brandy with a view to steadying her nerves, he took the bus to the railway station and caught a train for Borgholzhausen. He arrived an hour and fifteen minutes late for work, but the foreman, having learned of the circumstances, generously decided that his pay would not be docked. It was, after all, Christmas Eve.

By the time he got home, he was feeling somewhat better. The car had been insured and, God knew, he could use a new one. Perhaps the explosion had been a blessing in disguise. Wasting no more time in idle speculation as to why a car should suddenly blow up in that manner, he settled down to a merry Christmas with his lovely, twenty-six-year-old wife, Monika, and their two children, Hartmut, who was ten, and seven-year-old Sabine. The fact that the children were only home for the holidays made the occasion the happier. Karl-Wilhelm Lange was very fond of his children.

He was also very fond of his wife to whom he had been married for over nine years, but being a modern German husband, he realized that sexual jealousy and possessiveness were old-fashioned and not at all in tune with the new morality, so when a few friends dropped in after the children had gone to bed, he raised no objections when one of the men removed his wife's clothing and began to engage in sexual dalliance with her on the expensive and not yet fully paid for living-room sofa. With what was close to a resigned sigh, he removed his own clothing and joined a naked group on the living-room carpet who were engaged in trying to form the currently popular daisy chain. There were times when hard-working and weary Karl-Wilhelm secretly wished that things were a trifle more old-fashioned.

As wife swapping and group sex were considered to be normal by many modern, progressive people in Germany at that time, Christmas of 1974 at the Lange home could be regarded as having passed uneventfully.

After it was over, the children were taken back to the children's home where they normally lived, the juvenile authorities having decided that the Lange home was no place to bring up children and having removed them from their parents' care nearly a year earlier.

It had been not long thereafter that Mrs Lange had made her suicide attempt. It had been unsuccessful and, in any case, it had had nothing to do with her children being taken away from her. She had found that something of a relief. Unlike her husband, she was not very fond of children.

With the exception of Norbert, of course.

At fourteen, Norbert Schmidt was legally, technically, emotionally and, in some respects, physically a child. In one respect, however, he was not a child at all but a sort of super-adult, and that was sexually.

Monika Lange appreciated this. Norbert was her favourite sex partner.

Not, of course, that Monika was any more possessive or monogamous than her husband. Although Norbert was her favourite, she was cheerfully prepared to engage in sex with any reasonably presentable male—or female—who made application and this did not even exclude her husband. Monika was a very liberated woman.

Karl-Wilhelm Lange was without a car until after the New Year and had to ride the bus and the train back and forth to his job in Borgholzhausen so that he was home even less of the time than usual, although, at best, he was not home much, being a man who worked all the overtime he could get.

This was not because he preferred work to home, but rather was related to the fact that the house furnishings had been ruinously expensive and it was going to take a long time to pay them off. In addition, like nearly all Germans, he harboured somewhere in the back of his mind, a dream of one day owning his own home, and he paid religiously into one of the building funds set up for that purpose.

As he often said to his colleagues at the factory, he had himself started out from the most miserable beginnings and he was determined that his children should have it better than he had.

Lately, however, he had said less about this, as it appeared that, except for brief visits, there was not much chance that they would be released by the juvenile authorities until they were completely grown up.

Mrs Lange did not trouble her head with such speculation, but spent most of her days in bed with Norbert, frequently being too tired by evening to be able to cook Karl-Wilhelm's supper when he finally came home.

As for Norbert, like any healthy teenager, he managed very

well on sandwiches and soft drinks with an occasional chocolate bar for energy. He was a good-natured boy of simple tastes who had found school uninteresting and who was now attending special classes for children with educational problems. As these were not very demanding, it left him a good deal of time for Monika and he was usually still with her when Karl-Wilhelm came home from work.

Shortly after New Year, Karl-Wilhelm had a visit from a Detective-Sergeant Hermann Distel of the Bielefeld Department of Criminal Investigations. The sergeant, a large, blond man with an open face and a broad, smooth forehead, wanted to know why Karl-Wilhelm had blown up his car. The insurance company experts had, it seemed, found no plausible reason for the explosion and, following tests, had come to the conclusion that it had been the result of mixing nitro-carbon paint thinner with the petrol. They suspected that Karl-Wilhelm had planned to provide himself with a new car in this manner and at their expense.

Karl-Wilhelm indignantly denied this. 'Do they think I'm going to commit suicide to get a new car from the insurance?' he said. 'Why, I could have been blown higher than a kite or trapped inside and burned to death. Anyway, I don't do things like that. I work for my money.'

The sergeant stoically took down his statement on a small, portable tape recorder and went away. Two days later he returned and asked Karl-Wilhelm if he knew anyone who might want to murder him.

'I've run a check on you,' said the sergeant, 'and I believe you told me the truth about the explosion. I talked to the fire department people who put out the fire and they say that only a half-wit would have tried a trick like that with himself in the car. However, there's no question but that there was nitro-carbon paint thinner mixed with the petrol, so somebody must have put it in your tank the night before. The question is who.'

But Karl-Wilhelm had not the slightest idea. 'Who in Heaven's name would want to murder me?' he said wonderingly. 'I'm not off work enough of the time to make any enemies. I haven't had the slightest trouble with anybody.'

'Well, then,' said the sergeant. 'It must have been a vandal. We get a lot of stuff like that. Kids busting windscreens or slashing tyres just for the hell of it. Some young punk was coming by and had a bottle of paint thinner in his hand, so he stopped and dumped it in your petrol tank.'

'Christ!' said Karl-Wilhelm. 'I could have got killed! There ought to be a law against such things.'

The sergeant gave him a sharp look, but Karl-Wilhelm was quite serious. 'What about the insurance?' he asked. 'Are they going to pay or not?'

'I've reported to them that we've found no reason to believe that you were in any way responsible for the explosion,' said the sergeant. 'I expect they'll honour the claim now.'

The insurance company did honour the claim and by January 13, which eventually turned out to be quite an unlucky day although it was a Sunday and not a Friday, Karl-Wilhelm Lange had a new Opel Kadett and was planning to take Monika and Norbert for a ride. They were both beginning to look a little haggard from their exertions during the day and he thought a ride and some fresh air might do them good.

The ride went well and was beneficial to all concerned up until three-thirty in the afternoon when they stopped at a small country inn near the town of Stukenbrock for a snack. Among other things on the menu was goulash soup, a popular delicacy in Germany, and three bowls were ordered.

Monika and Norbert began to eat theirs immediately and, as far as Norbert was concerned, rather noisily, but Karl-Wilhelm paused to hold forth at some length on the subject of the children, Hartmut and Sabine, wishing that they could be present to enjoy the ride and the soup. Whenever there was anything pleasant, he almost invariably thought of the children.

Monika, who was perhaps slightly embarrassed to be reminded that she had a son only four years younger than her lover, interrupted and asked him if he had locked the car. She did not, she said, want to be blown up because someone had put a bomb in it or something.

Karl-Wilhelm thought he had locked the car, but he went out anyway to make sure. The new model had a lock on the petrol tank.

A moment later, he returned and, having announced that the car was, indeed, locked, fell upon his soup, but after eating less than a quarter of the bowl, summoned the proprietor.

'What do you make your soup out of?' he demanded indignantly. 'Old rubber boots? It tastes like a chemical factory!'

The proprieter responded with equal indignation and threats of violence, but, having tasted the soup in Karl-Wilhelm's bowl, he was forced to agree.

'I can't imagine what got into it,' he said, looking hard at Monika and Norbert. 'Yours was all right, wasn't it?'

'Delicious,' said Monika.

'Mmmph,' said Norbert. He was not strong on conversation and complicated questions confused him.

'I'll get you another bowl,' said the proprietor and he took Karl-Wilhelm's half-empty bowl out to the kitchen and poured it down the sink. He than brought back another bowl which Karl-Wilhelm ate with appreciation.

'That's more like it,' he said.

'Can't imagine what got into that soup,' muttered the proprietor.

On the way home, Karl-Wilhelm nearly ran his new car into a tree, being suddenly taken with such frightful cramps in the stomach that he could hardly hold himself upright. He was, however, able to bring the car to a halt, staggered out and, having vomited copiously and taken a little rest, felt good enough to drive the rest of the way home where he went to bed while Monika and Norbert retired to the living room for some sex on the sofa.

'It must have been that damn soup,' said Karl-Wilhelm irritably.

He was, however, a man with a strong constitution and by Monday morning he was feeling completely fit and set off for work cheerfully. Although business had been slow in some branches of German industry, the aluminium factory at Borgholzhausen was running at full stretch and there was plenty of overtime which was what Karl-Wilhelm liked.

Monika continued to spend most of her days in bed with Norbert, occasionally inviting in a few friends for the sake of variety. Norbert was, if anything, more vigorous than ever. He was now approaching his fifteenth birthday and it was difficult to imagine what he would be like once he had reached full maturity and the height of his powers.

As for Monika, she had been running at full steam, so to speak, ever since the birth of her youngest child. Before that she had been somewhat more conservative, although no stranger to partner exchange and group sex, activities which she had taken up even before marrying Karl-Wilhelm at the age of sixteen. Like him, she came from what is usually termed 'underprivileged' surroundings.

Following the incidents with the exploding car and the unpalatable soup, the remainder of January, all of February and the first two weeks of March passed without incident, Karl-Wilhelm spending most of his time in the factory and Monika spending most of her time lying down.

Norbert, although not strictly speaking a member of the

family, also spent nearly all his time in the Lange home, serving as a combination substitute husband and son to the vivacious, young wife and mother and providing the healthy physical exercise so essential during the long months of the North German winter.

Actually, there was not much else for Monika to do. She did not like housework, detested winter sports and, with the exception of Norbert, had no hobbies. The television programmes were hardly worth turning on the set for. It was a quiet time.

And then, on the late evening of March 15, misfortune struck once again for the Lange family and, as had so often been the case in the past, its target was the unfortunate Karl-Wilhelm.

It was shortly after eleven o'clock and Karl-Wilhelm was soundly sleeping, if not the sleep of the just, the sleep of the exhausted. He had just completed a week of ten- and twelve-hour days, it was now Friday and there was still one more ten-hour day to be worked before his day off on Sunday. He had come home late and had gone straight to bed the moment he finished cooking and eating his dinner. Neither Monika nor Norbert had been present when he arrived from work and he was too tired to give much thought to where they might be. Had he thought of it, he would no doubt have come to the conclusion that they were visiting friends or had perhaps gone to the movies.

He had not, however, been capable of thinking of anything except getting into bed and now he lay sleeping as if he would never wake up again.

As it turned out, he nearly did not.

At some time after eleven o'clock Karl-Wilhelm was abruptly roused from his sleep by agonizing pains in his head and neck. Struggling upright in the bed in the total darkness of the bedroom, he could feel something hot and warm running down the side of his face and into the collar of his pyjamas. His head was reeling and, as he raised a hand to his temple, he was astounded to feel something hard, cold and metallic sticking out of the right side of his neck just below his ear!

'Help!' roared Karl-Wilhelm, bounding out of the bed and charging through the house in the direction of the front door. 'Burglars! I've been stabbed!'

He had guessed very accurately that the thing sticking out of the side of his neck was the handle of a knife, but he was still not aware that there was also a six-inch gash in his scalp, which was laid open to the bone.

Monika and Norbert, returning from the movies, were horror-struck to find him reeling in the snow in front of the house and spattering blood in every direction. In the glow of the street lamps it looked black rather than red.

While Norbert helped him back into the house and got him lying down on the living-room sofa, Monika rushed to the telephone and called the emergency ambulance.

'Quick! Quick!' she shrieked into the instrument. 'My husband has been killed by burglars!'

Had this been an accurate statement, there would, of course, have been no point in the ambulance coming at all, but, as a matter of fact, Karl-Wilhelm Lange proved to be a difficult man to kill. Taken to hospital, he was relieved of the knife rammed completely through his neck, his scalp was sewn up and he was put to bed, where he promptly resumed his interrupted sleep, his last thought as he closed his eyes being that he would probably lose a day's work but that he might be able to take it as sick leave.

The following morning he received another visit from Detective-Sergeant Distel.

'You appear to be remarkably accident-prone,' said the sergeant. He sounded a little reproachful. 'Do you know any Indians?'

'There was an Indian advertising trips to the United States at the supermarket about two years ago,' said Karl-Wilhelm, 'but I didn't get to meet him personally.'

'That's the wrong kind of Indian,' said the sergeant. 'I mean an Indian from India.'

'I've only seen them on the television,' said Karl-Wilhelm doubtfully. 'I don't think there are many living here in Bielefeld. Why should I know Indians?'

'Because the knife somebody stuck in your neck is an Indian knife,' said the sergeant, holding it out. 'It's called a Kukri. Have you ever seen it before?'

Karl-Wilhelm looked curiously at the knife. It was crooked and had a thick, but very sharp blade which at the tip was sharpened on both edges.

'Never saw anything like it,' he said. 'I can't imagine why anyone would come all the way from India . . . ?'

'It was not necessarily an Indian who attacked you, Mr Lange,' said the sergeant. 'Now, I asked you this the last time. Is there anyone who could conceivably want you dead?'

Karl-Wilhelm thought hard. 'No,' he said, shaking his head. 'There just isn't anybody.'

'Well, so far, somebody has blown up your car with you in it, has stuck a knife in your neck and has hit you over the head with a hatchet,' said the sergeant. 'If it's the same person, he or she must, at the very least, have a strong dislike for you. Has there been anything else of this nature that I don't know about?'

'Was I hit over the head with a hatchet?' said Karl-Wilhelm, putting up a hand to feel his bandaged head.

The sergeant nodded. 'With the sharp edge, according to the doctor,' he said. 'And the hatchet was lying beside your bed. Your wife says it's yours. Was there anything else?'

Karl-Wilhelm thought some more. 'Well,' he said finally, 'there was the soup.' He explained about the strange-tasting goulash soup and his attack of indigestion after eating it. 'Didn't affect Monika and Norbert though,' he observed. 'I expect something must have fallen into mine accidentally.'

Sergeant Distel made no comment on this remark, but went back to police headquarters where he reported the results of the interview to his superior, Inspector Julius Wagner, a short, mournful-looking man with a fringe of mixed grey and black hair all the way around the perfectly bald top of his head.

'I think his wife is trying to kill him,' said the sergeant after he had concluded his report, 'but I don't know why. He doesn't have enough life insurance to make it worthwhile and nothing they own is paid for yet. Without Lange, Mrs Lange would have to go out and find a job and I doubt that she would appreciate that.'

'Maybe she has a lover,' suggested the inspector. 'You should investigate the background of the family. We don't simply want to sit here and wait until she or somebody else kills Lange. All these attempts you've been telling me about were potentially fatal. It's merely a combination of luck and a strong constitution that's allowed him to escape so far.'

'I have investigated the family background,' said the sergeant. 'Or rather, I had Walter do it. He's made up a report on what he found out which you can read if you like. It's a bucket of worms. A very modern marriage. Sex with anybody and everybody.'

'Well then, the woman probably became emotionally involved with one of her lovers,' said the inspector. 'All these liberal, progressive marriages, the people think they won't get emotionally involved, but they do.'

'I don't know if you'd call it emotionally involved,' said the sergeant, 'but her favourite now and for the past year has been a fourteen-year-old, mentally deficient boy with no money and no way of supporting her even if she was free from her husband and even if it were possible for her to marry a boy of that age.'

70

The inspector looked startled, shocked and finally faintly disgusted.

'You're sure of your facts?' he asked. 'The woman could be prosecuted for contributing to the delinquency of a minor.'

'I'm sure,' said the sergeant. 'There's no attempt made to conceal the relationship. The people are proud of being modern. Do you want to file charges on the delinquency bit?'

The inspector gave him a sardonic look. 'Hardly,' he said.

'You know about how far we'd get with a morals case the way the courts are nowadays. Anyway, that's not our department. All we're interested in is that nobody kills Lange or, if they do, that they're brought to justice. Leave me whatever paper and tape you've got on it so far and I'll see if I can think of anything we can do. You think it's the woman?'

The inspector, who like many police officers had a great deal more work than time, took the reports and tapes home with him and went through them that evening. When he had finished, he knew nearly everything that there was to know about the Lange family. The sergeant and the men under him were very thorough in their work and they left out nothing.

Karl-Wilhelm and Monika Lange had married on March 30, 1965. The bride had been sixteen years old and seven months pregnant. This was not very exceptional. Even as early as 1965 the combination wedding gown – maternity dress was not uncommon in Germany.

The Langes had, moreover, begun their marriage under the worst possible circumstances. Both came from large, under-privileged families in small villages outside Bielefeld and, although Karl-Wilhelm had turned out to be a hard and conscientious worker, there had been continual interference and meddling by both families.

This had apparently proved so irritating to both Karl-Wilhelm and his wife that in June of 1972 they had emigrated to communist East Germany.

They did not stay long. Although Karl-Wilhelm was a worker and the communist countries are the workers' acknowledged paradise, communists are also very old-fashioned and stuffy in their attitudes on sex. Partner swapping is frowned upon and group sex is regarded with horror. On December 6, 1972, the Lange family was deported by East Germany back to West Germany. No reason was given.

Apparently still trying to escape the relatives who, according to the report, spent more time in the Lange household than did

Lange himself and whose morals were, if anything, more avant-garde and liberal than theirs, the Langes fled to Africa on January 22, 1973. There they wandered about rather aimlessly for three weeks, finally wrecking the car and returning to Bielefeld on February 10 by ship and train.

Not long after the return from Africa, the attention of the Juvenile Office was drawn to the condition of the Lange children who were, it seemed, largely dependent upon themselves, their father being mostly in the factory and their mother mostly in bed with Norbert.

As no improvement appeared likely, they were removed from the custody of their parents and placed in a home for abandoned and neglected children. Karl-Wilhelm had been disconsolate about being separated from his children, but had agreed when it was pointed out that the move was in their best interests. They were allowed to come home on holidays and for some weekends when Karl-Wilhelm was there to look after them.

On October 24 of that same year Monika Lange had carried out her unsuccessful suicide attempt, swallowing an undetermined quantity of sleeping pills. Her stomach was pumped out and she was apparently none the worse for the experience. When asked as to her motives for wishing to end her life, she had replied that it was a mess and she thought it better to put an end to it.

'I'm inclined to agree with her,' said the inspector, handing the Lange file back to the sergeant. 'I hope the modern way of life never becomes compulsory. I doubt I have the physical capacity for it.'

'Few do,' said the sergeant. 'Do you also agree with my theory that Mrs Lange is trying to kill Mr Lange?'

'I think my attitude is about the same as yours,' said the inspector. 'I don't see who else would want to, but I can't understand why she wants to. She wouldn't gain anything from it, either financially or any other way. Lange apparently doesn't care who she sleeps with, and he works like a madman to pay for everything while she lies around on her back. According to the juvenile people, she neither cooks nor cleans the house. Lange does it, but he isn't there enough for the Juvenile Office to think it adequate for the children.'

'If it was the other way around, that is, if Lange was trying to kill his wife,' said the sergeant, 'that would make some sense. As it is . . .'

'Exactly,' said the inspector. 'Still, there seems to be little doubt that someone really is trying to kill Lange and they don't seem in the least concerned that the police have been called in. After all, the business with the soup took place only twenty days after the car blew up. To me that would indicate a degree of stupidity seldom found even amongst our least competent criminals. No one but a moron would make a second murder attempt while the first was still being investigated.'

'Norbert Schmidt is more or less certified as not having all of his marbles,' observed the sergeant non-committally.

'So much so that I don't think he has the intelligence to plan such things,' said the inspector. 'However, the important thing is to prevent Lange from being killed, whether by his wife, or Schmidt or anybody else for that matter. In view of the fact that the police being called in doesn't seem to discourage our would-be murderer, we're going to have to move rapidly. I want you to put tails on Mrs Lange and Norbert round the clock. Then, I want you to put a couple of our best men on finding out where Mrs Lange and Norbert were the night Lange was stabbed, where the knife came from and so on. Even though it isn't actually a murder case yet, we're going to treat it like one.'

Both Mrs Lange and Norbert Schmidt had been questioned as to their whereabouts on the night of the attack which had left the sturdy Karl-Wilhelm with his head split open and a knife sticking out of his neck, but still very much alive, and they had replied that they had been to a movie. The film showing was one of the series of so-called 'Schoolgirl Reports,' a semi-pornographic production and one of the more successful box-office hits of the German cinema, which was largely confined to pornography in any case.

'We asked them what happened in the film and they told us,' said the sergeant. 'No doubt about it. They both saw the film. However, whether they saw it on the night they said they did, that's something different. It's been running for a couple of months now.'

'Well, we've had no luck with the knife,' said the inspector. 'It seems to be untraceable and the business with the exploding car and the soup are too far back now for us to hope for much there. I'd say that our whole case, if there is one, hangs on that evening when Lange was stabbed. If we can show that Mrs Lange and Norbert really were at the movies that evening, we can eliminate them as suspects and start looking for somebody else. Right?'

'Right,' said the sergeant. 'We'll concentrate on the night of March the fifteenth until we get something one way or the other.'

The investigation, consequently, settled down to the painstaking, methodical detailed work for which the German police are so justly famous. Teams of interrogators went from house to house not only in the district where the Langes lived, but also to every house along the route between the Lange house and the cinema which Mrs Lange and Norbert were supposed to have attended.

In the end, it turned out that Mrs Lange's face and unusual taste in sex partners were her undoing. She was a woman whom men, and women, noticed and several persons had noticed not only her but also her odd companion who looked too old to be her son, but, by many people's standards even in modern, progressive Germany, too young to be anything else.

Mrs Lange and Norbert had indeed gone to see the 'Schoolgirl Report' and had enjoyed it very much, but they had gone to the afternoon showing and not the evening one. They were, consequently, brought to police headquarters where this was pointed out to them.

Norbert had, as usual, nothing to say, merely nodding his head in happy agreement with everything. Monika Lange, however, sighed and said, yes, it was true, she and Norbert had planned to do away with Karl-Wilhelm. It was she who had personally stabbed him in the neck with the knife after attempting to stun him with a blow from the hatchet. Norbert, less active in this than in some other respects, had contented himself with the passive role of a spectator.

Having confessed to this attempt on her husband's life, Monika Lange went on to admit to the poisoning of his soup in Stuckenbrock and the addition of a bottle of nitro-carbon paint thinner to the petrol in the tank of his car. For good measure, she added that she had poisoned Karl-Wilhelm's food on a number of other occasions, but he had failed to take notice of it and, generally, it had not even upset his stomach.

By the time of the last attempt she had become almost desperate and regarded her husband's continued survival as a challenge. It was, she said, intensely annoying to keep on trying to kill somebody when they didn't even pay any attention to what you were doing.

She had purchased the knife a week earlier at a souvenir shop on the perhaps naïve assumption that the police would think the murderer a foreigner who had left the country and would stop looking, and she had coached Norbert on the time of the movie they had seen until the boy really believed they had gone in the evening rather than the afternoon.

'But why did you want to kill your husband in the first place?' asked the inspector. 'How did you plan to live? Even if you felt that your marriage was a failure, why didn't you simply ask for a divorce?'

'He stood in the way of our love,' said Mrs Lange vaguely. 'Norbert and I . . . you understand . . . ?'

At this point, several of the officers present were overcome with spasms of uncontrollable laughter and hurriedly left the room. If there had ever been a man who had not stood in the way of his wife's love for another man, woman or boy, then it was Karl-Wilhelm Lange.

Nonetheless, this was the only reason that Monika Lange was able to offer and, on February 14, 1975, she was convicted, on the basis of her own confession, of attempted murder and sentenced to four years' imprisonment. Norbert, who was a minor and, in any case, scarcely competent to stand trial, was not charged at all.

Karl-Wilhelm, who had in the meantime received a divorce and who was now able to see a great deal more of his children, pleaded for clemency for his ex-wife from the court. In his opinion, Monika's actions had been motivated by too many reports in the popular press of women who murdered their husbands because they stood in the way of their love for another. Such women often garnered huge amounts of publicity, received offers to appear on television or in the movies and, although in some cases illiterate, became the respected authors of bestselling books.

As for punishment for the crime, that was nearly as old-fashioned and out of style as monogamy. The average time spent in jail would scarcely be enough to finish writing a book.

Monika Lange never expressed herself on this point, either during her trial or after, but if a career as a celebrity was her aim, she failed. Practically all of the publicity in the case went to her indestructible husband and she received no movie offers nor has she yet written a book.

6

IMPOTENT

On the night of Saturday, July 7, 1979, a full moon shone down on Swansea, the Welsh port of 175,000 inhabitants, located where the broad reaches of the Bristol Channel open out into the Atlantic.

It was a romantic moon and in the red Austin 1300 parked in the narrow road, locally known as Lovers' Lane, on the outskirts of the city, there was romance.

The seat of the Austin had been let down into a reclining position and a lovely, thirty-year-old woman lay naked upon it. Lying on top of her was her lover of the same age, a teacher of history at one of Swansea's junior schools. He too was naked.

Experienced lovers, the couple were approaching their mutual climax when there was movement in the darkness outside the car. Although the moon was full, the oaks and beeches bordering the road, which descended on a slope to a small lake, screened the car from its light.

Looking over her lover's shoulder, the woman saw the movement, but before she had time to react in any way, red fire flashed out of the darkness followed by the deafening sound of heavy-calibre pistol shots fired at close range through the open window of the car.

A terrible blow seemed to smash her left shoulder and between her thighs the body of her lover went abruptly rigid and then terrifyingly limp, his low sighs of pleasure cut off as sharply as with a knife.

Frightened and horrified beyond hysteria, the woman struggled to disengage the upper part of her body from the corpse of her lover, jerked loose the handbrake and pushed the gear lever into neutral. Her mind, hyperstimulated by fear, had instantly grasped at the knowledge that the car was parked on a slope and if it could be set in motion, it might roll away from the gunman outside.

It worked! The car gave a lurch and began to roll rapidly down the steep road. Inside it, the woman fought wildly to control the direction, but she could not see and she could not free herself of the body of her lover who was lodged between her thighs, his dead weight pinning down the lower part of her body. A hundred yards down the road, the car swerved off into the shallow ditch, tilted over on its side and came to a stop.

The impact had separated her from the corpse and she pushed open the door and scrambled out. She was naked and her shoulder was bleeding badly, the warm blood running down over her breasts and belly, but she was still alive and she was going to run for it.

She ran, cursing the moon which made her pale, naked body glow like a fire in the darkness. She could hear the sounds of feet coming down the road and she marvelled that the killer had not already seen her and opened fire.

There was too much undergrowth in the forest for running and she dared not force her way through it for fear of making sounds that would betray her to her pursuer. Worse, the blood streaming from her shoulder seemed to be draining her strength and she was afraid that she might faint. The only chance was to find somewhere to hide and she picked the first clump of dense bushes that she came to and plunged into it, worming her way in as far as she could go.

She was not lucky. It was a thorn bush and the sharp points stabbed into her naked body from every side, but there was no possibility of changing bushes now. There were, it seemed, two men close behind her and she could hear them talking, the one demanding in a querulous voice where the bitch had gone and the other growling that she had to be found and finished off.

As they passed the bushes, a ray from the moon shining through an opening in the leaves above lit briefly the face of one of the men. It was a hard face, ruthless and determined, and it was disfigured by a hideous scar running from eye to jaw-bone across the right cheek. To her astonishment, it was a face that she had never seen before.

Lying as silent and motionless as a wounded doe in the thicket, the words in her mind kept repeating themselves like a stuck phonograph record. Why did he do it? Why did he do it?

A little distance off, the killers coursed back and forth through the forest like hunting dogs searching for their quarry. They called each other 'Eddie' and 'Alfie' and they seemed determined to finish what they had begun at the car, but they did not have the noses of hunting dogs and the quarry remained undetected.

After what seemed like centuries, they gave up and one of them

77

voiced the opinion that she had been fatally wounded at the car and had probably dragged herself off some place to die.

From their remarks, it was obvious that they believed her companion to be dead and she did not doubt it.

Even after they had gone, she waited for a long time before coming out, partly because she was afraid that they had not really gone and that it was only a trick and partly because she had to gather her strength. It was a walk of nearly half a mile to the nearest farm and she did not think it likely that she would encounter any cars along the way.

As a matter of fact, she did encounter a car, but she was suddenly struck by the terrifying thought that the killers might be in it and she threw herself into the ditch and hid until it had passed.

Eventually, she reached the farmhouse and beat feebly on the door with her fists.

The farmer's wife who opened it was so startled to see a naked woman covered with blood and dirt and crying hysterically on her doorstep that she nearly shut the door in her face.

Even after she had been let in, she could not speak coherently and the farmer and his wife had no idea of what was wrong with her. She was, however, obviously badly injured and because of her unclothed condition, they thought she had probably been attacked by a sex criminal. While the wife laid her down on the sofa, covered her with a blanket and attempted to comfort her, the farmer called an ambulance and the Swansea police.

Not much later, the woman was on her way to hospital and the first police cars were beginning to arrive at the area. Although she had not said so, or anything else coherent, it was assumed that considering the circumstances, whatever had happened, it had probably been in the nearby Lovers' Lane.

The ambulance had not yet reached the hospital when the first patrol car came upon the red Austin tipped on its side in the ditch.

The man was still inside it but, as the patrolmen were unable to find any signs of respiration or heartbeat, they left him there and called for an ambulance, a doctor and someone from the Department of Criminal Investigations over the radio-telephone. There was a good deal of blood inside the car and the corpse had what they thought was a bullet wound in the head.

As a matter of fact, the ambulance which had picked up the woman had called ahead to the hospital to report that she had what looked like a bullet wound in the shoulder, and this information had been passed on to police headquarters. As a result, members of the Swansea Department of Criminal Investigations had been alerted and were already preparing to leave for the scene.

One of the first to arrive was a detective inspector, a senior investigations officer who immediately took charge of the operation although, so far, he did not know what the operation was. The fact that the victims had been partially or wholly undressed at the time and the location where the attack had taken place all pointed to a Lovers' Lane bandit type of crime; the car lying on its side in the ditch might also mean that there had been a freak accident of some kind.

Although the man was unquestionably dead, the duty medical expert from the Coroner's Office had not yet arrived and there was no certainty as to whether the wound in the head had been caused by a bullet or by striking some hard object inside the car.

The inspector, consequently, had no choice but to wait for the doctor's arrival and, in the meantime, he sent his assistant, a detective-sergeant who had arrived only shortly after himself, to telephone the hospital in Swansea to find out whether the doctors could give an opinion as to the nature of the woman's wound. If it had been caused by a bullet, then the man had probably been shot as well.

While the sergeant was busy doing this, the inspector, a very broad, stocky man of slightly less than medium height, had one of the patrolmen present shine a flashlight into the Austin while he attempted to locate the ownership papers of the car.

He was not successful in this but he did recover a man's wallet from the pocket of a jacket lying, together with other items of male and female clothing, on the floor of the back seat. A driver's licence and other personal papers were inside and served to establish, at least tentatively, the identity of the victim.

The doctor now arrived and so did a half-dozen police detection specialists. They immediately began going over the car, photographing the corpse and the entire vehicle from every angle, and, as soon as they had finished, the body was brought out and laid on a plastic sheet.

The doctor, a comparatively young man with an open, pleasant face and sandy brown hair, made a brief but careful examination. The victim, he said, had died within the past two hours of a heavy-calibre bullet fired into the back of his head. He had, apparently, been engaged in sexual intercourse and had ejaculated at the moment of death or very shortly before.

The result of this medical examination was little different from what the inspector had anticipated, as the sergeant had already returned to say that the hospital reported the woman to be suffering from a painful but not dangerous bullet wound in the shoulder and a great many scratches from the thorn bush. The bullet had been extracted, the patient was resting comfortably and her husband had been notified.

The inspector, who had not expected that the couple in the red Austin would prove to be man and wife, observed that the notification of her husband was hardly necessary as it was very probably he who had fired the bullets.

This was a logical assumption and the sergeant, a blond, round-faced man who wore horn-rimmed spectacles, was sent racing off with a team of detectives to take the woman's husband into custody before he could make his escape.

To their surprise, he had made no attempt to escape, but had, instead, rushed to the hospital immediately upon being informed that his wife was there, and it was at the hospital, pacing up and down in the corridor outside her room, that the sergeant found him.

The thirty-four-year-old man appeared to be more astounded than they when informed that he was being charged with the murder of his wife's lover and the wounding of his wife, but offered no resistance to arrest. He requested, however, permission to return home and make some arrangements for his children to be looked after in his absence.

Accompanied by the sergeant to a neat cottage in the nearby town of Llanelli, he telephoned his mother who agreed to stay at the house until either he or his wife returned. The three children, a boy, nine, a girl, seven, and another boy, five, were all sound asleep and were unaware that anything had taken place.

Following the arrival of their grandmother, their father was taken to police headquarters, formally charged with the shootings and placed in the detention cells. He vigorously denied all knowledge of the crimes and insisted that he had had no motive for them.

This struck the inspector as a strangely naïve statement. The man had had one of the most common motives for homicide anywhere in the world. His wife had had a lover and he had shot both of them.

Although it was not possible to question the woman immediately, the investigations soon showed that she had been having an affair with the history teacher for over a year at least.

The young wife, the inspector thought, had probably been

80

impressed by the handsome bachelor's position as a teacher. Her husband was only a docker working at the port and he had not had the educational advantages of his rival nor was he as handsome.

The couple had married on May 5, 1970, and, although it had probably not always been easy to support a family of three children on a docker's wages, they appeared to have been happy.

At least, until the history teacher came along.

How they had arranged matters that the husband had not become suspicious before, the inspector could not imagine. Lovers' Lane was in rather heavy use and a number of witnesses were found who reported having seen the red Austin belonging to the school teacher parked there every Friday night for the past year or more, and invariably with the same couple in it. The lovers had been, it seemed, persons of very regular habits.

In the meantime, the chief suspect was being interrogated and not responding in a manner at all satisfactory to the police.

He still insisted that he was innocent of the crimes and said that he had not left the house on that evening until he had received the telephone call from the hospital to say that his wife was there. He did not, he added, own a gun, nor even know how to fire one.

To the inspector's dismay, this appeared to be true. Obtaining a pistol in Britain is not an easy matter and there was no evidence that the man had ever owned one legally, nor was there any evidence that such a heavy-calibre illegal weapon had changed hands in the area within the past few months.

There was, moreover, confirmation of his statements. Questioning of the neighbours in Llanelli produced testimony from no less than three persons who had seen Griffiths moving about inside his living room at almost exactly the same moment that the shootings had taken place miles away.

The police were, therefore, forced to admit that the docker could not possibly have fired the shots that had wounded his wife and killed her lover. This did not, however, mean that he was innocent.

No one else had had a motive. The teacher had not had a jealous girlfriend. Indeed, apart from the docker's wife, he had had no girlfriend at all. The wife had not had a second lover. As a busy housewife and mother of three young children she had scarcely left the house at all, with the exception of Friday nights.

This striking regularity in marital infidelity seemed to the inspector so unusual that he suspected it might offer a clue to the motive for the murder, although he did not, at the moment, know what that was. The lovers had gone to Lovers' Lane on Friday evenings with almost military consistency, but on this single occasion when they had gone on a Saturday, the shootings had taken place. The inspector thought that this must have significance and that, if he could understand what it was, it would clear up the still unexplained aspects of the case.

The ideal solution, of course, would be identification of the man, presumably hired by the husband, who had actually pulled the trigger. No one realized at this time that there had been two men and two guns, for it had been assumed that both victims had been shot with the same weapon, and the bullet extracted from the woman's shoulder and the one recovered during the course of the autopsy from the man's head had not been subjected to ballistic comparison. Had they been, it would have become apparent that they had not been fired from the same weapon.

Nevertheless, the inspector felt confident that once he had been able to take a statement from the surviving victim, all would be revealed and, as soon as she had been pronounced physically and psychologically fit for questioning by her doctors, he came personally to the hospital to carry out the interrogation.

In some respects the interview was a success. The woman had had a clear glimpse of one of the killers' faces and she could describe him exactly. The information that there had been two men and that they had fired without any attempt at robbery or other preamble was also valuable.

In another respect, however, it was highly confusing.

Her husband, said the woman, had known where she was and what she was doing on that evening and he had been the only person in the world who did.

This was tantamount to saying that no one else could have told the killers where to find them, and the inspector demanded and, after a certain amount of embarrassed hesitation, received an explanation.

Beginning at the beginning, the woman said that her marriage had been a love match, made when she was only twenty years old, and over the years their love for each other and for their three children had never ceased to increase. They were like two parts of a single person. Neither could nor wanted to live without the other.

The inspector, conscious of the fact that she had been shot on her husband's orders while having sexual intercourse with her lover, raised his eyebrows but said nothing.

The woman, apparently divining what was passing through his

mind, turned an attractive pink, but insisted that what she said was true. It was for this reason that she found it so hard to believe that her husband had had anything to do with the shootings. After all, she said, he knew her lover well, liked him very much and, if they had been in the car having relations that night, it was more her husband's fault than hers. She had not wanted to in the first place and, if it had not been for his relatives, they would have gone on Friday night as usual and not on Saturday.

The inspector's eyebrows practically disappeared over the top of his head. The case was obviously far more complex than he had suspected.

Indeed it was and it was some little time before the entire matter had been explained and the inspector had all of the astounding details. When he did, however, he was overcome with a feeling of profound sadness, for he realized that he was in the presence of tragedy and of a love which surpassed by far the normal bonds between man and wife.

Briefly, the docker and his family had, indeed, been supremely happy. They had not been rich, but the man had worked hard and, with overtime, they had managed to buy, pay for and furnish their snug little cottage. They had had three fine, healthy children, all of whom were turning out well, and the years of their marriage had only served to bring them more closely together. It had been a marriage that any could envy and that many had.

And then, on January 4, 1977, disaster had struck. A telephone call had come from the waterfront. There had been an accident. The cable of a crane lifting a cargo net filled with heavy crates had snapped. The husband had been one of the dockers standing beneath it. He had been crushed. He had been rushed to hospital. The foreman who made the call did not know whether he was alive or dead.

In fact he had been alive, but his back had been broken and for six months he lay in a rigid cast. The doctors were not certain that he would ever walk again.

But he did and, when he left the hospital, it was under his own power and with help from no one. Eventually, he was even able to return to his job.

The doctors proclaimed it a miracle. An extremely serious back injury had healed without any trace of ill effects.

Except one. Unfortunately, said the doctor, certain nerves in the lower part of the body had been irrevocably destroyed. The patient was healthy and normal in every respect but he had no more sensation in his genitals than in his toe-nails. He was totally and permanently impotent.

This had apparently troubled him a great deal more than it did his wife. She had pointed out that they had already had their children and that conventional intercourse was not the only manner of achieving sexual satisfaction, if she felt herself in need of it.

The husband, however, was not convinced. He believed that he was no longer a complete man and he was terrified that his wife would eventually become involved with someone who was sexually normal and leave him. He was prepared to do anything to keep her and, in his desperation, he came up with a strange and unorthodox solution to the problem.

His wife, he said, should take a lover, not a lover for love and romance or even anyone she particularly liked but merely someone who appealed to her sexually and could satisfy her needs.

His mildly alarmed but bemused spouse had not been very enthusiastic about this idea. She was a respectable wife and mother and she could not see herself sneaking into cheap hotels, with someone she pictured to herself as looking like an Italian waiter, for a little illicit and probably depraved sex. She was not, however, greatly concerned, as she felt it extremely unlikely that a suitable candidate would present himself for the post.

And then, within less than three months from the time her husband had come up with his bizarre scheme, her eldest son brought home his history teacher from school. He was new in the town, knew no one and the boy had asked if he could invite him to dinner.

The husband had taken one look at the man and had announced that he was exactly what they were looking for. He was the right age. He was a bachelor. He was a stranger in town so there would be no gossip. He was not the type to appeal to his wife from the point of view of personality, being bookish, polished, intellectual and slightly effeminate. He was a little too handsome.

But sexually! That was something different. The husband was convinced that his wife would find him an utter delight in bed and, in the end, she was forced to agree that there was something about him that a woman might not find totally repulsive, although entirely on a physical plane of course. The difference in educational levels and general outlook precluded anything else.

This was precisely the husband's opinion and precisely what he wanted to hear. The only question that remained, he said, was to determine whether the fellow liked girls. If it turned out that he was more attracted to his own sex, well . . .

The history teacher was asked to dinner again. And again. And again. After a time, he became such a friend of the family that he sometimes drove the wife to do her shopping. One day the drive took them along a deserted country road and the wife, having suggested that they park for a moment, more or less fell upon him.

He did like girls.

There is no way of knowing what the history teacher's feelings were when the attractive young housewife who had just deceived her husband with him announced that they must now hurry home and tell him all about it, but they probably included a certain amount of terror. The docker was a very large and very muscular person, although of a mild and gentle character as are so many large, strong men.

On arrival, however, his feelings must have been even more extreme when the husband expressed great satisfaction and produced a written contract which he had drawn up in advance.

It was a simple document and not very long. In it the first party agreed to engage in sexual relations with the second party once weekly on Friday evenings and to remain totally faithful to her husband otherwise. She contracted not to leave her family or to permit herself to become emotionally involved with this partner or any other man.

The second party was bound to provide adequate sexual services once weekly on Friday evenings and to make no sexual approaches at any other time during the week nor to attempt to persuade the first party to leave her husband and family.

As for the husband, he agreed to permit the regular sexual contacts between the parties named in the contract.

The encounters were to take place in the teacher's car in a suitably discreet place and manner, this place being common knowledge to all three parties concerned.

The three parties had signed the contract and, according to the first party, it was still in a tin box in the bedroom where all of the family's more important papers were kept.

The inspector immediately telephoned the sergeant telling him to go to the cottage in Llanelli to look for the contract and then returned to ask why, if the contract specified Friday nights only, she and the second party had been in Lovers' Lane on a Saturday night? Was it not true that they had become, after all, emotionally involved? And was it not true that her husband had suspected this and had decided to deal with the violation of the terms of the contract in his own manner?

The woman wept, saying that she could not believe that her husband would have done anything to harm her. In any case, it was not true. She could not speak for the teacher but she still loved her husband and she had no intention of leaving him for anyone else.

Asked, however, who else could possibly have known that she was in Lovers' Lane on that Saturday night, she was forced to admit that no one had known except her husband.

Had it been a Friday night, a number of persons might have known, for there were witnesses who had seen the history teacher's red Austin parked there on Fridays, but this particular week had been the sole exception. The docker and his wife had been invited out on Friday evening for dinner with relatives and the regular Friday night rendezvous had had to be postponed by one day.

This irrefutable evidence was fatal to the accused. The contract had been found in the tin box as the wife had said and it verified her statements in every detail. The husband himself was forced to admit that no one else could have known where the sexual encounter was taking place that evening, but he still denied having hired the killers. He had not, he said, believed that there was any emotional attachment nor had he thought that his wife was planning to leave him.

This was, however, an unsupported statement and, as there was a great deal of material evidence implicating him in the crimes, he was formally indicted on charges of premeditated homicide and inciting to homicide and ordered to be held for trial.

He was still sitting in the detention cells when, on December 23, 1979, two days before Christmas, a very nervous little man with a receding, unshaven chin and one glass eye made contact with a detective sergeant in the city of Glasgow, far to the north of Swansea. The little man was a police informer and he said that he had something to report.

As he had reported a good deal in the past and much of it had proved to be accurate, his statements were taken seriously. There were, he said, two brothers in Glasgow who were claiming they had killed a man and wounded a woman somewhere in the west of England earlier that year. He gave their names. One was thirty-four-year-old Edward Hodkins, generally known as Eddie. The other was twenty-six-year-old Alfred Hodkins, otherwise known as Scarface because of a scar across his right cheek.

Neither name was unknown to the police. The Hodkins brothers were hardened, professional criminals who specialized in armed robbery, but did not consider themselves too good for simple theft.

As the informer also mentioned where the brothers could be located, they were quickly taken into custody and found to be carrying .45 calibre automatic pistols on them. However, as the police had been aware of the sort of men with whom they were dealing, they did not have the opportunity to make use of them.

Being professionals, neither of the Hodkins brothers admitted to anything, but their guns were test-fired by the Ballistics Department and the results distributed throughout Britain and particularly in the west. At the same time, a circular was sent to all police units citing the statement of the informer that the guns had been used in the murder and wounding of a man and woman in the west country.

Swansea is, of course, in the west and the inspector there, immediately noting the possible connection to his own case, ordered a comparison of the ballistics tests taken in Glasgow with the bullets extracted from the bodies of the Lovers' Lane victims.

The results were positive. It was the Hodkins brothers who had fired the shots on that Saturday night in July in Lovers' Lane outside Swansea. The inspector had found his hired killers.

Only they were not hired killers. Brought to Swansea and confronted with the results of the ballistics tests, the Hodkins confessed to the shootings but said that they had never laid eyes on the impotent docker in their lives. They had not even known the identity of the two persons they had shot.

It had been a simple error, they said. They had been planning a hold-up and needed a getaway car. As the people who parked in Lovers' Lane usually got out of the cars in the summertime to go and have intercourse in the woods, they thought this would be a good place to steal one.

They had not even realized that there was anyone in the Austin until they were standing directly outside the wound-down windows, and they had been so startled that they had fired instinctively without thinking. They were sorry that they had shot the couple. It had been unintentional.

It probably had been, but that did not influence the jury and on June 5, 1981, the Hodkins brothers were sentenced to twenty years' imprisonment each.

The docker was released and rejoined his family on Christmas Eve.

It was a happy Christmas.

7

IMITATION

It was the last week of October of the year 1979 and the end-of-season nostalgia which invades the Côte d'Azur once the hordes of summer visitors have departed hung invisible but present over the waterfront of the city of Cannes. The sun still shone bright and yellow in the flawless blue of the Mediterranean sky and the little waves still lapped gaily at the white sand of the beach stretching for nearly a mile, with the famous esplanade – the Boulevard de la Croisette – running parallel from the Pointe de la Croisette to the port; but it was over. The season was finished.

The man walking down the Croisette that afternoon was like the city. Although he was trim and lean and his step was firm, he was seventy-seven years old and for him too, it was over. His life was finished.

He had known this for some time now, ever since Marie-Ange had been taken away to the hospital. As long as they had been a couple, it had been possible to ignore the passage of time. There had been other things to think about and, whatever others might find lacking in retirement, he had found it good.

Of course, there had been no problem with money. Not that he was rich, but he had worked all his life in the big car-manufacturing plant outside Paris and his pension was quite adequate for their needs. When it was time, they had sold the apartment in Paris and moved to Cannes where the sun shone and there was a lot that was interesting to see and do. They had had no children and they could do what they liked. They had been happy.

Until something had begun to go wrong with Marie-Ange's mind. She was two years younger than her husband, but the doctor said it was senility.

Whatever it was, it destroyed her quickly, even if not entirely. She was still alive, but she could not take care of herself and it had eventually been necessary to put her into a hospital which handled such cases.

Financially, it had not been a burden (the state medical

insurance had taken care of the bulk of the cost), but Oliver and Marie-Ange Tuaillon had been married for just over fifty years. They had been very close. Oliver was still strong, healthy and vigorous physically, but, from the moment that Marie-Ange entered the hospital never to come home again, he was in mind and spirit a corpse.

The doctor had said that she could not be expected to last out the year and Oliver did not expect to either. As it turned out, he would not, but his passing would be a little less peaceful than he or anyone else could have anticipated.

Oliver Tuaillon, whose life had passed so uneventfully up until this moment, was going to live that last, golden summer passionately, recklessly, dangerously, and this was his last day, Thursday, October 25, 1979.

There had been nothing suicidal in this careless exposure to risk. The adventure had begun already in April and Marie-Ange had not died until August 19. Up to that time he had been pretending to himself that she would recover and come home, although the doctor had told him quite plainly that she would not.

The affair had, therefore, nothing to do with the death of Marie-Ange. He was not deliberately going to join her and it was an idea that probably would not have occurred to him. He was not Romeo. He was a retired foreman from a car factory.

No, the whole thing had begun quite casually and accidentally on that April 4, when the weather had already turned warm and sunny but the tourists had not yet arrived to clog the streets and crowd the bars and cafés.

It was the best time of year for a local resident to take a turn down the Croisette and Oliver Tuaillon had done just that.

It was what they would have done had Marie-Ange not been in the hospital, but she was and, undoubtedly for that reason, Oliver did not enjoy the walk. Half-way down the Croisette, he came to a halt in front of a bar and, after a moment's hesitation, went in and ordered a small glass of white wine, a 'petit blanc'.

Being a Frenchman and having spent most of his life in Paris, Oliver was no stranger to bars and cafés, but this one struck him as decidedly unusual.

Or rather, it was not the bar that was unusual, but the customers. They were all young. They were all female. And, to Oliver's not very discerning eye, they were all beautiful!

They were all also very modishly dressed in a cheap sort of way and made up to a point just short of grotesque. After a little reflection, he came to the conclusion that they must all be prostitutes. The café was their business headquarters or, perhaps, their union hall. Having worked all his life in the car industry, he assumed that they were unionized.

It was an understandable error. Among foreigners, the French bear a reputation of being extremely sexy and even a little debauched. In reality, they are moral and conservative to an astonishing degree. In the declining years of the century and, perhaps, of western civilization, a majority of the French still enter marriage with no previous experience on the part of either husband or wife.

Oliver and Marie-Ange had married over fifty years earlier and both had been virgins. Sex instruction was confined to some rather nervous conversations with the appropriate parent. Nonetheless, they had managed very well, so well, in fact, that Oliver had never felt the urge to engage in the casual sexual encounters deemed so necessary by enlightened persons today. He had never been with a prostitute or, for that matter, any woman other than Marie-Ange.

Oliver Tuaillon, therefore, knew nothing about sex other than what he and Marie-Ange had experienced so pleasantly together and sexual thoughts were probably not uppermost in his mind when first one and then another and finally the whole group of lovely, young girls came to seat themsevles uninvited at his table. He was so lonely that he would not have minded if they had been street-cleaners. That his new friends were beautiful young girls was merely an added, if inexplicable, attraction.

There may be men of seventy-seven who consider themselves sexually attractive to young girls, but Oliver Tuaillon was not one of them. What he undoubtedly thought was that the young ladies were hoping to stick him for the drinks.

But, in this, he was mistaken. The young ladies were more than half drunk and extremely jolly. They giggled. They told jokes which Oliver Tuaillon could not follow. And they bought not only their own drinks, but his as well.

They were also remarkably informal and presently Oliver noticed that one of the most beautiful, a tall, striking blonde named Sylvie, was making unmistakable sexual overtures to him.

This did not surprise him so very much. The girl was, after all, in the business. It was, however, a little flattering to be propositioned at his age, even if it was commercial.

Old, tired, mourning Marie-Ange and, perhaps, a little drunk, Oliver had let matters take their course and had eventually ended up startled, a little dismayed and more than a little exhilarated to find himself alone in his apartment with the ravishing Sylvie, who had stripped to the waist and was urging him to toy with her breasts.

Oliver had done so, expressing at the same time his fear that that was about the extent of his capabilities, but Sylvie had said, 'Nonsense!', she knew tricks that would make his hair stand on end and, indeed, she did, although it was more than his hair which stood.

When it was all over, Oliver felt gratified in more ways than one. Sexual contact is the most intimate of all human contacts and he was in great need of human contact. He was pleased and surprised that he had been capable of it at all. And he was grateful to Sylvie who, it seemed to him, had shown great delicacy in the matter and had not even undressed other than to bare her breasts.

He therefore hastened to reward her generously for her expert services and was amazed and a little alarmed when she gave back part of his money, but asked if she might stay the night. She was, she said, momentarily out of a room and, as she could not afford a hotel, she would otherwise have to sleep in the park.

There was, of course, no question of that, but, at this point, Oliver must have realized that he was entering into a situation of high risk.

It was not so much that Sylvie was a prostitute, but that she was young. In France, the most deadly enemy of the old are the young, and rarely a week passes without a newspaper report of some old person or couple murdered following preliminary torture designed to extract information concerning the hiding place of their savings. Many of the French still do not trust banks and keep their savings in cash at home.

Oliver Tuaillon was not one of these. He and Marie-Ange had savings, over a hundred thousand francs in all, but they were deposited in the bank. If he were to be tortured to make him tell where the money was hidden, he would not be able to and he would then, of course, be tortured to death.

As Oliver could and did read the newspapers, he knew all about this and he knew the dangers of letting a young person stay in his apartment. That Sylvie was a girl made no difference. She was not only stronger than he; she was bigger.

Nonetheless, Sylvie moved in and, as might have been expected, showed no inclination to move out. Oliver's three-room apartment was spacious, modern and comfortable. It was probably the best place she had ever lived in her life.

It was also rent-free and even the board was provided. Oliver bought all the groceries and even handed over a reasonable cash allowance. Sylvie had found a home.

So had her friends who came to see her every day bearing wine, sausages and other comestibles and potables. Life was virtually one continuous party. It was a gay time. For Oliver Tuaillon, the great adventure had begun.

Unfortunately, it was not quite all wine and song. Sylvie, it developed, had a temper and, being a physical sort of girl, she was inclined to use her fists when she lost it. She could use them like a man and there was a good deal of weight behind them. Oliver, going out to do his shopping, found that he was attracting amused glances from the shopkeepers with his black eye or swollen nose. Europeans love to gossip and everyone in the neighbourhood knew that a young girl had moved in with the old man, although not much was seen of her.

Most of their disputes were over Sylvie's use of the apartment as a place of business. She would go out, hang around the bars and then bring home a customer, frequently a tourist. Oliver was then required to wait in the kitchen while the guest was entertained, first in the living room and then in the bedroom, assuming that a financial agreement satisfactory to all parties had been reached.

Oliver objected to this not so much because he minded his apartment being turned into a whorehouse, but because he was afraid that the clients might steal something. Actually, they never did, but Sylvie's friends, Yvette, Fifi and Desirée, showed a tendency to carry off everything movable in the apartment. They were usually prevented by Sylvie who wanted to keep the things for herself.

Still, it had not all been bad and Oliver, enjoying the unaccustomed sensation of belonging to a carefree group of attractive young women, sometimes wondered at his good fortune. There were not many men of seventy-seven leading the life that he led.

Unfortunately, he would not be leading it for very long and the walk along the Croisette on the afternoon of October 25 was to be his last. On the following morning, a retired lady in an apartment overlooking Tuaillon's noticed that her neighbour's feet were sticking out off the end of his bed and that he had his shoes on. The feet were quite motionless.

Two hours later, they were still motionless and the lady, who had often amused herself when the offerings of the television were dull by watching the activities of the old man and his merry harem of what she had instantly recognized were prostitutes, came to the conclusion that something was wrong. Not only had the old man been lying very still for a very long time, but there was no sign of his girlfriends in the apartment.

The lady thereupon called the police and, having a rather dramatic turn of mind, reported that her elderly neighbour had been strangled.

Considering that she had seen nothing but his feet, this turned out to be an amazingly accurate report. Oliver Tuaillon had been strangled.

But not to death. Although Dr Jérome Delafoix, the Cannes coroner, at first thought so, the subsequent autopsy showed that the actual cause of death had been a blood clot on the brain.

'Much the same thing,' said the doctor. 'The blood clot was caused by the beating he received or by the strangulation or both. It's murder any way you look at it.'

The coroner had come personally to the office of Inspector Henri Fauchon, chief of the Cannes Department of Criminal Investigations, to discuss the case and ask what the inspector intended to do about it. All of the towns along the French Riviera are highly sensitive to bad publicity and homicide does not associate well with the concept of a carefree holiday resort.

The inspector replied that they were investigating and that they already had a lead. Tuaillon was known to have been living with one or more young prostitutes and it was obviously one of these who had killed him. The motive had undoubtedly been robbery as everything of any value in the apartment had been taken.

'Pretty rough prostitute,' said the coroner doubtfully. 'That was an old man, but he was in good physical condition. He was beaten and strangled to death with bare hands. With that sort of strength, your prostitute could have made more money as a docker.'

'She's not my prostitute,' protested the inspector mildly. 'And anyway, it's known there were several of them. It was probably more than one woman who did it.'

'That wasn't the impression I got from the body,' said the doctor, 'but maybe so. What I can't understand is what he was doing with a whole troupe of prostitutes in the first place.'

'What anyone does with prostitutes, I suppose,' said the inspector. 'His wife had died recently and he didn't know any other girls and he needed relief . . .'

'At seventy-seven?' said the doctor. 'And a whole squad of them? If he'd had the energy for that, they wouldn't have been able to kill him. He'd have been too tough.'

'Well, the fact is he was consorting with a half-dozen or so prostitutes, or so they appear to be according to the descriptions we have so far,' said the inspector patiently, 'and he was murdered.'

'But more probably by the prostitutes' pimp than by the prostitutes themselves,' said the doctor, 'if you ask me.'

'I don't,' said the inspector who was becoming a little weary of the discussion, 'but we're investigating that angle too.'

He was, as a matter of fact, investigating every angle he could think of. Cannes is not a very large city. Although it may have close to a quarter of a million visitors in it during the months of the high season, the local residents number no more than 70,000. It was not often that the Department of Criminal Investigations had a homicide to investigate.

If the Cannes Homicide Squad is small, consisting at this time of no more than a detective sergeant named Jean-Louis Donat, the Vice Squad is enormous. What Cannes lacks in murderers it makes up for in prostitutes, and a close watch has to be kept on them so that they neither skin the tourists out of their money nor provide bad service, either of which might cause the tourist to plan his future vacations elsewhere.

As questioning of the neighbours and trades people in the Avenue des Cèdres, which was where Oliver Tuaillon's apartment was located, had produced numerous amused or indignant reports that the old man had been living with a small crowd of whores, the sergeant was spending most of his time in the Vice Section, where his colleagues were engaged in trying to identify Oliver's companions, a task for which they were better qualified than the understaffed Homicide Squad.

So far, they had established that only one girl had actually been living in the apartment at 12 Avenue des Cèdres and that her name was Sylvie.

'Which probably means that her name is anything but that,' said the head of the Vice Section, no lowly sergeant, but a full inspector in his own right. 'The ladies usually feel that they need a professional name to give their activities a bit of glamour, something like movie actresses.'

'Well then, the information isn't of much use,' said the sergeant. In sharp contrast to Inspector René Brissac, the Vice Squad chief, who was plump, sleekly groomed and jovial, he was tall, thin, a trifle shabby looking and decidedly gloomy.

'Why, of course it is,' said the inspector. 'We have a reasonable description of the girl and we know her professional name is Sylvie. We don't have all that many big blondes working under the name of Sylvie and besides this is the low season. What we have now is local talent.'

The sergeant said nothing. He was wondering how he was going to collect enough evidence to obtain an indictment against this Sylvie, even if the Vice Section did succeed in identifying her. The apartment had been full of fingerprints and the Identification Section was still engaged in mounting them all neatly on cards for future reference, but none of the fingerprints had been recovered from a location which could show direct connection to the murder. All the prints showed was that the person who had left them had been in the apartment at one time or another and that was scarcely grounds for an indictment.

Had the sergeant been a man less devoted to his duty, he might actually have wished that Inspector Brissac and his men did not have too much luck in finding Sylvie, so that he would not be confronted with the problem of what to do with her when she had been found.

The sergeant was, however, a conscientious man and he was not, therefore, dismayed when Inspector Brissac presented him with a list of nineteen Sylvies, all of whom were blonde, but not all of whom were big.

The sergeant, who was reasonably certain of the minimum height of the suspect or, at least, potential suspect, threw out all of the undersized candidates and, having done a great deal of leg-work in the district, came up with two Sylvies who were big, blonde and had been tentatively identified from their pictures, as furnished by the Vice Section, as the girl who had brightened Oliver Tuaillon's declining days. The fact that some of the witnesses said it was one girl and some the other did not matter. They looked, in any case, much alike.

They were not, however, equally good suspects. One of the big blondes had been included accidentally on the list and was believed to be dead. Having become fearfully intoxicated on a hot day in July, she had jumped into the Mediterranean saying that she was going to swim to Africa and had not been seen since. However, as her body had not yet washed ashore, she was officially listed as missing and not dead.

The other possibility, whose name really was Sylvie and whose surname was Poos, was also missing, but apparently only since October 25. As this was the date on which Oliver Tuaillon had been killed, the sergeant felt that he had a solid lead and he pursued it with all the means at his disposal which meant sending out 'wanted' circulars with the girl's name, picture and description to every police force and community along the coast.

This produced not the slightest result which, in a way strengthened the suspicions, as Sylvie Poos was obviously going to some trouble to keep her location a secret. It was believed probable that she had dyed her hair and had taken to wearing sun glasses. As it happened, she was one of the Sylvies who was really blonde.

As a matter of fact, the sergeant had not been so interested in finding Sylvie Poos as in finding her companion and business manager, a loutish looking specimen who went by the name of Ali Boum-boum.

Although the name had a vaguely North African sound to it, Ali Boum-boum's real name was Gérard Lebeau and he came from the city of Lyon. It was said that he had adopted the North African name in order to discredit North Africans, whom he hated, by leading people to believe that a scoundrel such as himself was of North African origin. As far as his police record went, he was not actually such a scoundrel, as he had never been arrested for anything other than procuring.

Despite this innocuous reputation with the police, Ali Boum-boum was the sergeant's prime suspect. Sylvie Poos, his friend and means of livelihood, was also well known to the police and she was universally described as a cream puff, big, blonde, but soft to the verge of sloppiness and beyond. No one who had come into contact with her could imagine her beating and strangling to death anything more resistant than a string of boiled spaghetti.

Ali Boum-boum was, however, according to his own statements, terribly fierce and, although up until now his character had been regarded as more sluggish than fierce, there was always the possibility that he had been carried away by the thought of money and he had certainly had the necessary physical strength.

The amount of money might have been enough to galvanize even his indolent nature. The police now knew that Tuaillon had had over a hundred thousand francs in the bank and there was no telling how much he might have been keeping at home. As Inspector Fauchon remarked, an orthodox Frenchman would never put money into a bank that he could not afford to lose.

The case was, therefore, proceeding nicely except for one thing. No trace of the suspects could be found.

At least, not yet. The inspector, the sergeant and everyone else involved in the case were confident that Sylvie Poos and Ali

Boum-boum would eventually turn up. Both were French born and bred and the French are very attached to France. They do not like to leave it even if the police are on their heels, a fact which saves the French government a great deal of effort in arranging for extraditions. Given enough time, a French fugitive will nearly always return home.

In the meantime, the sergeant continued his investigations locally and learned at least the professional names of two more of Oliver Tuaillon's playmates. One, a redhead, was called Fifi. The other went by the name of Désirée and was a brunette.

In theory these latest discoveries provided enough points of reference for it to be possible to identify positively some one of the half-dozen or so girls who were believed to have frequented Tuaillon's apartment that summer. The girls had all been close friends and the combination of a big blonde, a medium-size redhead and a small brunette, when the professional names were known, should have been easy to sort out from the rank and file.

Curiously, it was not. In fact, it proved to be impossible.

'We have very good sources of information on matters such as that,' said Inspector Brissac, 'and there were no three prostitutes, a redhead, a blonde and a brunette with the trade names of Fifi, Sylvie and Désirée, operating in Cannes this summer. Your information is incorrect, sergeant.'

'Have your own people check it,' said the sergeant.

'I will,' said the inspector and did.

The information was correct. The three girls who had come most to Oliver Tuaillon's apartment had been the big blonde named Sylvie, who actually lived there, and her close friends, the redheaded Fifi and the brunette Désirée.

'But this is ridiculous!' said Inspector Brissac.

'Yes,' said Inspector Fauchon without any emphasis at all.

Sergeant Donat said nothing, but looked smug. He was following another lead which he had not mentioned to anybody and which he thought was not only the most promising but also the most obvious direction which the investigation should have taken from the very beginning.

It had occurred to the sergeant that Oliver Tuaillon would have had to meet his merry band of prostitutes somewhere and that this would almost surely have been the Croisette. In the first place, Tuaillon had lived less than two blocks from the great boulevard and, secondly, ninety per cent of the prostitutes made it their headquarters as there was no better place for business and social contacts.

Now, in France, prostitutes do not hang out in just any bars and cafés. They hang out in certain specific ones which cater to such trade and, like everyone else, they have their preferences.

Oliver Tuaillon, reasoned the sergeant, had wandered into a bar or café patronized by prostitutes who had come to the conclusion that he had money and that he could be separated from it. They had, therefore, struck up an acquaintance with the lonely old man.

All that sergeant had to do was find that bar or café. The girls would be regulars. The bartender or the waiters would know their names and what they looked like and they would know other prostitutes, pimps and even clients who could provide still further information on them. With enough information, they could be run to earth. So far, he had not found the bar or café, but he was sure that he soon would.

Although he was not telling anybody, the sergeant had a private axe to grind. He was hoping that, if he could solve this case, the most puzzling one in the history of the Cannes police, he would be promoted, and a promotion meant a transfer out of Homicide as the slot called for the rank of a sergeant. The sergeant was very anxious to get out of Homicide, as he found the work dull. In the three years he had been chief of the Homicide Squad, there had been exactly two corpses. In the Traffic Section from which he had come, they had often had more than that in a day.

The process, however, took time. There was an immense number of bars and cafés along the Croisette and they had to be checked as quickly as possible because the season was now very much past and many were closing for the winter.

The sergeant, therefore, worked day and night, literally, the night actually being a better time for canvassing bars. As he knew the town well, there were also some that he could skip because they were definitely not places that Sylvie, Fifi and Désirée would have patronized.

For a week, the sergeant walked his feet off without finding the slightest trace of the three girls and then, as he was approaching the depths of despair, he entered late one evening a bar which he had not checked out and which he had no intention of checking out. Rather, he was there because he was looking for a waiter who had until recently worked in another bar and who was supposed to have had a girlfriend named Sylvie.

As he headed down the long, narrow room in the direction of the bar, he passed a booth in which three girls were sitting and one of them called out, 'Hi, big boy! Are you looking for me or for a good time? It could be the same thing.'

'Hi, fellows,' said the sergeant and kept on walking. He was not Oliver Tuaillon and he knew what kind of a bar he was in. The three girls, a blonde, a brunette and a redhead, were no more girls than he was. This was a transvestite bar and the blonde, the brunette and the redhead . . .

The blonde, the brunette, the redhead!

The sergeant stopped so fast that he skidded on his heels, swung around and marched back to the table. 'Hello Sylvie,' he said.

And, of course, it was Sylvie, Fifi and Désirée, whose real names were respectively Jean-Paul Nestour, Pierre Blanc and Jean-Marie Idre. The vice squad had not identified them because they had simply been looking for the wrong sex.

The three persons in question were not too certain about their sex either. Fifi and Désirée described themselves as feminine, but Sylvie said that he or she was bisexual. All had had hormone shots to develop their feminine characteristics, although none had taken the final step of amputation of the male sex organs. All three earned their living as bar girls, prostitutes or entertainers and Sylvie had had a career as a striptease artist, appearing widely up and down the Riviera and in night clubs as far away as Spain, Belgium and Switzerland.

Taken to police headquarters by the triumphant sergeant, Fifi and Désirée promptly accused their friend of the murder. They admitted that they had stolen some things from the apartment, but said that Tuaillon had already been dead when they arrived. She had told them that there had been a quarrel and that she had been rougher with the old man than she had intended. As he was dead anyway, they might as well take whatever they could from the apartment.

Sylvie denied this for a time and said that her friends were trying to harm her out of professional jealousy, but, in the end, she came to realize the hopelessness of her situation and agreed that the version given by Fifi and Désirée was essentially correct.

'It was an accident,' she said. 'I didn't have any reason to kill him. He was paying for everything and he told me that he was going to have a will made out leaving me his money when he died. His death was a blow to me. I had to move out of the apartment and he hadn't even made the new will out yet.'

Jean-Paul Nestour, otherwise known as Sylvie, was charged with causing death without the intention of doing so and her friends were charged with theft and concealing knowledge of a felony.

They were tried in the early summer of 1980 and on June 13, an unlucky Friday, Sylvie was sentenced to twelve years' imprisonment while Fifi and Désirée, in return for having cooperated with the police, got off with one year each.

Possibly out of respect for the dead, the subject was never brought up at the trial which was, in any case, very short, but, following the sentencing, Inspector Fauchon, who was by nature curious, as befitted an investigations officer, went to ask Sylvie a question before she was taken away.

'How did Tuaillon come to get mixed up in the gay scene?' he said. 'There wasn't a trace of any homosexual tendencies in his background. If there had been, we'd have solved this case a lot faster.'

Sylvie, who had taken her sentence badly, looked at him sadly through tear-filled eyes.

'He wasn't gay,' she said. 'He was straight as a string.'

'But then . . . why? . . . you . . . that is . . . you mean he didn't know?' stammered the inspector incredulously.

'Of course he didn't know,' said Sylvie. 'Do you think I'm stupid? If he'd have known the truth about all of us, it would have killed him!'

8

RELIGIOUS

The three young women standing in front of the charge desk in the squad room of the Wetteren police station were nuns and the desk sergeant knew them by sight, if not by name.

Wetteren is, after all, a small place. Located roughly ten miles to the east of Ghent, Belgium and a little to the north of the main highway running from Brussels to Ostend, it is a quiet community of under twenty thousand souls with a small shopping centre, seven catholic churches, thirty-one taverns, a brothel and an old people's home. There is a cloister next to the Old People's Home which houses not only the nursing sisters, but also those engaged in teaching and other activities.

'Yes?' said the sergeant politely. He was intrigued over what might have brought three nuns to the police station. If there had been a burglary at the cloister, someone could have simply telephoned or, even if it had been felt that the report should be made in person, one nun would have sufficed. Why three?

To his astonishment, there was no immediate answer. The three nuns looked nervously at each other as if each was waiting for the others to speak and said nothing.

The sergeant cleared his throat. It was a Monday morning, January 16, 1978, and he was not feeling exactly at his most cheerful. Wetteren lies in the heart of Flanders and the weather was, of course, rotten, a grey, gloomy, depressing day with bitterly cold showers of mixed rain and hail sweeping one after another over the city.

'We think we want to report a murder,' blurted one of the nuns abruptly, her voice a squeak of nervous excitement and embarrassment.

The sergeant opened his mouth and then shut it again without saying anything. He did not know what to say. It was over thirty years since there had been a homicide in Wetteren. It occurred to him that the woman might be drunk or playing a practical joke, but how could that be? They were nuns.

'You mean you don't know whether you want to report it or not?' he asked cautiously.

'No, no!' said another nun. 'We mean we want to report what we think is a murder. Maybe it isn't. We hope it isn't.'

'Very well,' said the sergeant resignedly. 'Who has been murdered?'

'We think Mrs Maria van der Gunst,' said the nun who had spoken first. 'She was a patient at the Old People's Home.'

'She has just died?' asked the sergeant, his finger poised over the dial of the internal communication system.

'Oh no,' said the nun. 'She died on the fifth of July last year.'

The sergeant stared at her with a total lack of comprehension and then dialled.

'Franz?' he said into the telephone. 'Is the inspector there yet? Listen. I have what appears to be a report on a homicide. Could you come down and talk to the people? Would you do it right now? Right. I'll make out an F.I.R., if you think that's best.'

He hung up the telephone.

'Someone from the Department of Criminal Investigations will be down immediately,' he said. He took a printed First Information Report form out of the drawer of the desk. 'Now, may I have your names please?'

The nuns turned out to be named Franziska, Godlive and Pieta. They were all members of the Order of Holy Joseph living in the cloister and working in the Old People's Home. They were young, shy and looked remarkably innocent.

The story which they had to tell was, however, anything but innocent and the sergeant found it so shocking and improbable that his pen hung suspended and motionless over the form as he sat literally paralyzed, his mouth hanging open in astonishment.

According to the charges that the nuns wished, however reluctantly, to file, the murderess was the Mother Superior of their order and the directress of the Old People's Home.

The only conclusion that the sergeant could reach was that, for some unexplained reason, the three young nuns had gone insane simultaneously. He knew Sister Godfrida, the Mother Superior, by sight, a sturdy, stern-looking woman in her mid-forties and he knew that she had been at the convent for close to thirty years. She was not only the last person in the world to be suspected of murdering her patients; there was also no reason in the world why she would want to.

He was, therefore, on the point of summoning a doctor to take

103

the poor, insane nuns away when Detective-Sergeant Franz Gropa came down from the Department of Criminal Investigations and did so.

Upstairs in the office of Inspector Dyke Van Horn, the nuns repeated their charge with much the same effect as they had had in the charge room below.

'But why?' said the inspector, his eyes bulging slightly. 'Why in the name of Heaven would she do such a thing?'

He was a stocky man, somewhat under average height, with a high, broad, forehead and his brown eyes were abnormally deep-set. Having been involved in criminal investigations for nearly twenty years, he had thought that he had heard everything. Now, he realized that he had not, but he still had no idea of how much more he still had to hear.

The three nuns looked at each other again, their faces mirroring an inner struggle.

'We are sinning,' said Sister Godlive. 'There is a vow of silence on us.'

'Put on us by the director,' said Sister Franziska. 'But he is not our superior in the church.'

'Sister Godfrida is,' said Sister Pieta.

'Her sins are greater than ours,' said Sister Franziska.

Sister Godlive turned to the inspector.

'Sister Godfrida murdered Mrs van der Gunst because she wanted her money and jewellery,' she said.

The inspector made a mental note that she had now said that it was murder, not that she thought it was murder.

'An excellent motive for murder,' he said. 'One of the more common. But not with nuns. What would she do with the money?'

'Pay for her expensive meals in fine restaurants and for her wines and brandy,' said Sister Godlive.

'Buy her filthy pornographic magazines and her sex toys,' said Sister Pieta.

'And her drugs, her morphine, her heroin, her cocaine and the other things,' said Sister Franziska.

The inspector got up from his desk, walked all around it and sat back down again. A very strong feeling of unreality had suddenly invaded his prosaic, somewhat shabby office. Expensive restaurants? Wines? Pornography! Sex toys!! MURDER!!! In the convent of the Old People's Home?

Sergeant Gropa, a normally rather handsome, young man with an open, good-natured face and short-cut blond hair, was sitting at his desk with mouth and eyes wide open, looking like an idiot. Abruptly, he closed his mouth.

'Loudun!' he said opening it again.

The inspector considered the idea, eyeing the nuns a little warily. He was, of course, familiar with the case of possession or, depending upon your outlook, collective hysteria which had taken place in Loudun, France, and which had been made famous in the book *The Devils of Loudun*. There, an entire convent of nuns had gone into a sort of sexual frenzy, exhibiting their private parts to the gaze of the idly curious, and demanding sexual satisfaction on the spot. Had the Devil come to Wetteren?

If so, it was for a different form of manifestation. The young nuns showed no inclination to fling themselves on the floor and display their genitals. Rather, all three were pink with embarrassment.

So was the inspector and he got up again and went to gaze out of the window so that he could put his questions with his back turned.

'If what you claim is true,' he said slowly, 'this must have been going on for some time. Why do you come to us only now?'

'Because she came back,' said Sister Franziska.

'She was sent away to be cured of her drug addiction last year,' said Sister Godlive. 'But at Christmas we received a postcard from her. It said, "I shall soon be with you." We didn't believe it, but last Friday she came back and now it has all started again.'

'You mean your superiors knew that Sister Godfrida was a drug addict?' said the inspector. 'Do they know that you have come to the police?'

'No,' said Sister Pieta. 'In fact, we were specifically forbidden to speak of these matters outside the convent. Everyone there knows about Sister Godfrida and what she is doing, but no one can say anything because we are sworn to silence. They say that the reputation of the order must be preserved at all costs.'

'But we have talked it over among ourselves,' said Sister Godlive, 'and we decided that our vows are to the Church and to God. What Sister Godfrida is doing is an offence to God and, even if our superior forbids us, we should disobey and try to stop her before she kills still more of the old people.'

'You are suggesting that she has killed others besides Mrs van der Gunst?' asked the inspector.

'Yes,' said Sister Godlive. 'Many others perhaps. This has been going on for nearly seven years. Ever since she had her brain operation.'

For the first time since the nuns had entered the office, the inspector began to have a feeling that this conversation was not, perhaps, as insane as it sounded. Sister Godfrida had had a brain operation. Perhaps it had left her deranged in some manner or other. It was, at least, possible. Otherwise, the whole story made no sense. You did not become the Mother Superior of a convent if you were on hard drugs and addicted to gourmet foods, expensive wines and pornography.

'Very well,' he said. 'How do you think that Sister Godfrida murdered Mrs van der Gunst?'

'She gave her an overdose of insulin,' said Sister Franziska without hesitation. 'She was an old woman, eighty-seven, and she had diabetes. Even if there had been an autopsy, it would not have shown anything because she had been receiving insulin anyway, but there was no autopsy, of course.'

'I don't know if an autopsy now would show anything or not,' said the inspector. 'I would like you to speak with our medical expert. Do you mind if I call him?'

The inspector wanted Dr Fons Shryker's opinion on whether an overdose of insulin would show up in an autopsy, but he also wanted him to meet and speak to the three nuns. What they had been saying was so incredible that the possibility that they themselves were on drugs could not be excluded.

Dr Shryker, a slender, elegant sort of man with rimless spectacles and a small moustache, came to the inspector's office, confirmed that an overdose of insulin could probably not be determined in the autopsy of a person who had been taking insulin in any case and certainly not when the victim had been buried for close to half a year, spoke at some length with the nuns and then, after they had left, expressed the opinion that they were not only sane, but telling the literal truth in so far as they knew it.

'But, my God!' said the inspector in dismay. 'This is a terrible case for us to handle. How can I go to the Prosecutor and tell him that I want to investigate the Mother Superior of the convent because she is murdering the patients in order to spend their money on gourmet meals, fine wines, sex toys, drugs and pornography? Even if he doesn't send me for psychiatric observation, how would we ever prove such things?'

'If it's true, she must be clinically insane,' said the sergeant. 'Wouldn't a psychiatric examination show that? Even if we couldn't prove homicide, we could at least get her committed to some institution where she would be out of harm's way.'

'You couldn't force her to submit to a psychiatric examination.'

said the doctor. 'She'd have to cooperate and, in any case, I'm not certain that you could get her committed purely on the basis of the examination and the accusations of three nuns.'

'I'm sure we couldn't,' said the inspector, 'because, if they're telling the truth, then the Order would do everything possible to cover the thing up. They wouldn't cooperate and, even if she would, they wouldn't let her.'

'Then what do we do?' said the sergeant. 'We can't simply forget about it. Those nuns have lodged an official complaint, even if there's no F.I.R. on it. We have to take some action.'

'I'm quite aware of that,' said the inspector a little testily. 'We will take action, but, at the moment, I don't know what action to take. Maybe we could start by making a very discreet investigation of the charges. See what you can do with that, but handle it personally. I don't want a word of this to get out.'

Sergeant Gropa was a well-trained and clever investigator, but he had no easy task in assembling background material on Sister Godfrida without anyone in Wetteren suspecting that he was doing so. She was, after all, a rather conspicuous figure in such a small community and she had been a member of her order for twenty-nine years.

The early history was unexceptional. The daughter of a devout, lower-income family, she had entered the Order of Holy Joseph at the age of fifteen, apparently more at the wish of her parents, who lived in the neighbouring village of Overmere, than at her own. Her name had been Cécile Blombeek. She was now forty-four years old, a plump, grim-looking woman who wore rimless glasses, and most of her career had been as a nursing nun. In 1971, she had herself been operated on for a brain tumour. The operation had been a complete success.

Or had it?

For the sergeant soon began turning up reports of less banal activity following it. Sister Godfrida had been seen two years earlier at an extremely expensive restaurant in a very stylish seaside resort on the Belgian coast with another nun, Sister Mathieu, who was considerably younger and not a nurse but a teacher. The nuns had been wearing not their habits, but chic trouser suits. Both had been more than a little drunk and had shown a tendency to fondle each other.

'Good God!' said the inspector when he had read this part of the sergeant's report. 'Don't tell me that she's a lesbian as well!'

'It appears to be a close friendship,' said the sergeant cautiously. 'I have other reports from people who spotted her in restaurants in Ghent and Brussels and, generally, she was with Sister Mathieu.'

Whether he wanted it or not, this was what the inspector needed. It was confirmation that the story told by Sisters Franziska, Godlive and Pieta was not a complete fabrication. There had been something strange in the comportment of Sister Godfrida following her operation and, if that much were true, then the rest might well be. The case which had, up until now, remained unofficial and untitled, became the 'Investigation into the Suspected Homicide of Maria van der Gunst on or about July 5, 1977'.

That grounds for suspicion of homicide existed did not solve the problem of how the police were to prove it, and it seemed to the inspector that short of a voluntary confession or being caught red-handed in a second murder there was little hope of a solution to the case.

The best he thought might be done was to assemble enough evidence of erratic conduct on the part of Sister Godfrida from the other nuns for her to be quietly removed from contact with patients in the Old People's Home and, if necessary, committed.

The only source from which he could obtain such information was, however, from persons under her authority and he was not at all sure that the others would be as willing to violate the injunction of silence laid upon them as had been Sisters Franziska, Godlive and Pieta.

There was not even any certainty that he would be able to get further statements from those three.

'I'm afraid the only way to handle this,' he told the sergeant, 'is to make an open, official case out of it, have the body exhumed and autopsied and bring in the nuns for questioning. If we're able to establish our case, we'll then proceed to the arrest and interrogation of the suspect.'

'And, if none of them talk?' asked the sergeant.

'In that case, our position will be very difficult here in Wetteren,' said the inspector.

'The population will undoubtedly consider us to be communists, atheists or insane and the Order of Holy Joseph will be forced to take legal action against us for defamation. Under the circumstances, I suspect that the commissioner would have to take action.'

'Meaning that neither of us would remain in criminal investigations,' said the sergeant in alarm. 'Why do it then? I do not like walking a beat in the factory district.'

'Because it's our job,' said the inspector. 'And besides, I may be in an old people's home myself one day. I would hope that the police would be making some effort to see that I was not murdered by drug-addicted, lesbian nuns.'

Actually, the inspector did not have much to fear even if he did end up in an old people's home, for the case of Sister Godfrida was without question unique in Belgium and probably in all Europe.

In the opinion of Dr Shryker, her case was the result of an unusual combination of circumstances which would, it was devoutly hoped, never be repeated and which had originated with the brain operation seven years earlier.

'An operation like that is a tricky thing,' he told the inspector. 'There is still not enough known about the brain, but we do know such an intervention can result in profound, if not immediately obvious, personality changes.

'This is apparently what happened with Sister Godfrida. Physically and mentally, the operation was a success, but, psychologically, it was a disaster. Certain tendencies that had been latent became dominant. Certain inhibitions were suppressed. An alteration in the psychological balance obviously took place and resulted in a woman who looked like Sister Godfrida and who had superficially the same personality, but who was, in fact, a totally different person.'

That Sister Godfrida was a different person from the one she had been before her operation was already certain, for the evidence that had now been assembled showed that prior to that time, she had been a very ordinary sort of Mother Superior at the Old People's Home. A hard worker and a strict disciplinarian, she had been considered demanding but fair, not asking more of the nurses under her than she was prepared to perform herself.

There was no hint of any improper behaviour with the other nuns or with the patients and to everyone who knew her, the thought of her indulgence in gourmet meals, expensive wines, drugs and pornography was simply laughable.

Following the operation, things had changed abruptly. Sister Godfrida had been given morphine to still the post-operative pain and it had proved, in her case, fatally addictive. She became willing to do anything to get it, and the manner in which she went about this was described in the testimony of another young nun, known as Sister Ursule.

In her statement to the police she said, 'I came to the patient's room at approximately ten o'clock in the evening. He was a man in his sixties and still vigorous.'

'Sister Godfrida was standing beside the bed and she had lifted the skirts of her habit and was showing him her body. I heard her say, "If you pay me well, I will make you happy."

'She then asked him for three thousand francs and he agreed. He was lying on the bed in a dressing gown and she put her hand inside of it. He also began touching her body.

'I thought that I had gone insane or was having a vision sent by the Devil, so I went back to the duty room and took a small glass of brandy to clear my head.

'This happened in the summer of 1972 or 1973 when I had not been long in the order. I did not tell anyone about it, but later on, there were many such things and Sister Godfrida would offer herself to the patients, both men and women, even if others of us were present. She did not seem to care.'

She had little reason to care. Sister Godfrida's activities were not motivated solely by commercial considerations and her fellow sisters were made the same offers gratis although 'offer' was not precisely the right term as Sister Godfrida was not only insistent, but remained a strict disciplinarian in this respect as well.

'When we came on duty,' ran the nearly identical statements of a number of the young novices, 'Sister Godfrida would make us kneel on the floor and kiss her feet. She said she had no objection if we did it higher up. She pulled up our habits and jabbed us in the buttocks, the thighs and our private parts with a hypodermic needle. If anyone complained, she beat them with a dog whip.'

The inspector need not have feared for lack of testimony. Once the ice had been broken, the statements poured in from every side.

Sister Godfrida had consistently approached the nun on night duty with homosexual requests. Sister Godfrida had beaten nuns, novices and patients alike. Sister Godfrida had visited the younger nuns and novices in their beds and had sought to engage in lesbian relations with them.

On this last point, there was a slight disagreement. All of the Sisters insisted that they had repulsed their sex-mad superior personally, but were quite certain that the others had been forced to yield.

On another point, however, there was total unanimity and this was the almost public love-making between Sister Godfrida and Sister Mathieu and the great feasts and celebrations they had held in the convent itself. The most extravagant foods and the finest of wines were served, but only for Sisters Godfrida and Mathieu.

110

The others were restricted to a diet of bread, boiled potatoes and water, accompanied by the comforting thought that mortification of the flesh was part of the religious experience. The patients in the Old People's Home fared no better, but, being old, had little appetite in any case.

Even taking into account the vow of silence which had been imposed on the members of the Order, it was a tribute to the nuns' devotion to their vocation that nothing had previously come out regarding the incredible goings-on in the convent and Old People's Home. The Sisters had clung loyally and desperately to their vows and it had been only the suspicion of murder which had finally brought them to speak out. As the inspector later learned, the decision to go to the police had been made by a large number of the nuns and not merely the three who had acted as spokeswomen.

From the inspector's point of view, of course, Sister Godfrida's gourmet tastes, her fine wines and even her pronography and sex-toy collections were of no official interest. Even her lesbian assaults on the younger Sisters was not something on which he could take action. Theoretically, homosexuality is illegal in Belgium, but female homosexuality taking place within a convent would be extremely difficult to prove and, in any case, none of the victims was prepared to file charges, all insisting that, although others had been subjected to the most vile indignities, they themselves had escaped unscathed.

What the statements did indicate, if not prove, was that there was a basis for the accusations of murder. Obviously, for Sister Godfrida to have been murdering her patients, she would have to have been mad as a hatter and the accounts of her conduct indicated precisely that.

Even so, the inspector proceeded with the utmost caution. The descriptions of the Mother Superior's behaviour were simply incredible and he could hardly believe them himself. Supposing she denied everything and claimed that the nuns had mounted a conspiracy against her? She was known to be a strict disciplinarian. There was even a possibility that it really was no more than that, although the inspector did not believe it. There had been too many cross-references in the nuns' statements and practically no contradictions at all.

What he needed was some form of material evidence and the most likely place to look for it was in Sister Godfrida's finances. Drugs she might have been able to obtain by stealing from the elderly patients, many of whom were prescribed some kind of narcotics or others, but fine restaurants, wines, clothing and pornography all cost money. Did Sister Godfrida have any legitimate source of such funds?

It was quickly determined that she did not. There are orders which permit their members to own property, make investments and even play the stock market if they wish, but the Order of Holy Joseph was not one of them. Sister Godfrida was paid only a token salary, barely enough to buy a single second-rate pornographic magazine a month. Moreover, she did not come from a family where there was a possibility of an inheritance.

There was one other means by which she could have come into possession of money and that was by earning it by prostituting herself to the patients. But, although many of the Sisters had reported sexual activities between the Mother Superior and her charges, not all had reported seeing money change hands. In at least one case, the patient with whom Sister Godfrida had allegedly engaged in sex in one form or another was completely penniless and a charity case.

This did not, however, mean anything. Sister Godfrida's sexual exertions could not have all been commercially orientated for she had briskly pursued practically every nun in the convent and none of them had been in a position to pay for her services.

The inspector's conclusion was that Sister Godfrida was a woman who was not averse to turning a profit from sex, but if there was no money in it, she was prepared to do it for nothing.

As for earning enough from the patients to finance her exuberant life-style, it was soon shown that this would have been impossible. Few of the patients were persons of means and the majority of them were beyond the age where sexual offers, however tempting, either would or could be accepted. From statements taken from the patients later, it turned out that many had been horrified or had doubted their own sanity and had refused. The refusal had not, however, always been accepted. When the spirit moved her, Sister Godfrida was not a woman to take no for an answer.

The patients had been, of course, completely at her mercy and justifiably terrified of their chief nurse, for she had not hesitated to use the dog whip on them that she used on the nuns and the novices. As a matter of fact, she had used it rather more freely on the patients, as they then complained of pain and were prescribed morphine by the doctor. The morphine was, of course, appropriated for Sister Godfrida's personal use and the patients were given aspirin, if anything.

In the end, the inspector came to the conclusion that he had enough evidence to present his case and he moved to take the suspect into custody in as discreet a manner as possible. He did not think that there would be an indictment because Sister Godfrida would obviously be sent for psychological observation and he was confident that she would be declared unfit to stand trial.

Her recent conduct provided ample support for this belief. Although she had known for some time that the investigation was going on and that she herself was the object of it, she had in no way altered her behaviour and had continued beating nuns and patients, making sexual advances and living a life of luxury enjoyed by few members of the holy orders.

Whether Sister Mathieu, who had been one of the main beneficiaries of her friend's extremely modern and liberated attitudes, came to the conviction that the ball was over and that it was time to disassociate or whether the quarrel had had some other cause, the two women had engaged in a savage sort of fist fight in the convent, ripping off a scandalous amount of each other's clothing before being separated by the thunderstruck nuns. The conflict had been so violent that it had been necessary to summon a carpenter to repair the damage to the furniture.

A court order and the permission of the relatives had, in the meantime, been obtained for the exhumation of the corpse of Maria van der Gunst, but, as the doctor had feared, the subsequent autopsy failed to establish anything definite. Mrs van der Gunst had been diabetic and had been taking insulin for many years. There were traces of it in her body, but whether the quantity taken had been correct, could no longer be determined.

This troubled the inspector as there was now no evidence of homicide at all other than the unsupported statements of the nuns and, if Sister Godfrida were to prove uncooperative, it would be impossible to obtain an indictment.

He need not have worried. Whatever other failings she might have, Sister Godfrida was a truthful woman and, when asked by the inspector if she had had anything to do with the death of Maria van der Gunst, she replied, 'Yes indeed. I sent her to Heaven because she was too noisy. She disturbed my sleep.'

In response to the inspector's relieved inquiry as to how she accomplished this, she confirmed what the nuns had said and stated that she had given the old woman an overdose of insulin.

The case was, for all practical purposes, over. There had been homicide. The murderess had been identified and had confessed.

It was unlikely that she would stand trial, but she could, at least, be restricted from causing any further harm.

As the inspector was, however, interested in knowing how many homicides he had solved in the case, he continued the questioning.

He did not find out and no one ever will, for only Sister Godfrida knew and she cannot remember. In two other cases, those of eighty-two-year-old Pieter Diggmann and seventy-eight-year-old Léonie Maihofer, she was certain. She had sent both of them to Heaven with insulin overdoses in February of 1977. On anything prior to that time, she was vague, but a subsequent study of the medical records and death certificates from the Old People's Home led a medical commission to believe that Sister Godfrida had been responsible for approximately thirty deaths among her patients, thus assuring her a place among the great non-military, non-political mass murderers of all time.

As had been anticipated, Sister Godfrida was ordered to be sent for psychological observation, very promptly declared unfit to stand trial and quietly committed to a mental institution where she is expected to remain for the rest of her life as the psychiatrists fear that her condition is incurable.

Sister Godfrida accepted this all humbly, cheerfully and uncomplainingly, declaring herself submissive to God's will.

It was only to be expected of her. She is, after all, a nun.

9

REFRESHMENTS

The 1960s were a time of magic. With the dawning of the Age of Aquarius, Youth rose up to overthrow the authoritarian restraints of society and the State. The stuffy precepts of Christian morality were thrown out the window and every man, woman and child was free to do his or her own thing.

Pornography became not only respectable, but chic. The right of teenagers of either sex to engage in prostitution without parental interference was established. The rights of law-breakers were so jealously guarded that the very concept of law-breaker practically vanished. Gallant, but, regretfully, unsuccessful attempts were made to arrange for the legalization of all of the narcotic substances known to man. With thundering drums and screaming electronic trumpets, the media led the way into the twenty-first century . . . about forty years too early.

After that, things were, of course, much, much better everywhere in the world, as anyone who had survived to the eighties can easily confirm by simply reading the newspapers.

This great revolutionary wave of the future began, as so many things begin, in the United States and, after the usual lag of two or three years, arrived in Europe where it was variously received depending upon the national character. Not being French, it was practically ignored in France where a student–worker alliance of short duration was occupied with a traditional burning down of the city of Paris, but in West Germany, it was warmly greeted. Not having had it too good in the twentieth century, the Germans were, presumably, eager to get out of it.

Unfortunately, the young Germans did not understand the basic purpose of revolution and, long after the now balding heros of the American youth revolt had become wealthy stock-brokers, respected journalists or bestselling authors, they were still running around shooting people.

They were, of course, eventually all killed by the authorities or assassinated by their friends, proving that it does not pay to do things too thoroughly, a common German failing.

Their achievements, however, stand! Pornography is now so common in Germany that it is difficult to make any money out of it. Thousands of what were formerly termed criminals have been treated and released, some many times. The use of drugs is so widespread that children young enough to have only barely mastered the alphabet are writing bestsellers detailing a life of prostitution before puberty for the purpose of financing their addiction.

Great as these contributions to our modern, enlightened society may be, they pale into insignificance when ranged next to the strides that were made in the liberation of the German woman.

Thoroughness is not an exclusively male attribute among the Germans and, during the sixties, a great many young and less young women took the sexual revolution so seriously that they became positively dangerous.

Male sex activity is, unfortunately, limited by certain physical considerations which, pornography to the contrary, quickly terminate any marathon attempts, an evolutionary precaution, perhaps, to provide time for the male to eat and sleep and not die of exhaustion.

Not so the happy female! As anyone who patronizes the lower-priced establishments of carnal delights knows, it is quite possible for the lady to enjoy an apple without interrupting business and it is said that in Italy spaghetti is sometimes eaten, although probably without sauce.

The liberated German ladies of the sixties were not, however, interested in apples or spaghetti, even though the latter dish is quite popular in Germany, but applied themselves with grim, Teutonic thoroughness to the task at hand, so that sex in the sixties soon came to resemble more a contest of athletic endurance than a pleasurable attempt to ensure the survival of the species, however thwarted by chemical or mechanical means.

To this day the waiting rooms of Germany's psychiatrists are filled with anxious males who have found that, in one respect at least, they are the weaker sex and have never been able to get over it.

A curious irony of fate. For the past two thousand years at least, the human male had incessantly sought to convince the human female that true freedom and equality of the sexes lay only in the female accepting promptly and enthusiastically the sexual overtures of the casual male acquaintance.

In the sixties, male logic prevailed and the victors rushed

116

joyously in . . . to be shortly carted off to the clinics as sexual nut-cases.

Of course, even in the sixties, these tragic conditions did not apply to all Germans and there were many happily married young couples who, although enjoying free, untrammelled sexual relations, did not put undue emphasis on them, but kept their minds on their jobs and other activities.

Such as the two strikingly handsome young couples who, on the evening of Saturday, November 5, 1966, at approximately nine o'clock, were driving from the city of Kempten in the extreme south of Germany to the nearby town of Marktoberdorf where a dance was taking place.

Seated behind the wheel was Wilhelm Leinauer, a twenty-six-year-old motor mechanic with blond hair and finely chiselled, classic features. He was the owner of the car, a not particularly new model.

In the front seat next to him was twenty-four-year-old Mrs Christel Müller, a dainty, dark-haired woman of such beauty that even in Germany, which has more than its share of handsome women, men and women turned to look at her in the street.

In the back seat, her husband, twenty-five-year-old Manfred Müller, a man as handsome as his wife was beautiful, sat next to lovely, blonde Viktoria Leinauer, the same age as himself and the wife of the driver.

It was a typically gay foursome of young, beautiful people on their way to an evening of entertainment. The Leinauers and the Müllers knew each other well, intimately said some, and in Germany in the mid-sixties that meant something.

Just outside Marktoberdorf the road from Kempten crosses the Wertach, a not terribly large river, but, at this point, some fifteen feet deep with nearly vertical banks, and it was here that the trouble with the steering arose.

'It's pulling to the left,' said Leinauer, turning off the pavement just short of the bridge. 'I'd better take a look.'

He got out of the car and started around to the back, presumably to get the tools out of the boot. Christel got out too and came to join him.

Suddenly, the car began to roll!

'Look out!' shouted Wilhelm and Christel simultaneously. 'The car's moving! Jump! Jump!'

But Manfred and Viktoria could not jump. The car was a two-door model and, as they struggled to push forward the seats, it nosed over the steep slope leading to the river bank less than fifteen feet away and shot downward at a speed that threw the terrified couple back into the seat cushions. Neither could swim, and a plunge into the swift waters of the Wertach meant certain death. Even if Wilhelm and Christel had dived after them, the banks would have been too steep for any of them to get out and, in any case, Wilhelm and Christel could not swim either.

But the car did not take the final plunge. As the front wheels tipped over the edge of the bank, the body fell and the rear axle hooked on to a low tree stump, bringing the car to such a sudden halt that Manfred and Viktoria were thrown violently forward into the front seat.

An instant later, Christel and Wilhelm were at the doors and had helped them to safety. It had been a close call, but no harm had been done except to the car which had to be taken away by a break-down truck. The repairs were not expensive as Leinauer did them himself. He quickly found what the trouble had been. One of the hydraulic lines leading to the brakes had burst. He did not find out why the steering wheel had been pulling to the left.

Actually, the business with the car was only one of a number of mysterious incidents which had come to plague Viktoria Leinauer during that magic year of 1966 when all the world was being made anew. Twice, she had gone to bed in the evening only to wake up in the middle of the afternoon of the following day feeling remarkably groggy and fuzzy headed. Wilhelm said that she had been sleeping so soundly in the morning when he got up to go to work that he had not had the heart to wake her.

On another occasion, her brand-new electric iron which she had had for only a month suddenly threw out a shower of sparks, burned her hand slightly and would have electrocuted her outright had she not been wearing thick, felt slippers and standing on a rug.

Or so said the repairman from the shop where she had bought it.

There had been a false connection which had conducted the current into the metal parts of the iron and made them deadly. He wanted to know if she had been fooling around with it.

Viktoria, who had had a rather painful shock despite the felt slippers, was indignant and used such language that the repairman went away without another word and someone else from the shop brought her a new iron with the apologies of the management.

She insisted on him testing it before he left. It worked perfectly.

Viktoria and Wilhelm had mentioned these strange happenings to their friends the Müllers, who had wondered greatly, but were unable to offer any explanation. Manfred was, in any case, home only at weekends. A trainee for a government post, he had been sent for a training course to Neustadt on the Wine Street, over two hundred miles to the north-west, on November 1 and would remain there until February 1 of the following year when he would be transferred to Fürstenfeldbrück just outside Munich and only about forty miles from Kempten and home.

In any case, there were no more incidents after the near-tragedy with the car and the end of the year passed with no more than the usual parties, some of which were, however, remarkably lively. There is nothing like a group of beautiful, young, thoroughly liberated women to put life into a party.

Following the end-of-the-year celebrations, there were no more parties, nor would there be any until the carnival season which takes place before Lent and is known in southern Germany as Fasching. By that time, Manfred would be in Fürstenfeldbrück.

So too would another promising young trainee for a government post with the Weather Bureau. His name was Albert Blumoser, he was twenty-three years old, easily as handsome as Manfred with whom he would share a room at the school and he came from the town of Erding to the north-east of Munich and, therefore, on the opposite side from Kempten. The two young men had not known each other previously, but they immediately hit it off together very well.

And then, on February 10, 1967, a Friday, there was another mysterious event, although this time a pleasant one. Manfred Müller received in the mail a small, but heavy and interesting-looking parcel wrapped in brown paper and addressed correctly to Mr Manfred Müller, 808 Fürstenfeldbrück, Fliegerhorst Weather Service School. The return address was given as B. Schiller, 673 Neustadt/Weinstrasse, Bahnhofstrasse 5, which puzzled Manfred greatly as he did not know anyone by the name of B. Schiller in Neustadt or anywhere else for that matter.

'It must be somebody I ran into when I was in Neustadt and didn't get the name,' he told Blumoser, 'but, for the life of me, I can't think who it was. Let's see what's in it.'

What was in it was a small, stoneware jug with a bucolic design of flowers and unidentified objects growing out of a hobnailed boot. A label on the opposite side identified the contents as gentian-bitter, a drink pleasing to Germans, and, possibly, some others, and another label draped around the neck confirmed, a little unnecessarily, that this was a German product.

For Manfred Müller, the mystery was only increased. The jug

was the sort of souvenir article that a moderately drunken tourist might buy to send to an aunt from whom he expected to inherit nothing. He could not imagine who might have sent him such a thing, but it had to be a joke.

Apart from the jug, the parcel contained a small stoneware mug intended no doubt to spare the recipient the indignity of drinking directly from the bottle and a small box of not particularly good cookies. Written on the paper in which it had all been wrapped was, 'Greetings from the Palatinate!' which was the district in which Neustadt on the Wine Street was located, and 'To be drunk with gusto . . . but alone.'

Totally bemused, Manfred Müller put jug, mug, cookies, wrapping and all into his locker and went off to Kempten to spend the weekend with his wife and their friends. It passed pleasantly and without incident.

On Monday, Manfred Müller and Albert Blumoser returned to the school in Fürstenfeldbrück and, on Tuesday, Albert began to come down with a cold, no unusual affliction in February.

'I'm going downtown to buy myself a bottle of rum,' he told his room-mate. 'It may not cure the cold, but at least I won't be able to notice the symptoms.'

'You'll catch your death of pneumonia going out in this weather,' said Müller. 'Anyway, rum isn't the thing for a cold. What's good for a cold is gentian-bitter.'

He had been making sporadic attempts to get rid of his mysterious present ever since returning from the weekend in Kempten, but without success. Gentian-bitter was apparently not as popular with young Germans as B. Schiller had thought.

'All right,' said Blumoser. 'Why not? It can't do any harm and I can't feel any worse than I do now', giving vent with these words to two of the most tragically inaccurate statements ever pronounced in consecutive order.

Müller, equally unsuspecting and intent only on getting rid of as much of the contents of the souvenir flask as possible, hastened to get it out, filled the little mug to the brim and handed it to the cold sufferer. Fetching another glass, he poured himself out a drink as well, but, in the meantime, Blumoser had tipped back his head and drained the mug in a single draught.

Manfred Müller moved to follow his example, but rather than tossing back the contents of his glass at a gulp, he took a cautious sip. The fact was, he was not overly fond of gentian-bitter.

The cautious sip was justified. This was by far the worst

gentian-bitter that he had ever tasted or would even have been able to imagine.

It was, in fact, so bad that he spat it straight out on the floor, an involuntary action which saved his life for, in the same instant, Albert Blumoser let the mug fall and staggered backward, clutching at his throat. He was gasping for breath and, before Müller's astonished and horrified eyes, the skin of his face began to turn blue. His knees buckling, he fell to the floor and by the time Müller had recovered from his astonishment and had rushed forward to bend over him, he had already lost consciousness.

There is an emergency ambulance service attached to the Ludwigshöhe Hospital in Fürstenfeldbrück and in less than fifteen minutes Albert Blumoser was in the operating room and the doctors were working feverishly to save his life.

The effort was in vain. Within less than half an hour from the time that he had drunk the gentian-bitter Albert Blumoser was dead. He never regained consciousness.

In the meantime, someone at the school had summoned the police. It had not been Manfred Müller, who was in a state of shock. He had called the ambulance and had run out into the hall shouting for help, but it had not occurred to him to notify the police. In the surprise and confusion following Blumoser's collapse, he had failed to connect the strange-tasting gentian-bitter with his room-mate's condition.

By the time the police arrived, however, he had, and he explained exactly what had taken place and how the bitter had come into his possession.

The flask was still standing on the table where Müller had put it down and so was his nearly full glass. The mug from which Albert Blumoser had drunk lay on the floor. The carton in which the flask had arrived and the wrapping paper, including the note extending greetings from the Palatinate, were standing next to the waste basket.

As the first police officers to arrive were merely two patrolmen from the nearest available patrol car, their only action was to remove everyone from the room and take up stations at the door. At the moment, no one knew what had taken place other than that one of the trainees at the school had drunk something and was reported by the hospital to be in serious, if not critical, condition with something which was definitely not alcohol poisoning.

As the switchboard at police headquarters was maintaining constant contact, by an open telephone line, with the hospital, it was quickly learned that Blumoser had almost no chance of surviving, and a team from the Department of Criminal Investigations left immediately for the scene to determine the circumstances. The patrolmen who had already arrived were also in contact with headquarters but they did not know what had happened, nor, for that matter, did anyone at the school.

This initial team from the Fürstenfeldbrück Department of Criminal Investigations was made up of Inspector Julius Wagner, a stocky, square-built man with sandy, blond hair parted in the middle, and Detective-Sergeant Walter Hoffmann who was young, dark, slender and had a moustache and a short, neatly trimmed goatee.

After listening to Manfred Müller's account of what had transpired, the officers took a look at the room from the doorway, but did not enter it.

Following this brief inspection, the sergeant called the hospital, was informed that the victim was dead and, on instructions from the inspector, called for a team of technicians to be sent out from the police laboratory.

While the inspector waited for them to arrive and spoke with the director and members of the staff of the school, the sergeant took Manfred Müller down to police headquarters to make a tape recording of his statement and for questioning as to who might have wanted to murder him.

It was not yet certain that murder had been intended. There was still the possibility of a tragic accident, but, if the act had been deliberate, it had been directed against Manfred Müller and not his room-mate. It was Müller to whom the parcel had been addressed.

While this was going on, the Fürstenfeldbrück coroner had been notified and had rushed to the hospital where it was quickly determined that Albert Blumoser had died of a massive dose of prussic acid mixed nearly half and half with the gentian-bitter.

As a matter of fact, the proportion had been rather more than half and half in favour of the prussic acid which had tended to settle to the bottom of the flask during the time it had been standing undisturbed in Manfred Müller's locker. Enough had, however, remained with the gentian to do the job.

With this finding, later confirmed by a laboratory analysis of the remaining contents of the flask, the possibility of an accident was practically ruled out and the case was officially declared to be murder.

122

Murder, however, of the wrong person. Although it was obvious that the prussic acid had been intended for Manfred Müller, the police, in order to leave no stone unturned, carried out an investigation into the background of the victim. The results were conclusive. There was no one in the world who had had the slightest reason to wish to harm Albert Blumoser. Moreover, apart from his parents, there had been hardly anyone who knew that he was taking the training course at Fürstenfeld-brück. He had not taken part in the course at Neustadt on the Wine Street and, in so far as could be determined, knew no one in the Palatinate.

Neither, however, did Manfred Müller and, in any case, it was quickly determined that the parcel containing the poison had not been mailed from the Palatinate, but from the main post office in the city of Stuttgart, less than a hundred miles to the north of Kempten.

Nonetheless, the police in Neustadt were contacted with a request to locate the B. Schiller whose name and address were on the package and take him into custody. Not in the least to Inspector Wagner's surprise, the Neustadt police reported promptly back that they had a dozen or so B. Schillers living in the city, but that the address given did not exist.

The B. Schillers in Neustadt were checked as a matter of routine and were cleared of all suspicion in connection with the case and, in the meantime, the Fürstenfeldbrück investigators, who had not expected that the poisoner would write his real name and address on the parcel containing the poison, had gone on to more promising leads.

One of these was the fact that the writing addressing the parcel to Manfred Müller, the writing conveying the greetings from the Palatinate and the writing of the return address were all different. The department's handwriting expert reported that the two addresses had been written by a man, but that the greeting was in a woman's handwriting.

A part of this mystery was solved almost immediately. The postmark showing the exact time, date and place that the parcel had been mailed, the sergeant went up to Stuttgart and easily located the post-office employee who had been on duty at the time. The return address was his handwriting.

At almost exactly midnight of February 6, said the postal official, a woman whose age he was unable to estimate other than that he thought her to be under thirty, had appeared at the window of his counter carrying a package. She had had long, blonde hair, had been wearing dark sunglasses and her right arm had been in a sling.

As she handed in the parcel, the postal official had remarked that there was no return address on it and had pushed it back. German postal regulations are strict and mail without a return address is not accepted.

The woman had apologized and had asked if he would write the return address on for her. She had, she said, broken her right arm and she could not write with her left hand.

The postman had, of course, complied and had written on the parcel the return address which she dictated.

'I'm afraid we're going to have a lot of trouble with this case.' said the inspector when he had finished listening to the sergeant's report. 'The woman was obviously disguised. Who wears sunglasses at midnight in a post office? And it seems probable that there was nothing wrong with her arm either. She simply didn't want her handwriting on the parcel so she made use of what was actually a rather clever trick.'

'Which probably means that the woman's handwriting on the greetings from the Palatinate isn't hers either,' said the sergeant.

'Not necessarily,' said the inspector. 'Even the most carefully plotted murders and, I think, this is a carefully plotted murder, sometimes display the most childish mistakes.'

'There was certainly a mistake in this one,' said the sergeant. 'She murdered the wrong man. On the other hand, I don't think that my trip up to Stuttgart was entirely wasted. At least, we know that the murderess is a woman.'

'That we do,' said the inspector, 'and that knowledge also gives us an insight into the motive. Müller isn't rich enough to make murder for money a possibility, so it was either his wife or his girlfriend who was trying to murder him.'

'He has a girlfriend?' said the sergeant.

'Not to my knowledge,' said the inspector, 'but he's good-looking enough to have one and that sort of thing is very popular today. We're in the middle of the sexual liberation trend.'

'Promiscuity for the People,' said the sergeant. 'It's all right as long as nobody gets jealous or mad. I suppose I'll be going to Kempten?'

'Right,' said the inspector. 'They already expect you. I talked with the head of their Department of Criminal Investigations on the telephone this morning. You'll have full cooperation and you won't even have to do any work. They'll carry out the actual investigation. You'll just serve as liaison to me.'

'What about the lab work?' said the sergeant. 'Am I taking the carton over with me?'

'Everything,' said the inspector. 'They've been able to trace the carton the flask was in. It originally contained Chantre brandy and it was shipped by the firm of Dachser & Company in Memmingen on July 29 of last year to the Schaenmayr Liquor Store KG in Kempten. What happened to it there, you have to find out.'

So far, the investigation had been progressing smoothly. The identity of the person who had written on the return address had been established. The probable sex of the poisoner had been established. And it was known that the carton containing the poisoned gentian had come from Kempten, Manfred Müller's home town.

And there, everything came to a halt. The carton, that most promising of leads, had simply been discarded on a rubbish heap by the Schaenmayr Liquor Store who had had no further use for it. They were able to identify it by the large number seventy-three scrawled with blue crayon on the top, which was an area code number used by the wholesale firm in Memmingen, but what had happened to it after it had been left on the rubbish heap they could not say. The rubbish heap was within two blocks of Manfred Müller's house, but within the same distance and closer to a hundred or so other houses.

'Mrs Müller could have picked it up, of course,' said the sergeant, reporting in at the inspector's office just before going off duty. He was driving back and forth between Kempten and Fürstenfeldbrück every day and running up a shocking bill in petrol mileage. 'But so could anybody else in Kempten. I think it's an indication, maybe, but as a lead, it's dead.'

'And Mrs Müller?' asked the inspector. 'What's she like?'

'Wow!' said the sergeant. 'You wouldn't believe it, if you saw it. This is her second marriage and, from what the neighbours and acquaintances say, it's a question in my mind why she bothers to marry at all. A very, very liberated girl, Mrs Müller.'

'And her husband holds the popular view that all women should be liberated except his sisters and his wife,' said the inspector, 'so Mrs Müller, finding this attitude irksome, went out and bought a quart of prussic acid . . .'

'Not in Kempten, she didn't,' said the sergeant. 'That's classified as a highly toxic substance and it can only be sold to registered users who have an authorization. They checked it out over there. No sales other than the legitimate ones.'

'Strange,' said the inspector. 'Well, if she couldn't buy it in her own home town, it's not likely that she'd have been able to anywhere else either. We'll have to let that go for the time being. What about romantic entanglements, either hers or his?'

'There, we have too much material,' said the sergeant. 'Mrs Müller is a swinger, that's certain. She's been making out with half the male population of Kempton and surrounding communities both before and after marriage. It's not certain that Müller knows everything, but he must know that she's not sitting home knitting socks. As a matter of fact, they seem to be turning up some evidence that Müller was in on the fun and games too. He and his wife are very close friends with another couple named Wilhelm and Viktoria Leinauer and the gossip has it that they switch around a good deal.'

'Wife swapping. The poor man's sport of the sixties,' said the inspector. 'But that's not too good for our case. If they're all sleeping with each other already, why bother to murder one member of the party?'

'Beats me,' said the sergeant, 'but I'm not very progressive and there's a lot about this I don't understand. Kempten is going to start checking out Gerd Fischer tomorrow. He's Mrs Müller's first husband. Twenty-seven years old and sort of a spoilsport they say. Doesn't swing. Doesn't like wife swapping. Can hardly blame her for divorcing him.'

'In this department, sarcasm is authorized only for senior investigations officers,' said the inspector.

The sergeant, having been thus rebuked, went home to his dinner, and the following day returned to Kempten where the Department of Criminal Investigations was trying to find out how Gerd Fischer had felt about his ex-wife's second marriage and whether he had, by any chance, access to prussic acid.

'It begins to look good,' the sergeant told his chief that evening. 'Fischer was decidedly unhappy over the divorce. Didn't want it. And he made threats against his wife at the time. None that they've been able to find against Müller, but of course, Müller wasn't on the scene at the time of the divorce. It wasn't as if he was named a correspondent in the divorce case or anything like that. There was definitely bad feeling though and Kempten is working on the theory that Fischer may have wanted to murder Müller in order to get his wife in trouble. They figure that, if the murder was that carefully planned, the motive could have been a sophisticated one too.'

'Sounds reasonable,' said the inspector. 'But then who was the woman who took the parcel to the post office in Stuttgart?'

'No answer to that yet,' said the sergeant. 'Fischer is living with a young woman, but she doesn't have long, blonde hair. She had short, brown hair and there's nothing wrong with her right arm.'

'The blonde hair could have been a wig,' said the inspector.

'That's what they think in Kempten,' said the sergeant.

In the following days, the Kempten Department of Criminal Investigations came to think so more than ever. Evidence was uncovered that Fischer had been even more bitter over his wife's second husband than he had been about her divorce from him. He had, it seemed, been hoping even after the divorce to win her back, a hope which evaporated with her second marriage.

Equally conducive to suspicion, Fischer, although not an authorized buyer of prussic acid, had had access to the poison as he had worked at one time in a galvanizing plant, one of the places where prussic acid was used commercially. The flask of gentian-bitter had not been large, and only half the content had been prussic acid. It was an amount that he could easily have taken from his place of work without its loss being noted.

There was, of course, no proof that he had, just as there was no proof that the Müllers and the Leinauers were swapping partners, but the Kempten police felt that the combination of indications was now strong enough for direct action to be warranted.

They did not, however, take into custody Gerd Fischer, but rather the young lady with whom he was living. She had the reputation of being a remarkably respectable young woman and the police thought that, if it was she who had delivered the parcel to the Stuttgart post office, it had been without any knowledge of what was in it. Fischer had perhaps told her that it was a joke of some kind and, although she would now know that it had been a somewhat lethal sort of joke, she could not come to the police without incriminating herself, even assuming that she was prepared to denounce her companion.

It had been hoped that if she were placed under interrogation, she would quickly cave in and at least admit to mailing the parcel, but, in fact, she did no such thing and denied any knowledge of the crime. Samples of her handwriting were compared with the note from the parcel and found not to correspond.

In the end, the police were forced to release her and she departed leaving their carefully constructed case in ruins for, in the course of the interrogation intended to establish her whereabouts on the night that the parcel was mailed, she had incidentally established that Gerd Fischer, whether he had anything to do with the murder or not, had had nothing to do with mailing the parcel. At the time it was mailed, he had been not in Stuttgart, but in Kempten.

'Well, that's too bad,' said the inspector when he heard of the collapse of the case from a downcast sergeant who was getting tired of driving back and forth between Fürstenfeldbrück and Kempten. 'But it is a possible explanation of where the prussic acid came from. Mrs Müller may have obtained it from a galvanizing plant or some other industrial facility.'

'Mrs Müller doesn't work in a galvanizing plant,' said the sergeant. 'Mrs Müller doesn't work at all.'

'But perhaps she has a friend who does,' said the inspector.

'Then, why doesn't he come forward?' said the sergeant. 'The case has been headlined in every newspaper in the country. He must know about it.'

'Supposing,' said the inspector, 'that you worked in a galvanizing plant and you were on close, let us say intimate, terms with a very beautiful, young, married woman and she came to you one day and said, "Could you fix me up with a pint or so of prussic acid? I want to use it to water the geraniums," and you did fix her up with a pint of prussic acid from the plant and not long after you read in the newspapers that somebody had tried to murder your friend's husband with prussic acid, but had murdered somebody else instead. Would you rush straight down to the police with your story?'

'I'll tell them over in Kempten you said to check the galvanizing plants,' said the sergeant.

'Should have done it in the first place,' said the inspector.

The Department of Criminal Investigations in Kempten agreed. The commercial users of prussic acid in the area should have been checked first of all. It was not, however, too late.

The task was actually rather simple. Who among the Müllers' friends and acquaintances had worked in a place that used prussic acid?

The answer was equally simple. None.

The investigators were not, however, discouraged. During the course of their investigations an interesting fact had come to light. Wilhelm Leinauer was reputed to be a very close friend of Christel Müller, and another close friend of Leinauer's, although perhaps not quite on the same level, was thirty-year-old Konrad Reisacker who owned a small metal treating and galvanizing plant. Reisacker was authorized to buy prussic acid and maintained a stock of it at his plant.

Brought to police headquarters, Reisacker, who was an honest man, happily married up until now, the father of several children and frightened nearly out of his wits, instantly broke down and told all.

His troubles had begun, he said, when he met Wilhelm Leinauer during the course of one of the sex parties, formerly called orgies or debauchs, but now *de rigueur* with the smart, young set, in the city of Ulm. Reisacker had come along, but Leinauer had been accompanied by Christel Müller who, he said, had comported herself in the most shameless manner he had ever seen in his life.

The reason that Reisacker was attending a sex party in Ulm and not in Kempten was because neither this nor any other sex party was liable to be attended by Mrs Reisacker, a deplorably unliberated woman who did not believe that the expression of her personal freedom required her to engage in sexual relations with strangers.

Worse yet, she did not believe that Mr Reisacker required this sort of contact for the development of his personality either. In fact, she had given him to understand that, regardless of the medias' enthusiasm for the new morality, any deviation from the narrow confines of conventional monogamy, however out-of-date that might be, would result in dire consequences.

Reisacker, who was very attached to his wife and children, had taken this greatly to heart and, if his statement to the police could be believed, had wandered but this once from the path of righteousness.

Following the sex party, his friendship with Leinauer had continued in Kempten, although they had not seen each other very often. He was not worried about Leinauer exposing him to his wife because Mrs Leinauer had not been present at the party either, nor had Mr Müller. He had assumed that Leinauer and Mrs Müller were on intimate terms, but thought that this was probably true of any male that the lady encountered, in view of her behaviour at the party.

In any case, he had not connected the matter with Christel Müller nor with anyone else when Leinauer turned up one day at the plant and asked if he could have some prussic acid. A weasel, he said, was getting his chickens and he intended to poison the beast.

Leinauer had brought along an empty stoneware flask which had contained gentian-bitter and Reisacker filled it roughly half-full of the deadly liquid, enough, he had remarked, to poison all the weasels in Germany.

Leinauer had said that he only wanted to poison one, and he had seen no more of him until he had come around on February 9 to say that, if anything turned up in the newspapers about prussic acid, it would be best to keep his mouth shut unless he wanted Mrs Reisacker treated to a blow-by-blow description of her husband's activities at the sex party in Ulm.

He had, of course, realized immediately that something terrible had taken place or was going to very shortly and his worst fears had been confirmed when he picked up his newspaper on February 15 to see a picture of the stoneware flask which he had personally filled with poison and the headlines, POLICE SEEK PRUSSIC ACID MURDERER!

Although he had acted innocently, he had also acted contrary to the law, for he was not supposed to let the lethal fluid out of his hands and he was uncertain what his responsibility involved. It was possible, he thought, that he himself might be charged with the murder or, at least, held responsible for it to some degree.

In addition, there was the matter of Mrs Reisacker. Although he did not think that Leinauer would be at liberty long enough to expose him once he had told his story, a police investigation would surely bring out all the details including the sex party in Ulm. As there would be nothing that the newspapers would enjoy publishing more, he could expect to find himself facing a divorce suit as soon as his wife got around to reading them.

Happily for Konrad Reisacker, his wife turned out to be less stern than he had feared and, although the truth did come out including some scarcely believable details concerning the sex festival in Ulm, she did not file for divorce.

Nor was the law very harsh. Recognizing that there was no intentional wrongdoing on Reisacker's part and considering the difficulty of his situation, he was given a stiff fine for negligence in handling toxic materials and released, partly out of recognition for his wholehearted cooperation with the police.

What disciplinary action was taken by Mrs Reisacker was not reported, but it is believed that Reisacker seldom makes trips out of the city, or even the neighbourhood, alone any more.

As for Wilhelm Leinauer and Christel Müller, they were both taken into custody before Reisacker had even finished making his statement.

Both denied all connection with the crime, but, upon being confronted with Reisacker's testimony, Leinauer changed his mind and confessed. He and Christel had prepared the death package together and Christel had turned it in at the post office wearing a blonde wig and sunglasses so that she could not be recognized.

Christel Müller did not give up so easily, but continued to maintain that her former husband, Gerd Fischer, was behind the murder attempt on Manfred Müller. However, her position had now obviously become untenable and she eventually added her confession to Leinauer's

Although lovers who conspire to murder someone and are caught usually end up accusing each other of bearing the sole responsibility, Wilhelm Leinauer and Christel Müller did not. Both admitted that they had plotted Müller's death together and both said that it was because he had stood in the way of their love.

He had certainly not stood very much in the way of it, but they said they thought that he would have opposed a divorce.

This raised a sinister question. Viktoria Leinauer would also have opposed a divorce and she not only said so in no uncertain terms, but insisted that her husband had known that she would never give him his freedom to marry Christel Müller.

In view of this, the incident with the car which had nearly rolled into the river with Viktoria and Manfred in the back began to look less like an accident, as did the strangely wired electric iron. Mrs Leinauer's marathon stretches of sleep also came to mind.

Wilhelm Leinauer and Christel Müller, however, denied that there had been any plot to harm Viktoria Leinauer and she apparently believed them as she clung to her husband, informing the newspapers that she regarded him as morally innocent and that it was the shameless hussy Christel who was responsible for everything.

Manfred Müller also stuck to his wife, saying that he forgave her and that he could not believe the stories of her wanton conduct at the sex parties. A keen amateur photographer, he owned a large collection of pictures he had taken of his wife and, in order to raise money for her defence, he began selling the ones that were merely erotic to the newspapers and the frankly obscene poses to friends, well-wishers and collectors of such art. Some of the pictures brought in as much as a thousand marks each.

Even the best defence could not, however, do very much under the circumstances and, after having been found guilty of manslaughter and conspiracy to commit murder, Wilhelm Leinauer and Christel Müller were sentenced to twenty years' imprisonment each.

10

INCOMPETENT GYNAECOLOGIST

It was precisely six twenty-five in the morning, a point in time which would later have a certain significance, of May 27, 1981, and a fine, clear autumn day in the city of Sydney, Australia, when twenty-eight-year-old Christine Lane was awakened by the sound of someone hammering violently on the front door of her bungalow at 41 Clarke Avenue in the north-east sector of the city.

Startled, she threw a glance at the alarm clock, leapt out of bed and, scuffling into her slippers, ran to peer out of the window which overlooked the front door.

A tall, handsome, red-haired woman whom she recognized as her neighbour, thirty-one-year-old Pauline Mitchell, was pounding on the door with her fists and wailing hysterically. She was barefoot and dressed in a largely transparent nightgown which reached barely to her hips.

Reassured that some criminal was not trying to break into the house, Christine ran down to the front door, opened it and staggered back as the weeping, hysterical woman fell into her arms.

'It's Jimmy!' sobbed Pauline. 'There's something the matter with him! He's lying on the floor by the bed and there's blood coming out of his mouth!'

Christine Lane pushed her neighbour into the living room and sat her down on the sofa. Returning to the front door, she saw that the door of the house across the street was standing open and, after a brief hesitation, crossed the street, entered the house and found her way to the bedroom. The brief hesitation had been because it had occurred to her that fifty-one-year-old James Mitchell might have been attacked by an intruder, possibly a burglar. The owner of a chain of prosperous garages, Mitchell was, if not rich, very well-to-do.

She saw no sign of any intruder in the house, but, in the bedroom, Mitchell was lying, as his wife had said, next to the bed with the blood running from his open mouth. There was an alarmingly large pool of it already and Mitchell was either unconscious or dead, for he lay motionless and his eyes were closed.

Christine had once taken a Red Cross course in first aid, but she saw immediately that, whatever was wrong with Mitchell, it was beyond her limited knowledge and, without approaching the man, she ran back into the living room and dialled the telephone number of the emergency ambulance service.

Mitchell, it turned out, was dead. The ambulanceman made a hurried check for signs of respiration or heartbeat and found neither. What he did find was a deep wound in Mitchell's left side.

To the ambulanceman, it looked like a knife wound and he reported it as such to the communications desk of the Sydney police, which he contacted immediately over the ambulance's radio-telephone. Unless he was greatly mistaken, he said, this was homicide.

The co-ordinator at the communications desk asked him to remain on the scene until someone from the police arrived and sent two of his nearest patrol cars racing in.

The first arrived within less than five minutes and the officers promptly confirmed the ambulanceman's report. The man was lying dead on the bedroom floor and it looked like homicide.

It was by now five minutes to seven and the inspector in charge of the duty Homicide Squad had just arrived at his desk and was fortifying himself with a cup of coffee and a cigarette in preparation for the day's work. A large, intelligent-looking man with a smooth, pink complexion, he listened silently to the co-ordinator's report, swallowed the remains of the coffee in a gulp, stuck a fresh cigarette in the corner of his mouth and, having alerted his assistant, a sergeant who was drinking coffee in the outer office, set off immediately for Clarke Avenue.

On the way in the car, he briefed the sergeant, a young, very lean and muscular man whose most striking characteristic was an almost total lack of facial expression. This did not take long. The co-ordinator had not even known the identity of the supposed victim.

This was quickly established upon arrival for, by now, most of the neighbours in the street had collected in front of the house and Christine Lane came forward to say that it was she who had called the police and that the widow of the dead man was in her living room across the street. Everyone knew by now that Mitchell was dead.

While the sergeant went to take a statement from Mrs Mitchell, the inspector entered the house and looked at the corpse, but did not approach it. He then went across to join the sergeant, as he thought the widow might be able to provide some indication of the identity of the murderer.

Pauline Mitchell said she had no idea who might have killed her husband. She supposed that it must have been an intruder, possibly a burglar. She was a sound sleeper and had noticed nothing until the sound of her husband's body falling on to the floor beside the bed had awakened her.

She had been puzzled to find her husband not in the bed and had thought that he might have got up to go to the bathroom. However, the lights were not turned on and, when he failed to respond to her calls, she had become frightened, had turned on the light and was about to get up when she noticed her husband's feet sticking out beyond the end of the bed.

She had leaned across the bed and, looking down, had found herself staring directly into his face. He was bleeding from the mouth and she had thought he had injured himself falling out of bed.

Unable to rouse him, she had run across the street to Christine Lane for help. She had not seen anyone in the house and the front door had been locked as usual.

The inspector told the sergeant to tape-record Mrs Mitchell's statement and went back to the police car where he telephoned headquarters and ordered out a team from the police laboratory. The Coroner's Office was to be alerted, as James Mitchell had obviously not died a natural death and the body could not be moved until someone from the Coroner's Office had seen it.

The Coroner's Office had already been informed and one of the assistant coroners arrived in Clarke Avenue a short time later.

Having proceeded to an examination of the corpse, he reported that Mitchell had died of a single knife wound which had either penetrated the heart itself or severed some of the major arteries surrounding it. Mitchell had been dead for less than an hour and, in his opinion, had been stabbed while he was asleep.

The doctor, a tall man with steel-rimmed spectacles, then departed for the police morgue to wait for the arrival of the body so that he could perform the autopsy.

A police ambulance was already waiting to take it away but it could not be moved until the technicians from the police laboratory had seen it and had had the opportunity to examine the scene of the crime as it had been found.

The detection experts were, however, unable to find anything of significance at the scene or on the body. All that they were able to determine was that Mitchell had been stabbed while sleeping on his back. The death throes had been enough to roll him over the edge of the bed and on to the floor.

By this time, the Mitchell's family doctor had been called to the house and had given Mrs Mitchell a strong tranquillizer, so that she was able to accompany the inspector in an inspection tour to determine whether anything of value was missing.

Nothing, it seemed, was, although there was a substantial amount of money in the house and Mrs Mitchell had some valuable pieces of jewellery.

This did not surprise the inspector. Although others had suspected a burglar, he, with his professional experience in such matters, had never entertained the idea for a moment. Burglars break into houses for money. Sometimes they injure or murder someone in order to avoid capture or identification, but no burglar in his right mind would stab a sleeping man to death in his bed. Rather, he would be overjoyed that he was sleeping. The fact that nothing had been taken confirmed the inspector's suspicions that, whatever the motive for the murder, it had been a personal matter and not simply theft.

Having found nothing at the scene, the inspector terminated operations there, sent the body to the police morgue and returned with the sergeant to his office at police headquarters.

'I want you to begin,' he told his assistant 'by setting up a team to investigate Mitchell's relationship with his employees. He was the owner of a big chain of garages and he surely must have had trouble with some of his employees at one time or another. Find out if anyone had been fired lately and if any threats were made.'

'You're convinced it was an employee?' asked the sergeant.

'Not at all,' said the inspector. 'I'm not convinced of anything at this stage. In addition to the team on the employees, I want you to assign a group to tracing Mitchell's private activities. A rich man in his early fifties could have mistresses or be involved with someone's wife.'

'Mrs Mitchell is stunning, twenty years younger than he was and, according to her statement, they've only been married since May seventh of 1976,' said the sergeant.

'That's five years,' said the inspector. 'Rich men in their fifties become bored quickly.'

'And Mrs Mitchell?' said the sergeant. 'You don't want to take a look into her private affairs?'

'Yes indeed,' said the inspector. 'I want you to take charge of

135

that part of the investigation yourself. I am afraid we may find that Mrs Mitchell has a lover.'

The inspector's fears were not well founded. Pauline Mitchell came from a little town named Ravely where her parents still lived. There was one other child, also a daughter, named Barbara, who was now fourteen. Mrs Lois Hewitt, now fifty-six, had apparently decided on a second child at the very last moment. Otherwise, the Hewitts were unremarkable, respectable, middle-class people.

Pauline herself had had several casual affairs with men of her own age, but had never married until she met Mitchell. At the time, she had been working as a waitress in the chic Sydney restaurant, the Mikado, where Mitchell regularly came to eat and had met him there in early 1976. They had been married on May 7 of that same year.

'I'm happy to report that we haven't found any trace of a lover,' said the sergeant, reporting in to the inspector. 'As a matter of fact, she would have had to be feeble-minded or sex mad to risk such a thing. Mitchell was devoted to her and there was nothing that she couldn't have if she wanted it. What's more, I've talked to two of the men she had affairs with and they both say that she isn't particularly interested in sex. She's normal, but she doesn't have the sort of emotional character to murder her husband for a younger man.'

'You can never be certain what women are capable of,' said the inspector, 'but one thing is certain. She didn't stab him herself. I have the complete autopsy report and they were able to fix the time of death very exactly at six-twenty a.m. plus or minus five minutes. She wouldn't have had time to get rid of the knife and get across the street to Miss Lane's house. According to the cast of the wound, it was a sort of hunting knife with a single-edged blade seven inches long. It went in between the ribs and sliced open the lower part of the heart. Mitchell probably died without even waking up.'

'So it wasn't Mrs Mitchell or her lover,' said the sergeant, 'and, as far as we've gone with the matter, it doesn't appear to have been any mistress or husband of a mistress of Mitchell. Pauline seems to have been about the first serious affair that he ever had with a woman. Socially, he was a rather shy, retiring sort of man and there's no indication that he ever had a mistress before he married Pauline or after.'

'Which brings us back to where we started,' said the inspector. 'He had trouble with one of the employees and the man took his revenge. How is the team investigating the employees coming along?'

'Slowly,' said the sergeant. 'There are quite a number of them. Besides, we have to investigate not so much the ones who were still working for him as the ones who weren't. I'll report as soon as we have something concrete.'

The something concrete turned up two days later in the form of twenty-two-year-old James Cox, a motor mechanic, who had worked for one of the Mitchell garages for two months in the spring of 1981. He had been fired by Mitchell personally for smashing up a customer's car which he had borrowed without authorization.

Cox was not, of course, the only employee who had ever been fired by Mitchell, but he was the last and he had taken his dismissal very badly. According to some accounts, he had attempted to attack Mitchell with a screwdriver and had been knocked sprawling by the garage owner who, despite his age, was a powerful, active man.

Two of Cox's fellow employees, none of whom seemed to have liked him much, reported that the young mechanic had made threats against Mitchell and had said that he would get even, drawing his finger across his throat in a widely understood gesture.

The police did not doubt the sincerity of his intentions because they already had an acquaintanceship with James Cox. Despite his youth, he had already assembled an impressive record of charges including assault, assault with a deadly weapon and motor-vehicle theft. In all cases, Cox had pleaded guilty and had made a sufficiently good impression on the court to be let off lightly. Slightly built with blond, curly hair and a smooth, as yet nearly beardless, face, he looked far younger than his actual age and, emotionally, probably was.

His judges had treated him like a naughty boy, but the police were not in agreement with this assessment of Cox's misbehaviour. They thought that he was dangerous.

'There's a tendency in the courts today to excuse anything that anybody under the age of twenty-five does as a boyish prank, no matter how often they do it,' grumbled the inspector. 'Well, get out a country-wide pick-up-and-hold order on him. I suppose there's no trace of where he's got to?'

The sergeant shook his head. 'We're checking the garages to see if he's taken another job,' he said, 'but it's going to take a while. Of course, there's no guarantee that he's still in Sydney. In his place, I don't think I would be.'

James Cox was undoubtedly in agreement with the sergeant's attitude, for no trace of him could be found anywhere in Sydney. In the meantime, the investigation into the murder of James Mitchell had come to a virtual halt, as it was assumed that Cox was the murderer. He had had a motive. He had quarrelled with Mitchell shortly before his death. He had a record of acts of violence, some involving a knife. And he had even had a possible opportunity of obtaining a copy of Mitchell's keys to his house by taking an impression when they were lying around in the office or sticking in the ignition of his car. He was a known thief and he might have been planning to burgle his employer's house, a plan which, following his dismissal, had been altered to one of revenge.

The Mitchell murder case was, therefore, not exactly listed as solved, but it was not being very actively pursued either when the inspector received a strange letter from a twenty-nine-year-old woman who signed herself Mrs Joan Headley. Mrs Headley, it seemed, was what is known as a woman scorned and she was trying to do something about it, namely stick her erring husband with a murder rap.

In her letter Mrs Headley said that her thirty-five-year-old husband Peter had been having an affair with Pauline Mitchell. The Headleys owned a small vacation cottage on the coast half-way between Sydney and Ravely and she was certain that he had been taking Pauline there. Astonishingly, she added that Peter and Pauline had had an affair over fifteen years earlier and that they were the parents of an illegitimate child.

The charges in this letter seemed improbable to the investigators as they had gone into Pauline Mitchell's background rather thoroughly and had found no trace of any lover named Peter Headley nor of any illegitimate child. It was, of course, true that they had not gone back quite fifteen years, for Pauline would, at that time, have been only sixteen years old.

However, Mrs Headley stated that her husband worked in one of Mitchell's garages and this, at least, was true. There was a Peter Headley working in one of the Mitchell garages and he had worked there for a number of years.

Had the letter been anonymous, the inspector would probably have thrown it in the waste basket, but, as Mrs Headley had signed her name and given her address, he sent the sergeant to investigate.

The sergeant returned looking confused. Mrs Joan Headley, he said, was a perfectly respectable, ordinary housewife and she was as mad as a wet hen. She was convinced that her husband had had an affair with Pauline when Pauline was still a teenager and that she had given birth to a child. She did not know what had happened to the child, but she suggested that Pauline might have murdered it.

This was not, however, what troubled her. She had been told by a friend that Peter had called at the Mitchell house when Mitchell was not home and that he and Pauline had driven away together.

'Did you get the name of the friend who told her?' interrupted the inspector.

'Yes,' said the sergeant, 'Christine Lane.'

'You mean the woman who lives across the street from the Mitchells and who called the police?' said the inspector.

'The same,' said the sergeant. 'Of course, it's logical that, if Headley did come to the Mitchell house, she would be more likely than anyone else to see him, but it's apparently a pure coincidence that she happens to be a friend of Joan Headley. Anyway, Mrs Headley went down to the Headleys' vacation cottage and found traces that some woman had been there, presumably with her husband. She's sure that it was Pauline Mitchell and she thinks that Pauline and Peter planned the murder so that Pauline would inherit the garage chain. Peter could then get a divorce and marry Pauline and everybody would live happily every after with the exception of Mitchell and Mrs Headley.'

'She doesn't seem to have a very high opinion of her husband,' said the inspector.

The sergeant shrugged. 'Perhaps she knows him too well,' he said. 'I suppose you want to follow it up?'

'Definitely,' said the inspector. 'I'm not prepared to buy the whole story, but there's something to this. You could make a start by going out and confirming that part of Mrs Headley's statement with Christine Lane.'

'I already have,' said the sergeant. 'It's true. She says that she saw Headley at the Mitchell house on three occasions and that the first time was the tenth of June last year. She didn't mention it to Joan Headley until a few months ago because she thought that Mitchell might have sent Headley to his house to pick up something, but, when she saw Headley and Mrs Mitchell driving away together, she came to the conclusion that something funny was going on. She knows Headley and she apparently doesn't have a much higher opinion of him than does his wife.'

'Well then, why the devil didn't she come forward and say something?' said the inspector. 'Surely, she must have realized that this would make Headley a suspect.'

'She said that she was never questioned about it and that she didn't think it was her business to make accusations against people when she had nothing concrete to base them on,' said the sergeant. 'She should have been interrogated at the time when the other neighbours were, but we apparently missed her because she was down as the person who had called the police.'

'It's careless slips like that that can ruin an investigation,' said the inspector severely. 'We've been running all over the country hunting for Cox and this Peter Headley has been sitting right here under our noses. Well, what are you waiting for? Go get him and bring him in.'

'And charge him with what?' asked the sergeant. 'The murder of James Mitchell? We haven't a scrap of evidence that he was involved. We haven't even any evidence that he was having an affair with Mrs Mitchell. His wife is obviously jealous and all that Christine Lane can say is that she saw one of Mrs Mitchell's husband's employees call at the house. You're not going to get an indictment on that, particularly as both Headley and Mrs Mitchell are certain to deny it.'

The inspector thought it over. 'You're right,' he said finally. 'We'd have to show at the very least some relationship between Mrs Mitchell and Headley other than what could be normally construed as that of an employee and his employer's wife. Even the alleged affair when she was a teenager . . .'

'What about the illegitimate child?' said the sergeant. 'Mrs Headley insists that they had one and, so far, she seems to be telling the truth. Maybe she's right about that too.'

'She may be,' said the inspector, 'but, for the life of me, I don't see how we could trace an illegitimate child born fourteen or fifteen years ago.'

A strange look suddenly passed over the sergeant's normally expressionless features.

'Barbara Hewitt is fourteen,' he said.

'Barbara?' said the inspector. 'That's Mrs Mitchell's sister.'

'Is it?' said the sergeant.

'We'd never find out now,' said the inspector. 'Mrs Hewitt would stand by her daughter and the child probably doesn't know.'

'Headley would know,' said the sergeant.

'Do you think he's going to tell you?' said the inspector.

140

'Wouldn't there have been a doctor in attendance?' said the sergeant. 'Could a girl just have a baby like that at home and pass it off as her mother's?'

'It's possible,' said the inspector. 'It's not so very many years ago that nearly all women had their babies at home and with no more help than some other woman or a midwife. Mrs Mitchell is a big, healthy woman. She was probably a big, healthy teenager. However, try the Hewitt family doctor in Ravely. He may know something that would help us.'

The Hewitt family doctor in Ravely did, indeed, know something. He had, he said, always assumed that Barbara was an adopted child. In any case she was not the daughter of Mrs Lois Hewitt because she had been born on May 4, 1967, and he had performed a complete hysterectomy on the supposed mother on March 10, 1966.

'In short, if Mrs Hewitt had a baby in May of 1967,' said the sergeant to the inspector, 'she did it without ovaries or a womb, which should get her into the *Guinness Book of Records*.'

'It's more likely to get her daughter into jail,' said the inspector. 'Well, I think that's enough. Bring in Headley and Mrs Mitchell and we'll see what we can do with interrogation. We should be able to play one off against the other.'

The inspector was not too optimistic. Peter Headley and Pauline Mitchell were arrested and brought to police headquarters where they were asked if they knew each other. Pauline denied that she had ever laid eyes on Headley in her life or heard the name. Headley said that Pauline Mitchell was his late employer's wife. He had seen her once or twice when she came into the garage.

Pauline was then confronted with the evidence that her mother could not have given birth to Barbara at the time that she was born and was asked if it was not true that she herself was the girl's mother.

This proved to be too much for her nerves and she broke down and confessed that Barbara was, indeed, her own daughter.

She had, she said, had an affair with Headley when she was sixteen years old and he had abandoned her when she became pregnant. She had borne the child at home and her parents had accepted it as their own. Barbara had not been told.

She still denied any contact with Headley after marrying James Mitchell.

Headley was now confronted with Pauline's statement concerning his fatherhood of the girl known as Barbara Hewitt indicating that, contrary to what he had said, he knew Pauline Mitchell very well indeed.

The evidence of having made a false statement to the police led Headley to make an admission of his own in an attempt to re-establish his credibility. He had, he said, run into Pauline Mitchell by accident at a supermarket on June 10, 1980, and they had resumed their affair of some fifteen years earlier.

The inspector now had proof that both suspects had been lying to the police and he played them off so cleverly one against the other that Pauline Mitchell quickly broke down and incriminated Headley as the murderer of her husband.

She had, she said, not wanted to resume the affair, but Headley had forced her, threatening her with exposure of the true parentage of Barbara. She had been afraid that, if Mitchell found out the truth, he might hold it against her or even divorce her and she did not want to lose him.

She had, therefore, accepted sexual relations with Headley on several occasions, both at her own home in Clarke Avenue and at his vacation cottage between Sydney and Ravely.

Headley had, however, she said, not been satisfied with sex, but had wanted to divorce his wife and marry her. As a first step in this direction, he had murdered Mitchell.

The tape of this confession was played to Peter Headley who became more hysterical than Pauline had been. It was not he, he screamed, who had planned Mitchell's murder, but Pauline. She had wanted to inherit the garage chain and Mitchell's money and she had promised to share with him if he would put her husband out of the way.

And that was as far as the investigation ever went. The police had two conflicting confessions and, despite a great deal more interrogation, they were never able to extract anything else. Pauline said that it was Peter. Peter said that it was Pauline.

The jury believed them both. On July 27, 1981, they were found guilty of premeditated murder and sentenced to life imprisonment.

11

CHILDREN'S HOUR

It was a police inspector who found the body. The body was, however, that of his own daughter-in-law and the inspector was not on duty, but retired.

It was a Sunday evening, July 20, 1980, and the time was approximately seven o'clock when fifty-eight-year-old Inspector Edward Young, until recently attached to the police force of Orpington, a medium-sized community on the south-east fringe of London, passed with steadily crunching footsteps up the long, curving drive leading from the impressive entrance gates to the magnificent Victorian manor house which his son had bought in 1971. A hundred yards outside the entrance gates was the bus stop and a mile and a half beyond that the town of Orpington itself.

Practically speaking, the bus stop served only the manor, which stood in the midst of extensive grounds, surrounded by a low wall. There were no other houses nearby.

Young was carrying a bouquet of red roses in his hand. He always brought roses when he came to invite his son and daughter-in-law to dinner.

Thirty-seven-year-old Harold Young might not be there. As the head of a flourishing painting and decorating business, he could be off on one of the business trips which sometimes took him away from home for as long as two weeks.

His wife, Barbara, a year younger, would, of course, be home. There was no reason for her to be out on a Sunday. She would, however, be alone. Phyllis, the Youngs' only child, was now twelve years old and at boarding school.

The front door of the house was never locked and Edward Young rang the bell, pushed the door open and went in without waiting for a response. He and his wife were on excellent terms with their son and daughter-in-law and there was no need for formality.

Barbara was in the big downstairs living room. She lay on the Chesterfield sofa, the dressing gown that she had been wearing open and fallen away to expose her more-than-slightly-plump body. Her left knee was bent and rested against the back of the sofa.

The right leg trailed on the floor as did her right arm and hand. She looked as if she were sleeping, but Edward Young was an inspector of police. He realized immediately that she was dead.

However satisfactory a wife and daughter-in-law Barbara might have been, she had never been a pretty woman, and her large, round face was positively hideous now. The staring eyes were wide open and bloodshot. The skin of the face was dark, almost bluish, and her tongue protruded from her mouth for, to a layman, an amazing length. The black strangulation marks on the skin of the throat were plainly visible.

A man with no professional experience in such matters might have become excited, might have rushed forward to see if there were any signs of life, might have covered the exposed body, but former Inspector Edward Young did none of these things. Instead, he bowed his head for a moment in what could have been a prayer and then walked steadily out to the telephone in the entrance hall where, having dialled a familiar number from memory, he identified himself and asked to speak to someone who will be known here as Inspector John Brentwood.

Mrs Brentwood said that her husband was out in the garden but that she would call him. She, of course, knew Young well. He and her husband had been friends and colleagues for over twenty years.

When Brentwood answered, Young told him where he was and that his daughter-in-law had been murdered. He would remain at the manor until the police arrived.

Brentwood, a large man with a fine pink-and-white complexion and a luxuriant head of iron-grey hair, was startled out of his usual calm and nearly shouted into the telephone that he was coming personally and at once. As chief of the Homicide Squad, it was normal for him to be summoned if a murder took place, but there were not a great many murders in Orpington and this one involved an old friend and a woman that he knew. He and his wife had dined more than once at the Youngs' Victorian manor. There had always been jokes about how fortunate it was that Harold had failed his police examinations and had been forced into the painting and decorating business, which had made him wealthy. On a policeman's pay, he would have been lucky to afford a cottage, let alone a Victorian manor house.

Harold had replied that, although he was grateful for his good fortune, he still wished that he could have become a policeman and followed in his father's footsteps. Successful as he was, with a firm now employing over thirty full-time painters and decorators, his heart was really not in the business.

Barbara had never had much to say on the subject. With her broad, pudgy features and her fat, dumpy body, she seemed slightly embarrassed by her own unattractiveness, showed little interest in clothes, wearing the same dresses for years on end, and was not a very good conversationalist.

There were people in Orpington who wondered why Harold had married her. It had not been because she was pregnant. Their child had been born two years after the wedding.

Nonetheless, despite her lack of physical charms in the conventional sense, there was a certain something to Barbara Young which many men found appealing and it was universally agreed that she was the most respectable and conservative of wives and mothers.

As this was nearly the last woman in Orpington that Inspector Brentwood would have expected to be murdered, he did not immediately alert the station or his assistant, but went directly, swiftly and discreetly to the Young manor to see for himself what had taken place. Young, he knew, was no alcoholic, but he might have had a few drinks too many, or perhaps retirement had unsettled his mind. The report of a murder could be a mistake.

It was no mistake and the inspector saw it immediately that he entered the living room. Barbara Young was dead, obviously murdered, and the investigation would have to begin as of that minute.

He, therefore, went back out to his car and called the communications centre at police headquarters. Outlining briefly the situation, he issued orders for a detachment from the police laboratory to be sent to the scene, the Coroner's Office to be notified and his assistant, whose name might have been Detective-Sergeant Charles McCrae but wasn't, informed that a homicide had taken place and that the investigations was under way.

He then took Young's statement on his portable tape recorder. Young was a personal friend, but Inspector Brentwood was a meticulous man and regulations called for an official statement taken as early as possible from the person reporting the discovery of the body.

Young's statement was, of course, short. He had come over to see his daughter-in-law and invite her and his son to dinner some time during the coming week.

He could, of course, have telephoned, but the weather had been nice and he enjoyed the trip out to the manor house, of which he was very proud as it was a highly visible symbol of his son's success. He had come out on the bus and had been one of only two passengers on it. Being a frequent visitor to the manor house, he knew the bus driver well and had chatted with him on the way out.

As a police officer, Young carefully included all of these details. He knew why the statement was necessary and he knew that it would be checked. The person reporting the discovery of the body of a homicide victim is not infrequently the murderer.

The taking of the statement having been completed, the two former colleagues, both confirmed pipe smokers, lit their pipes and sat silently smoking in the police car. There was nothing either could say. All that could be done was to wait for the arrival of the specialists and identification experts from the laboratory, who would now attempt to determine who had murdered Barbara Young and, if possible, why.

Detective-Sergeant Charles McCrae, a hard-muscled man in his late thirties with a heavily pock-marked face and curly, dark blond hair, was the first to arrive, but left again immediately without seeing the body, as Inspector Brentwood asked him to drive Edward Young home. There was no point in the latter remaining any longer at the scene and, however calm and composed he might appear to be, the discovery of his daughter-in-law's corpse had undoubtedly been a severe shock.

While the sergeant was gone, a doctor from the Coroner's Office turned up and proceeded to an immediate examination of the corpse. Like the inspector, he had been summoned from his home and he was wearing gardening clothes and boots. A short, very broad man with a thoughtful, scholarly sort of face, he reported that Mrs Young had been dead for at least four hours and that, according to the indications, she had been engaged in sexual activity some time before her death.

Inspector Brentwood, startled, asked if he meant that she had been raped and was told rather bluntly by the doctor that, if she had been, she had enjoyed it more than rape victims normally do. It appeared, he said, that she had been sexually aroused herself. There was no laceration of the genitals nor any indication that intercourse had been accomplished through the use of force.

There was, he thought, enough semen in the dead woman's vagina to establish the blood group of her partner, but it was important that she be brought to the morgue as quickly as possible. He wanted to know if the ambulance had been summoned.

The inspector replied, rather absently, that it had not, but that he would now summon it. The body would be sent over the minute that the technicians from the laboratory had completed their examination of it and had taken their official pictures of the scene.

The inspector spoke absently because he was confused and astonished. He had assumed that Barbara Young had been killed by an intruder and, had she been raped, he would not have been in the least surprised. The fact that she had apparently engaged in voluntary sexual activity altered basically not only his concept of the case, but also his opinion of Barbara. Of all the women he knew, he could scarcely think of one who seemed less likely to have a lover than Barbara Young.

That lover struck him as a remarkable person. Modern England is far from prudish. A presentable man looking for sex partners could easily have found someone younger and more attractive physically than his friend's daughter-in-law.

The only explanation that occurred to him was that the man had not been presentable. He had been old or ugly or, for some reason or other, unacceptable to the many thousands of attractive young women running around London who accepted sexual invitations as casually as proposals for a game of tennis.

But, if the lover had been so undesirable, why had Barbara Young accepted him? She could not be starved of sex. Harold was a vigorous, active and more-than-averagely-handsome man. It was true that he was often away on business trips, but, surely, after fourteen years of marriage, Barbara's sex drive would not have been so imperative that she could not wait until he got home.

The whole thing made no sense at all and the inspector settled down to wait, nervously chewing on his pipe stem, for the technicians to complete their examination of the house.

The technicians went about their work carefully, and took a long time, but they found nothing that appeared to have any significance to the investigation with the possible exception of a long, brown wig and a good deal of make-up material. Mrs Young's own hair was straight and blonde and, as far as Inspector Brentwood could remember, he had never seen the woman wear make-up at all.

The investigation at the scene having been concluded, the body was sent off to the morgue for the autopsy and the inspector returned to his office where he found Harold Young waiting. Mr

Young said that he had come to confess to the murder of his wife. They had quarrelled. He had killed her. He was sorry.

The not overly surprised, but dismayed and saddened inspector asked if he cared to explain why and Harold Young said that he did not. It had been a private matter. He had confessed to the murder. It was enough.

The inspector did not think so. There are large differences in homicides and there are large differences in the punishments handed out for them. It is the duty of the police to establish not only the identity of the murderer, but also his motives. Otherwise, a fair and reasonable trial is not possible.

Harold Young was, however, obviously not prepared to discuss his motives, so it would be necessary for the inspector to find them out himself. He had no doubt that they would be connected with Mrs Young's sexual activity as suggested by the doctor, but he still had no inkling of the surprises that lay in store for him.

The autopsy report provided none of these surprises. It merely confirmed the suspicion that Barbara Young's last sex partner had not been her husband, for the semen recovered from her vagina was of a man with a different blood group from that of Harold Young. Otherwise, there was nothing new added to what the doctor had determined at the scene of the crime.

Death had been the result of manual strangulation, the hyoid bone at the base of the throat not being broken, but many of the tiny blood vessels in the whites of the woman's eyes having ruptured. The time had been late in the afternoon of the same day.

There was no indication that Mrs Young had managed to mark her murderer. No traces of skin or hair were found under the finger-nails and the doctor thought that she had probably lost consciousness rather quickly.

All of this was more confusing to the investigation than it was useful. At some time not long before her death, Barbara Young had been engaged in passionate sexual intercourse with an unknown lover, and she had then been strangled to death by her husband, presumably because of the former. The inspector could scarcely believe it.

Although he did not know it yet, he was going to encounter other things in this case which he would find even harder to believe. This became apparent when Sergeant McCrae, after making a number of discreet inquiries around the neighbourhood, came up with a possible candidate for the role of lover.

A possible candidate, yes, but hardly a probable one. His name was Simon Gilmour. He worked for a grocery store and delivered groceries to, among others, the Young house. And he was sixteen years old.

The inspector was incredulous. He wanted to know if the sergeant was saying that the wealthy and highly respectable Mrs Young had been having an affair with an adolescent grocery delivery boy twenty years younger than herself?

The sergeant said that, in so far as he'd been able to determine, that was the case. The boy had been seen in and around the manor a number of times when his presence could hardly have been in connection with the delivery of groceries.

More significantly, he had been spotted at least once climbing over the wall rather than using the front gate. The conclusion was that he had not wanted anyone to see him entering or leaving the grounds.

The inspector was inclined to disagree with the sergeant's theory. Gilmour, he thought, had more likely been sneaking into the house to steal something than to have sexual intercourse with the mistress.

The sergeant admitted that it was possible, but pointed out that Gilmour enjoyed a good reputation, was known as a hard worker, came from a good middle-class family and had no police record. He was hardly the type to become a sneak-thief.

The inspector remarked dryly that Mrs Young had been hardly the type to be murdered or to have a lover, and suggested that the sergeant continue his investigations.

The sergeant did, but failed to uncover any evidence of thieving by Simon Gilmour. Instead, he uncovered another mystery. In his efforts to find out whether Gilmour might have been spending more money than his legitimate income could explain, he came upon a curious circumstance. Gilmour had had, if anything, less spending money since the spring of that year and all of his teenage friends had been literally broke. Boys who had never before shown any interest in gainful employment had suddenly been going around looking for odd jobs to do, advances on pocket money had been taken and there had been a brisk business in small loans.

'What this is supposed to mean is beyond me,' said the sergeant, reporting on his discovery to the inspector. 'I thought at first that a pusher had moved into the area and that the kids were all on drugs, but it's not that. None of them are on drugs, but they're spending their money on something that they want to keep quiet. Whatever it is, it seems to have been going on since about April this year.'

'Strange,' said the inspector. 'And you think it has something to do with the murder of Mrs Young?'

'I can't see what it could have,' said the sergeant. 'Gilmour was the only one in the group who had any contact with the Youngs, whatever that was, and he's the one who seems to have been less broke than the rest. It's a strange thing though.'

'Very,' agreed the inspector. 'Well, if it isn't drugs or anything that's harming the boys' health . . . They don't look sick do they?'

'Gilmour looks a little haggard,' said the sergeant. 'The others seem to be perfectly normal.'

No progress having been made in this direction, the investigators attacked the problem from the other side by trying to determine Barbara Young's activities prior to her death. If she had had a secret lover, she must have met him somewhere and the circumstances must have been such that her husband could have learnt of the affair.

As in the case of Simon Gilmour, it was the sergeant who did most of the investigating and, as in the case of Gilmour, he promptly turned up another mystery.

Barbara Young, it seemed, had enjoyed, if that was the right word, a curious reputation with the local trades people. Although she was known to be rich, she had spent so little money that half of the merchants thought she was a psychopathic miser and the other half thought that her husband did not give her any money.

In April of that year, however, the proponents of both schools of thought were startled when Mrs Young suddenly began spending money like a drunken sailor. The sums were not large and the purchases were not major, but, for a woman who had exercised such caution in the past, the change in the behaviour was conspicuous.

'April?' said the inspector, looking at his assistant with alarm. 'April was when the local adolescents began to run short on pocket money! They were all boys, I take it, those adolescents?'

The sergeant confirmed that, as far as he knew, they were all boys.

'There's got to be a connection, Charles,' said the inspector, gnawing nervously on the stem of his pipe. 'You can't have a coincidence like that in a criminal investigation. It has to be . . . but no! That's ridiculous! My God! Surely . . . What do you think?'

'About April of this year,' said the sergeant slowly, 'the boys started spending money secretly somewhere. At about the same time, Mrs Young started spending money with the trades people. The only conclusion I can draw is that the money she was spending came from the boys.'

The inspector leaned forward, put his elbows on the desk and buried his face in his hands. 'Barbara,' he said. 'Barbara Young.'

His voice was muffled and the sergeant was not quite certain as to whether he was suppressing tears, laughter or both. He was, however, obviously in the grip of strong emotions.

'I've got it!' he exclaimed suddenly, lifting his head. 'She set up a gambling den there in the manor when Harold was away. The boys were gambling away their pocket money and she was taking a house cut on everything.'

'There would have been winners too,' said the sergeant. 'All the boys were broke. Besides, the house was searched and there was no gambling equipment there. All they could have done was flip coins.'

'Contact the juvenile authorities and have the boys brought in,' said the inspector. 'I don't want to know what happened, but we've got to have an answer to all this.'

Simon Gilmour, his close friend, James Evans, and an impressive crowd of other male adolescents whose ages ranged from fourteen to seventeen soon provided the inspector with more answers than he could use.

Had the boys been punks or rockers or one of the other weird aberrations of modern British youth, their cooperation with the police might have been less wholehearted, but these were merely decent, middle-class boys of whom a surprising number still exist in the United Kingdom despite the efforts of the media. Being taken to a police station for interrogation was not an experience to be used as proof that they were the criminals they claimed to be. It scared them.

And they talked. They talked frankly and at length and, because they had been greatly impressed by their experiences and the memory of them was still fresh in their minds, they talked in detail.

The remarkable and, to many, inexplicable series of events which had led to the death of Barbara Young and the inculpation of her husband for her murder had begun in April of that year and it had begun with Simon Gilmour.

Some time early in April, he said, he could not remember the exact date, he had delivered groceries to the Young manor and had found Mrs Young there alone. She had opened the door wearing a dressing gown beneath which there was obviously nothing, but Mrs Young, and the sight had excited him. At his age, he was, of course, easily aroused.

It seemed to him that Barbara Young had noticed this and, after he had put the groceries in the kitchen, she asked him suddenly if he was not tired and would not like to have a cup of coffee before leaving.

She had served him the cup of coffee in the living room and, taking a seat opposite, had crossed her legs so carelessly that he had been able to see her private parts. This had, naturally, put him into an unmistakable state and his hostess had asked him rather directly if he wanted to have intercourse with her.

Gilmour, unable to speak, could only nod and, to his astonishment, she had said, very well, if he would give her ten pounds, he could do with her whatever he liked.

He had paid the ten pounds and had been well satisfied. So too, apparently, had Barbara, for she had offered him a generous arrangement. If he would bring his friends, he could have one free treatment for every friend brought.

It was a fair offer and Simon was a boy with a certain degree of business acumen. He brought many friends. So many, in fact, that he was no longer able to say who or how many. Business had only been possible at those times when Harold Young was off on his trips, but on such days Barbara had often processed a half-dozen or more of the local teenage boys. At ten pounds each with only her sixteen-year-old procurer as overhead, the business had been distinctly more profitable than many small enterprises in the 1980s.

According to what she had told Simon, it was also a business which provided considerable personal satisfaction in addition to financial gain. Her husband, she said, was incredibly stingy, allowing her not so much as a penny for herself although he had piled up an impressive fortune in the bank. Even the household money was doled out grudgingly and years passed before she was allowed a new dress.

The sex allotment had been no better. Harold worked all the time and, even when he was at home, he was too tired to think of sex. Her love-life was non-existent.

The frolics with the teenagers had satisfied her requirements in many respects. She was getting a great deal of sex and, by her standards, a great deal of money. There was also something else. Although she did not say so and might not have known it consciously herself, she was getting even with Harold.

Barbara had gone about her project in a businesslike manner, buying the brown wig and the make-up materials to make herself more attractive to her young lovers and devising a system with Gilmour to indicate when she was alone and receiving. One of the upper storey windows could be clearly seen from the road and, if there was an ornamental lamp standing in it, it meant that Harold Young was on a trip and his wife's sporting establishment was open for business.

Gilmour's statement was confirmed by James Evans, also sixteen, who had been the first customer procured for the new business. He had found the woman old and unattractive but she had had such a powerful attraction for him sexually that he had spent every penny he could lay his hands on for her services. He had been hoping for an arrangement similar to Gilmour's and thought that he had been making progress in that direction when Barbara Young was murdered.

Similar statements were received from the other teenagers, most of whom said that they had found the service an improvement over the other entertainment facilities available in the area, but rather expensive. Although some denied this, it was apparently in all cases the first sexual experience for the young customers. No charges were brought, although Gilmour could technically have been accused of pandering.

The only question that remained was how Harold Young had learned of what his wife was doing, and the inspector came to the conclusion that someone must have told him. He could hardly have surprised Barbara in the act, for she had been cautious and Gilmour had been assigned to stand watch while she was taking care of his friends. If it was Gilmour who was being rewarded for his zeal, James Evans stood watch. In any case, Harold Young had not been a man to come home from a business trip unexpectedly and he had certainly neither suspected nor had reason to suspect that his pudgy, unattractive wife was running a sex school for teenagers in the manor during his absences.

The question was, who could have told him? No one knew except the teenagers themselves and they would have been the last persons in the world to approach the husband with such a tale. Moreover, even if they had, he would not have believed them. Whoever it had been, it had been an adult and one whom Young would believe and trust.

Practically speaking, this meant his father. Not many men have friends close enough to make a revelation such as the one which had been made to Harold Young. But how had Inspector Young himself known?

Inspector Young, it seemed, had learned of his daughter-in-law's misbehaviour completely by chance. He had come to the manor on the afternoon of June 6, bearing, as usual, roses, with the intention of asking his son and his son's wife to dinner. He had known that Harold was away on one of his trips, but this did not matter as he could leave the invitation with Barbara just as well.

Unfortunately, Barbara had been receiving and the young lookout had either been asleep, worn out by his own exertions, or too interested in watching to remain at his post.

The inspector had arrived undetected at the house itself and, in passing around it, had been galvanized by the sound of a woman rapidly and enthusiastically approaching a peak of erotic stimulation.

The inspector had recognized the voice and, as he knew with certainty that his son was not home, he was forced to the acceptance of something which was beyond his capacity for belief.

Hiding himself in some ornamental bushes, he waited and was presently rewarded by the sight of an adolescent boy emerging from the front door. For a moment, he felt relieved. This half-grown child could hardly be his daughter-in-law's lover.

Then, Barbara had stepped outside too. She was made up heavily, but inexpertly as she had had little practice, and she was wearing her brown wig. The inspector could barely recognize her. As he watched with bulging eyes, she gave her young lover a long, sensual goodbye kiss, a pat on the recently engaged parts and went back into the house.

The young man sneaked off through the bushes, climbed the low wall around the estate and the inspector presently saw him peddling off down the road on his bicycle.

From that day on, the inspector had consistently spied on his daughter-in-law whenever Harold was away on a trip and had come to realize the extent of Barbara's transgressions.

For over a month, he had wrestled with his conscience, trying to decide what was his best course of action. Should he approach Barbara and urge her to mend her ways? Should he speak to the parents of the teenagers? In the end, he had realized that there was only one thing he could do. He had to tell Harold, and he had told him.

Harold Young said in his statement that he had not been anxious for all this to come out, but as it had, he could say that he had confronted Barbara with the report of her unconventional behaviour and she had admitted it. Worse yet, she had been defiant, calling him an impotent miser and assuring him that even the admittedly clumsy teenagers were better lovers.

This had made Harold angry and he had strangled her.

Harold Young was by his own admission a murderer, but the court found that there had been substantial extenuating circumstances and a certain degree of provocation. As a result, when the sentence was handed out on December 15, 1980, it was for three years' imprisonment only.

12

EMASCULATED

It was eleven o'clock in the evening of January 15, 1977, a Saturday, and the bitter, black wind of the north Belgian winter was sweeping down over a deserted parking lot two miles to the east of the industrial and coal-mining town of Genk.

In the distance, the night lights of Genk cast a pale reflection against the rolling, black clouds of the winter night sky, pale because there were not many lights showing at eleven o'clock, even on a Saturday. Genk numbers no more than sixty thousand souls and most of them are working people who are accustomed to going to bed early.

Actually, the parking lot was not entirely deserted for there was one car parked there, a white Opel Manta, and inside the car, it was neither bitter nor cold. It was warm and cozy and it smelled of woman-flesh.

The man in the front seat half sat, half lay, his legs stretched out in front of him and his checked trousers down around his calves. Straddling his loins, the half naked woman moved slowly, sensuously, her blue-black hair falling in cascades over the face and shoulders of her lover.

The man groaned. 'Now . . .' he whispered. 'Now . . .'

The woman swung over to the seat beside him.

'No!' she whispered. 'You come to me. You are the man. You must dominate!'

The man rolled quickly over her, his body between her naked thighs. She wrapped her arms around his neck.

Suddenly, her legs hooked like clamps behind his knees. The arms around his neck tightened and finger-nails drove into the sides of his neck.

Three figures materialized out of the rain-swept darkness. The doors of the Opel Manta were pulled open. In the faint light from the dashboard, something flashed, cold, deadly.

The man roared and sought to pull away from the woman, but he was held helpless as in a trap. Blows began to rain over his head and back, and blood spurted.

156

Abruptly, the woman arched her back, released her grip and threw the man from her, rolling out of the door of the car in a single motion. Her skirt lay crumpled in the back seat and from the waist down, she was naked with the exception of her shoes and stockings. One shoe had come off.

The men were pulling her lover out of the car, hammering savagely at his face while the knife slid in and out in shallow torturing cuts. He had stopped bellowing now and fought silently and savagely, but his movements were hindered by the trousers around his ankles. He kicked one foot free.

'Pull his legs apart!' hissed the woman.

The men hesitated.

'Pull his legs apart!' screamed the woman in a horrible rasping voice that seemed to tear at her throat. 'Pull his legs apart! Pull his legs apart!'

She leaped forward and snatched the knife from the grip of the man holding it.

Her lover redoubled his struggles, kicking and twisting like a worm cut in half, but the hands were on his ankles and other hands held his arms fast. He was a strong man, but they were three. Slowly the thighs came apart.

'Ah!' cried the woman, her voice dripping satisfaction. 'Ah!' She moved forward, the knife held in the palm of the hand in the manner of people who know how to handle knives.

The man screamed in terror.

The woman leaned forward and cut.

There was a terrible cry, so terrible that the three men holding their victim released their grip and took an involuntary step backward.

'Come! Enough!' muttered one. He caught the woman by the arm. 'Leave him. We must go now.'

A great gush of blood had spurted over the hand holding the knife. Deliberately, the woman raised the hand to her mouth and licked her fingers. Then, without a backward glance, she followed the three men and disappeared into the darkness.

On the wet, icy-cold asphalt beside the parked Opel Manta, her lover lay clutching his groin with both hands. Between his knees the bloody scraps of meat which had been his testicles and penis formed strange, little heaps in the irregular, dully glinting lake of blood.

A quarter of a mile from the Zwartberg parking place stands Genk's St Jean Hospital, a modern, if not very large, institution which serves not only Genk but the countryside around it. Like any small hospital, it is quiet and perhaps a trifle unnerving in the early hours of the morning.

Anton Schleiman, a young administration employee doing the midnight to eight shift in the morning duty at the admissions office, had, therefore, not chosen his reading material very well.

The paperback was a slightly crude, but highly effective horror story of strange happenings in an insane asylum, with endless seas of gore, severed limbs and torn-out eyes and, although officially there were no mental cases in St Jean, it did not require a very strong imagination to conceive of some having been accidentally admitted along with the other patients.

Actually, the time and place were perfect for reading horror stories, for Schleiman was completely alone in the glass-walled admissions office, and outside the windows the wind was beginning to rise, sending showers of sleet-like bullets against the glass and wailing around the cornices like a thousand souls burning in hell. Throughout the building, there were the creaks and surreptitious, little sounds of a building caught in the icy grip of the winter wind, pouring down like a great river from the freezing, grey crests of the North Sea.

In other parts of the hospital, he knew, there were nurses and orderlies on duty, but they had no reason to come to the admissions office. He could be slowly tortured to death a thousand times over and no one would even know until it was too late.

Schleiman cast a nervous glance at the clock on the wall. It was nineteen minutes past two, less than six hours before he went off duty, but closer to seven before dawn. He lowered his eyes to his book again.

'There came a faint, scratching sound,' he read, 'as of razor-sharp claws drawn across the dark glass of the window. Suddenly . . .'

Schleiman went rigid. Over the whine of the wind outside had come what could only be described as a faint, scratching sound!

The book descended slowly into his lap and he pushed his chair back from the desk, every nerve in his body screaming, 'Run!'

But he did not run. In the first place, there was nowhere to run to. He could hardly rush in to the nurses' room pleading for protection. And anyway, protection from what? He had been reading a horror story and it had got to him. That was all. The sound of the scratching outside was, undoubtedly, a cat or dog looking for shelter and a hand-out.

So said his mind, but his body did not believe it. The mind was,

158

however, in charge and it drove him, stiff-legged as a dog looking for a fight, to peer through the glass of the door into the darkness outside.

Something was lying on the concrete slab in front of the door, something long and dark, much too long to be a dog. As he stood staring, transfixed, a blood-red hand rose into the light streaming from the office and the fingers extended slowly and feebly to draw downward across the glass. There was a faint scratching sound.

Schleiman's fear evaporated instantly. This was something he understood. Someone was hurt and had come seeking help at the hospital. From the bloody hand, Schleiman assumed that there had been a car accident somewhere within the immediate vicinity and he ran back to his desk to press the button which would summon male nurses and stretcher bearers on standby duty in their quarters a few hundred yards behind the hospital. There was no doctor or even a houseman on duty. St Jean is not an emergency hospital. If a doctor was needed, he would have to be summoned from his home.

Having called the male nurses and orderlies, Schleiman ran back to the front door and opened it. He did not, however, attempt to move the man although it was bitterly cold and the sleet was freezing on his bare legs . . . Bare legs? He saw suddenly and with astonishment that the man was naked from the waist down.

What kind of an accident could this be that tore off a man's trousers, but left his shoes on?

He had barely had time to pose the question when the stretcher bearers and orderlies came.

The man was lying face down and seemed to have lost consciousness, one hand stretched forward to the door and the other hidden beneath his body. Gently, the male nurses turned him over on his back.

Beneath the body, his right hand was clamped in a grip like death over his pubic area and between the fingers blood had oozed and partly frozen. The back of the hand was worn raw from being dragged over the ground with the full weight of the body on it.

'He's injured his genitals,' muttered a male nurse. 'Call out the duty doctor, Anton. This looks serious.'

Schleiman ran to his desk and placed the call. As he returned, the nurses and the stretcher bearers were cautiously prying the man's fingers away from his groin. Suddenly, they came free and a sort of groan of horror went up from the men.

There were no genitals. Penis and testicles had been sliced off close to the body. There was only a great, raw wound where they had been.

Schleiman and one of the stretcher bearers were immediately and violently ill, but the male nurses held their nerve.

'Pull yourself together,' snapped one of them, 'and help us get him inside. We've got to check the bleeding. I don't know how he's managed to survive this long.'

'Or why he would want to,' muttered the stretcher bearer who had not been sick. 'Wouldn't it be better to . . .'

'I didn't hear that,' said the nurse. 'Come on now. Get him on to the stretcher and up to the operating room. Careful! He's got other injuries as well. Anton, call the police. This is a criminal case.'

Schleiman went back to his desk only too willingly and a few moments later was endeavouring to convince a sleepy and sceptical desk sergeant that this was not a hoax and that he was neither drunk nor out of his mind. It was not easy. Genk is not the sort of place where people get castrated every day in the week.

In the end, the desk sergeant agreed to send a patrol car and, as one was in the immediate vicinity, it arrived within a matter of minutes.

The patrolmen were also sceptical and a nurse led them up to the operating room where the unconscious man was lying on his back on the operating table while other nurses and orderlies worked to stop the flow of blood. There was little they could do, for the wounds were no longer bleeding very much in any case.

The patrolmen looked, turned pale green and ran back down to their patrol car where they babbled an almost incoherent account into the shocked ears of the desk sergeant over the radio-telephone.

Very shortly thereafter, it was the turn of Chief Inspector Pierre Smal, the tall, long-nosed, balding head of the modest Genk Department of Criminal Investigations, to be shocked. A nervous, lantern-jawed man who would probably have been happier as an antique dealer than a police officer, it was seldom that he was turned out of bed at night and, until now, never at three in the morning or for such a reason.

He was, however, a very conscientious man and he immediately dressed and rushed to the hospital where he was, fortunately, unable to see the victim. The duty doctor had, in the meantime, arrived and was operating.

'But it's definitely deliberate castration?' said the inspector to the nurse on duty at the operating-room door. 'It couldn't be an accident of some kind?'

'It was deliberate castration,' said the nurse. 'His genitals were completely cut away.' A grim veteran of many years in hospitals, she was not as affected emotionally as her male counterparts.

'Can a man survive such a thing?' said the inspector incredulously.

The nurse shrugged. 'He has up until now. Great loss of blood, but he's getting a transfusion now. The doctor wasn't able to make a prognosis. He has other cuts and stab wounds and he's apparently been beaten. Personally, I think that the worst effects will be psychological, assuming that he survives at all.'

'I should think so,' said the inspector shuddering.

He went back down to the admissions office and called the station.

'I'm at the hospital,' he said. 'This is a terrible thing. I'm starting the investigation at once. Turn out Sergeant Eskens and everybody else on standby in the department and the lab. Tell them they're to report ot me here immediately.'

Not long after, detectives and laboratory technicians began to drift in, yawning and in some cases half-dressed. Finally, the chief of the Genk Homicide Squad, Detective-Sergeant Jan Eskens, a tall, raw-boned, man with a ruddy complexion and a soft, brown moustache and goatee, appeared.

'What happened?' he asked, looking in astonishment at the room filled with police officers. 'The desk said somebody got castrated. It isn't true, is it?'

The inspector assured him that it was true.

'This is probably a murder case,' he said. 'I don't believe a man can survive such a thing even if he is still alive. Now, the first thing we have to find out is who he is. I've gone through the clothes he was wearing and there's no identification in them. However, all he was wearing was a shirt, vest and shoes.'

'No trousers?' said the sergeant. 'What happened to his trousers?'

'That's what you're to find out,' said the inspector. 'He dragged himself to the hospital after it happened so it couldn't have been very far away. As he was bleeding heavily, he should have left a trail you can follow.'

'It's raining,' said one of the laboratory technicians. 'And it's dark.'

'Then use flashlights,' said the inspector. 'As for the rain, it's freezing. The blood traces should be frozen into it. Get moving.'

Electric lanterns were brought from the police vans and the investigations moved out into what had now become a full-scale sleet storm. There was some grumbling from the junior member of the department which, however, quickly died away beneath the choleric gaze of Sergeant Eskens.

As the inspector had predicted, the freezing rain had literally frozen the blood trail into place and, as the sergeant followed it with the beam of a flashlight, a detective dropped the little, weighted metal flags used in investigations work alongside it to mark the trail. They were hardly necessary for it ran straight as a string away from the hospital.

'He must have known exactly where the hospital was,' remarked one of the detectives.

'Either that or he could see the lights,' said the sergeant. 'There aren't many lighted buildings out here at night. He dragged himself a devil of a way in any case. We're close to three hundred yards from the hospital and the trail goes on.'

'Three hundred and twelve yards,' said one of the technicians who had been measuring. 'We're at the edge of the Zwartberg parking lot now.'

Minutes later, the white Opel Manta, standing with open doors, loomed out of the darkness.

'I think we've found it,' said the sergeant. 'Jean-Claude, run back and inform the inspector.'

By the time that the inspector arrived from the hospital, it had been definitely ascertained that the parked car was the scene of the crime.

'There they are, chief,' said the sergeant, shining his flashlight on to the spot where the man's genitals lay frozen into a thin sheet of ice. 'They cut him right here and he dragged himself all the way to the hospital.'

'Incredible!' said the inspector. 'In this weather and after the shock of such a thing! How could he find the strength?'

'Well, he's a coal miner,' said the sergeant. 'One of the Greek colony here working the mines. According to the papers in the car, his name is Alessandros Postolsikis. He's thirty years old, married and the father of two children.'

'His last two, I'm afraid,' said the inspector. 'Well, you'd better start the investigation immediately. Have the tents brought out and get this whole area under cover. You may have to use heaters to melt off the ice, but we want to get hold of those people before they clear out of the country altogether.'

'They?' said the sergeant.

'That's a strong man in the hospital there,' said the inspector. 'Do you think that any one person could have done this to him?'

The sergeant did not see fit to answer the question, but later, at the office in police headquarters, the department's medical expert did.

'At least three men,' he said, slipping off his ice-covered raincoat and hanging it on the peg beside the door. 'He was held practically motionless at the time.'

'There's hot coffee in the pot,' said the inspector, pushing his packet of cigarettes across the desk towards the doctor. 'Is he going to live?'

The doctor poured himself a mug of hot, black coffee and came to sit in the chair next to the inspector's desk. It was past seven o'clock in the morning, but, of course, still completely dark. Dawn would not come until eight-thirty and, what with the cloudy weather, would be hardly noticeable when it did.

'It will depend on his will to live,' said the doctor, lighting one of the inspector's cigarettes. 'They've patched him up and the bleeding has been stopped. He had a heart like an ox so, physically, I would say there's nothing to stop him. However, psychologically, he may simply not want to live any more.'

'I think he will,' said the inspector. 'The man must have an incredible will to live. Think what it must have been like dragging himself all that way to the hospital and in that weather. He must have known that he'd been castrated. When they found him, he was gripping the wound.

'That is, undoubtedly, what saved him,' said the doctor. 'That and the low temperatures. Otherwise, he would have bled to death. Do you know who he is yet?'

'A Greek coal miner named Postolsikis,' said the inspector. 'Jan has gone to contact his wife. He should be back any time. Then I think we may get some idea as to who did this.'

The inspector was, however, due for a disappointment. Helena Postolsikis, the young and attractive wife of the injured man, had no idea who might have castrated her husband.

'It was a terrible shock to her, of course,' said the sergeant. 'but most of the neighbours are Greek and the ladies are sitting with her. She's a courageous woman. Said it was, at least, better than if he's been killed and, thank God, they already had two children. She wanted to go to the hospital, but I told her it was no use, she wouldn't be able to see him yet.'

'Nor for some time, I suspect,' said the inspector. 'I just wonder when we'll be able to speak to him. He must know who did this. It certainly wasn't any group of casual strangers.'

'It must have been the male relatives of some woman he was playing around with,' said the sergeant. 'He was married, but he was having an affair on the side. They went out there to the Zwartberg for privacy. The relatives followed, sneaked up on the car and jumped him.'

'Yes, that's about the way I figure it too,' said the inspector. 'An act like that could only be revenge or jealousy. Did you get the names of his friends from the wife?'

'Some,' said the sergeant. 'I'll start checking them out as soon as I've had breakfast. They should know who he was playing around with.'

The sergeant went off to have breakfast and, a little later, the technician in charge of operations at the scene of the crime came in to report that the investigations there had been completed.

'Actually, the only things we found outside the car were his trousers and his genitals,' he said. 'We brought the car back into the garage as it was. There's a woman's skirt lying in the back seat and somebody was having sex relations in there last night. There are traces of fresh semen on the front seat.'

'That ties in with our theories on how it happened,' said the inspector. 'Postolsikis was having an affair with some woman and her male relatives caught up with them. Did you get any prints off the car?'

'Lots,' said the technician, 'but none that can be definitely linked to the crime. The important prints would have been those on the outside door handles because the people who did this must have pulled the doors open, but the rain and sleet obliterated them.'

At noon, the inspector called the hospital and was informed that Alessandros Postolsikis was still alive and it was believed that he would recover. He was, however, in a state of profound shock and the doctor would not permit questioning.

'When can he be?' said the inspector.

'Very difficult to say,' said the doctor. 'He's going to need psychiatric treatment first. The psychiatrist is coming this afternoon to begin studying the case, but he probably won't be able to talk to him today. It's going to be at least a week before he can make a statement.'

'We'd better have the people who did it before then or we won't have them at all,' said the inspector. 'They're probably Greeks and they'll go back to Greece.'

The sergeant confirmed the nationality of the suspects when he reported in at five that afternoon.

164

'The man who's responsible for this is Christos Papanastassiou,' he said. 'Another Greek coal miner, forty-one years old, father of three children and the husband of a twenty-nine-year-old woman named Evangelia Panteli, also Greek. They've been married for seven years, but Papanastassiou apparently couldn't keep up with his wife's sexual requirements. She's been chasing Postolsikis for over two years now.'

'Where did you get all this?' asked the inspector.

'Customers of the bar that Papanastassiou and his wife were running over by the Zwartberg until January of last year,' said the sergeant. 'He gave up coal mining and took over the bar in February of seventy-one. You know the place. It's called The Greek of Genk. Everything went fine apparently until a couple of years ago, when Mrs Papanastassiou got the hots for Postolsikis. From what they tell me, she practically raped him. He wasn't enthusiastic.'

'What was the matter? Isn't she good-looking?' asked the inspector.

'I haven't seen her yet, but she's supposed to be a bomb,' said the sergeant. 'No, Postolsikis seems to have simply been reluctant to play around with some other woman, but Mrs Papanastassiou wouldn't take no for an answer. There was a scandal about it in the Greek community. Mrs Papanastassiou and Postolsikis disappeared and were gone for nearly a month. When they reappeared, Papanastassiou got rid of the bar and moved up to Herstal just outside Liège.'

'And Mrs P. with him?' said the inspector.

'And Mrs P. with him,' said the sergeant. 'The people I talked to thought that was the end of the affair.'

'Well, they were mistaken,' said the inspector. 'Better get on over to Liège tonight and pick up Papanastassiou before he leaves for Greece. You can bring his wife in too while you're at it.'

The sergeant went to the address of the Papanastassious in the Herstal suburb of Liège, thirty miles to the south, but he did not expect to find them there. They would, he assumed, be on the train for Greece.

To his surprise, he found the family having supper and showing no signs of nervousness. Nor did they show any sign of nervousness or surprise when he informed them that they were under arrest and that they were to accompany him back to Genk.

For the sergeant, this was practically an admission of guilt, for innocent persons suddenly arrested for a crime of which they are innocent do not react so calmly.

Taken to the inspector's office in Genk, both denied all knowledge of the castration of Alessandros Postolsikis, although Papanastassiou admitted that he believed his wife to have had an affair with him.

'However, that is all over now,' he said. 'Evangelia came home in January of last year after they had run away to Greece. Alessandros did not want to continue. He was afraid his wife would find out.'

'And you have not seen Mr Postolsikis since January of last year, Mrs Papanastassiou?' said the inspector.

The woman shook her head silently.

'Then, why was your skirt lying in the back of Mr Postolsikis' car yesterday evening?' asked the inspector.

'It is not my skirt,' said Evangelia Papanastassiou.

'I think we can prove it is,' said the inspector.

He could and did, partially by microscopic comparison of tiny fragments of skin and body hairs caught in the fabric, partially by the statements of witnesses who had seen Evangelia Papanastassiou wearing the skirt, and partially by the statement of the owner of the shop in Genk where she had bought it. This caused her to change her statement.

'It is true,' said Evangelia Papanastassiou. 'It was I in the car with Alessandros. We were making love when my husband and his friends found us. They dragged me away. I do not know what happened.'

She identified the friends as twenty-six-year-old Anastosios Mickelis and thirty-four-year-old Konstantinos Kosmas and both were immediately taken into custody.

Finding themselves implicated as solely responsible for the castration of Postolsikis, the three men made statements of their own, which they had apparently previously agreed upon.

Evangelia, they said, had wanted to return to her husband, but Postolsikis had insisted on continuing the affair. Finally, she had agreed to one final rendezvous at the parking lot and they had driven her there. While they were waiting, they had heard terrible cries and, approaching the car, had found Postolsikis lying in a pool of blood. Evangelia had castrated him all by herself, but, as she had not mentioned this, they had thought he was not too severely injured and had gone away.

Evangelia said that this was a pack of lies and the inspector was inclined to agree with her. Postolsikis weighed over two hundred pounds, none of it fat, and he had the strength of an ox. Evangelia was rather delicately built and weighed less than a hundred pounds. The medical report had stated that the victim had been held motionless in a grip of iron while he was being emasculated. If the three men's statements were to be believed, it meant that Evangelia had held him motionless with one hand as she would have needed the other for the knife.

Eventually, Alessandros Postolsikis did recover and was able to make a statement to the police concerning the actual course of events on the evening in question. As the inspector had never doubted, it was the men who had done the holding and Evangelia who had done the cutting. Postolsikis was able to provide exact details, as the incident remained very clear in his mind.

All of the suspects finally agreed that his version of the events was correct and provided the additional information that Postolsikis had wanted to terminate the affair, but that Papanastassiou had demanded her lover's testicles as the price for accepting his wife back. Evangelia, feeling herself scorned by Postolsikis, had cooperated.

On March 3, 1978, Christos and Evangelia Papanastassiou were found guilty of mutilation and grievous bodily harm and sentenced to ten years' imprisonment. Anastosios Mickelis and Konstantinos Kosmas were convicted of aiding and abetting in the commission of a felony and sentenced to five years each.

After having served a part of their sentences, all were quietly deported to Greece by the Belgian government in order to save the expense of feeding them.

13

YOUNG

As murders go, it was a tidy one. There was no problem in identifying the victim, nor the murderess either for that matter. She was a well-behaved girl and she waited quietly beside the body, with the gun in her fist, for the police to come. There was nothing in the 6.35 mm automatic, of course. She had kept pulling the trigger until the magazine was empty. Five rounds. After a while she got tired of standing and she sat down on a bar stool. She kept the gun in her hand though.

Which was one reason that Walter Kleinbauer, bartender at the popular Racing Club Bar in the city of Freiburg, West Germany, stayed under the bar until the police arrived. Bartenders are often prudent, thoughtful persons and Walter did not know that the gun was empty.

Whether the gun was or not, the bar was empty, although before the shooting started, it had been practically full. Even in a place as small as Freiburg, nobody likes to stick around to get involved in a murder case.

Walter had had no choice, of course, so he had to go down to police headquarters and make a statement. Considering how fast and unexpectedly it had all happened, it was pretty complete.

'It was Sunday evening,' it read, 'March 17, 1968. Business was good. Lots of people in the bar. Sylvia came in about nine o'clock. I didn't think anything of it. She's one of the regulars. Usually with her husband though.

'It didn't strike me at the time. I was pretty busy. But, now that I think about it, she acted sort of funny. She didn't go to a table and she didn't come up to the bar either. She just sort of stood around at the back of one of the pillars behind the dance floor.

'Well, I guess if I thought about it at all, I figured she was waiting for Jürgen. That's her husband. He hangs out in the Racing Club. Like I say, I wasn't paying much attention. Christ! How could you expect something like that from Sylvia. She's only seventeen.

'Anyway, I guess it must have been around ten-thirty when Wolfgang came in. He's another regular. He gave me a big wave and started over towards the bar. When he did, Sylvia stepped out from behind the pillar and walked across towards him. I thought she was going to say hello. He's a family friend or, I guess, you'd have to say he was.

'Sylvia was fumbling around in her handbag like she was looking for her cigarettes and, all of a sudden, she pulled out this gun, points it at Wolfgang and starts pulling the trigger. They tell me it was five shots. I didn't count. It was enough anyway.

'She wasn't more than ten feet from him when she started shooting and I guess he took the lot in the chest. He just sort of hung there with his mouth open. He didn't fall over right away and he looked like he was trying to put his hands up or maybe say something. Then he fell all apart and flopped on his face.

'Sylvia just stood there. So did everybody else for a couple of seconds. It stuns you when something like that happens unexpected-like. Then the customers made a run for the door and I went under the bar. I don't know who called the cops. I didn't. I wasn't about to reach for the telephone when she was standing there with that gun in her fist. It was quite a while before they got there. By that time, she was sitting at the bar.'

'Mrs Sahl was sitting on the third bar stool from the west end of the bar when we entered the room,' said Detective-Sergeant Helmut Franck in his report to Inspector Wilhelm Weisacker, chief of the Freiburg Homicide Squad. 'She appeared to be dazed. I went up to her and asked her to give me the pistol. She picked it up from the bar and handed it to me.

'I then cautioned her on her legal rights and asked if she had shot the man on the floor. I did not at this time know his identity. She did not reply verbally, but nodded her head.

'I placed her under arrest and asked her to accompany me to police headquarters and she did so without resistance.

'Upon my return, Dr Leopold Schneider from the Freiburg Coroner's Office had arrived and had carried out an examination of the corpse. He stated that death had occurred within the past hour and had been the result of five pistol bullets fired into the chest and upper abdomen.

'He had also emptied the pockets of the victim and it was possible to establish from a personal identity card and other papers that the dead man was Wolfgang Hartmann, aged thirty-one, unmarried and a salesman by profession. He was carrying four hundred and thirty-two marks and some small change in a combination purse and wallet. He was not armed.

'Subsequent interrogation of the bartender and Mrs Sahl confirmed the identity of the dead man who, it was stated, was a regular customer of the Racing Club Bar. In later statements Hartmann was described as an intimate friend of Jürgen Sahl, a twenty-nine-year-old insurance salesman and the husband of the accused.

'On our way to the station, I questioned Mrs Sahl on her motives in the shooting and she stated that Hartmann had been her lover and was trying to blackmail her. She had killed him in order to save her marriage and to protect the future of her three-year-old son, Frank.'

'How heroic!' exclaimed the inspector. 'A courageous young wife and mother, fighting against the forces of evil to protect her child and save her marriage. Don't tell me that people learn nothing from television.'

He was a man with a naturally trenchant sense of humour and a great many years of criminal investigation work had honed it to a razor edge. He consistently questioned the integrity of even the most respectable, suspected the motives of practically everyone and rarely accepted a statement at face value. This one apparently struck him as improbable.

'We have a victim,' continued the inspector. 'We have a suspect. We have a motive. And we have a confession. There is only one problem. The girl is a minor. What is the maximum sentence she could get under German law?'

'Three years,' said Franck.

'And it would be a remarkable court that would give her that much,' said the inspector. 'In short, for a deliberate, cold-blooded murder, Mrs Sahl can expect a milder punishment than she might get for drunken driving. I want this case investigated very thoroughly, Helmut. The whole business is too much like a hunting licence for humans. See what you can do and keep me posted.'

The sergeant, who was not in the least surprised by this reaction, accepted his assignment with resignation. As the inspector's assistant, he could scarcely have expected anything else and he had already given some thought as to possible courses of action before making his report. A wiry, thoughtful, young man with medium-brown hair parted in the middle, he was gifted with the German passion for order and neatly tied-up solutions and he too felt that there was something decidedly peculiar about the murder of Wolfgang Hartmann.

There were, of course, two possible explanations for the murder. Either Sylvia Sahl had, as she stated, killed Hartmann on her own initiative and for her own reasons, or some other person had persuaded her, in view of her near immunity to punishment, to carry out the murder for some purpose of their own. The first thing to do was to determine whether Sylvia Sahl's motives were valid.

It seemed that they were. Sylvia had filed an official complaint with the police on Saturday, one day before the murder, in which she charged that Hartmann was attempting to blackmail her. No action had been taken however.

'And why not?' asked the inspector.

'She was supposed to contact us again immediately that Hartmann made another blackmail attempt,' said the sergeant. 'We were then supposed to set up a trap for him.'

'Do you believe it?' said the inspector.

Franck shrugged. 'It could be true,' he said, 'or she could have made the report to establish the motive in advance. I don't know.'

'Dig further,' said the inspector.

The sergeant dug further. He discovered that there really had been an affair with Hartmann, but that it had had no value for the purpose of blackmail. Despite her tender years and innocent appearance, Sylvia had had affairs with quite a few people and, at the age of fourteen, had found herself on the verge of unwed motherhood. Jürgen Sahl was the father, or so he believed, and he had proposed marriage.

Sylvia had said no. She enjoyed sleeping with Jürgen and she had no objection to bearing his children but she did not want to marry him.

'I don't think she knew what she was doing,' said a former school-mate and self-described best friend. 'She was just an innocent child. Sylvia didn't know anything about sex or even where babies came from, I don't think. She just did whatever Jürgen told her to. He was older and I guess she sort of respected him.'

'But you say she didn't want to marry him,' said the sergeant.

'She certainly didn't,' said Ute. 'She tried everything to get out of it. She didn't care about having an illegitimate child. She just didn't want to marry Jürgen. I think she thought she was too young to get married. Anyway, that's when she took up with Hartmann. He was Jürgen's best friend and she thought it would make Jürgen so mad he wouldn't want to marry her any more.'

'But it didn't,' said the sergeant. 'Or didn't he find out about it?'

171

'Oh yes,' said Ute. 'He knew all about it. It didn't bother him and finally Sylvia gave in and they got married.'

Franck did not delay in playing the tape of this interview to the inspector.

'We seem to have something here,' he said. 'If Sahl knew about his wife's affair with Hartmann, Hartmann could hardly have used the knowledge to blackmail her. She lied about the motive.'

'Of course she lied about the motive,' snorted the inspector indignantly. 'Innocent child! Didn't know where babies come from! The tripe you have to listen to in this business! Still, it's what I suspected. The husband was at the back of it. Now, get me a complete run-down on him.'

This new assignment turned out to be easy in some respects and impossible in others. The easy part was Sahl's record with the police. Assault, operating a vehicle without a licence, petty larceny, none of the offences were very serious but neither were they usual activities for an insurance salesman.

The impossible part lay in determining where Sahl got his money. From everything that Franck could discover, he appeared to be by no means short of cash, but it was not from insurance sales, as the company reported that he had never yet sold a policy nor been paid a commission. They were, in fact, surprised to learn that he was still working for them.

'The picture that you get from his police record is that of a petty hoodlum,' said the sergeant, making his report to the inspector. 'He's making money, but not big money, and he's not working for it.'

'Check with the Narcotics Branch,' said the inspector. 'There's easy money in smuggling hashish up here from the Middle East.'

'That sounds like a business that might appeal to Mr Sahl.'

The sergeant picked up the telephone and dialled a number 'Inspector Klein?' he said. 'Franck here. What do you have on a Jürgen Sahl, insurance salesman, over there in Narcotics?'

He waited for a few moments, said thank you and hung up the telephone. 'No record,' he said. 'They've been keeping an eye on him for some time. They think he and Hartmann were part of a ring bringing narcotics into Freiburg. They're still working on it.'

'So are you,' said the inspector. 'Go over to Narcotics and check out their material. I'll tell Klein that you'll be working from his office for a while. How's your security?'

'Okay, I hope,' said Franck, crossing his fingers. Plain-clothes investigation officers in German police departments are usually anonymous. Even his own mother did not know that he worked for the police. She thought that he was a special investigator for the tax office.

Such secrecy is common to many European police forces and an investigator whose identity is accidentally exposed to the public will normally be transferred to a desk job or even to another branch, as his usefulness is substantially reduced. Franck, who was a career officer and enjoyed his work, was anxious to avoid such a fate and was, consequently, cautious.

He had to be. In a city the size of Freiburg, security was not easy to maintain, but, being young, unmarried and knowing his way around, he could, by letting his hair and beard grow and neglecting personal hygiene, pass off as a student at the university, one of Germany's largest and oldest.

As a matter of fact, it was the presence of this respected institution of learning which caused the police Narcotics Section to be so large and active.

Although the media had not yet at this time succeeded in popularizing hard drugs, hashish and the so-called soft drugs were considered to be very chic, 'in' and a part of the wave of the future by the students. By others, they were considered to be a remarkably lucrative business.

At Narcotics, Franck found a warmer welcome than he had expected. He was a new face and a good many of the section's agents were already known to the pushers and, therefore, of little value for field work. Although Franck was working on a homicide case, it was hoped that he would, perhaps incidentally, solve some of the Narcotics Section's cases too.

'The problem is,' said Inspector Klein, 'they seem to have identified our agents. Every effort we've made to infiltrate the ring has failed. You're not in the Narcotics Branch and they couldn't be expected to know you.'

'What's been done so far?' asked Franck. 'Is there any contact at all?'

Klein shook his head. He was a powerfully built man with a close-clipped blond skull, who looked as if he should be in the riot squad rather than Narcotics investigations. 'At a standstill,' he said. 'We've had one or two students who asked for medical treatment for addiction and we got the name of the pusher. He's not important. Has a news-stand over by the Sociology Institute. What we want to know is where he gets it from. We put a tail on him and he met Hartmann twice and Sahl once, and Hartmann and Sahl together once, before he noticed that he was being shadowed. After that, nothing of course. We don't know that he gets it from Hartmann or Sahl, but he didn't meet anybody else.'

'What can I do?' said Franck. 'I don't know much about narcotics work.'

'Stop washing and let your hair grow,' said Klein. 'We'll provide you with credentials to show you're a registered student at the university and you can start attending lectures at the Sociology Institute. Try and find out who's on the stuff and get friendly with them. Sooner or later, you should get invited to a party where they're smoking. You'll have to smoke too. Pretend that you go for it and ask where you can get more. That should get you an introduction to Reichauer, the pusher that owns the news-stand. After that, you'll have to play it by ear.'

'And suppose I get addicted?' said Franck. 'Isn't that stuff habit-forming?'

Klein chuckled. 'Go and see the police doctor,' he said. 'He can tell you how great the risk is.'

Franck did. He was a serious young man and he was careful about his health. The doctor was, however, reassuring.

'Hashish is not organically habit-forming,' he said. 'The persons who become addicted to the so-called soft drugs are generally individuals who are either psychologically unstable or who have problems and are too weak to cope with them. Have you ever had any such problems?'

'I was engaged to a girl a couple of years ago,' said Franck, 'and she married somebody else. I was pretty upset.'

'How do you feel about it now?' said the doctor.

'I figure I was lucky,' said Franck.

'Go smoke the hashish,' said the doctor. 'You've got nothing to worry about.'

Somewhat to the sergeant's surprise, he found it relatively easy to gain entrance to the student groups that were taking drugs. The practice was widespread in the university town. Nor was it particularly difficult to obtain access to the pusher. Reichauer appeared not to suspect that Franck was anything other than the student that he pretended to be.

This was not so surprising considering the amount of trouble that the detective went to in order to make his role authentic. He religiously skipped lectures, moved only in student circles and never went near police headquarters. For his reports to Inspector Weisacker he called at the inspector's home late in the evening, coming in through the kitchen door.

'How are you getting on with Reichauer?' asked the inspector, pouring out a glass of beer for his assistant.

'I think I'm making some progress,' said Franck. 'I've been putting on the starving student act for him. I keep hinting that if I could make a little money some way I could buy more of his stuff.'

'Sounds promising,' said the inspector. 'I'll call Klein tomorrow and have him put an obvious tail on Reichauer. That way, he won't dare to make a pick-up himself and maybe you'll get the job.'

'What about Mrs Sahl?' said Franck. 'Is she still sticking to her story?'

'Like glue,' said the inspector. 'But I have the feeling she's beginning to have second thoughts. When it first happened she was getting a lot of sympathy as the gallant little wife and mother, fighting for her marriage, but I saw to it that the newspapers got the information on how her husband knew all about the affair. There's not so much sympathy now.'

'I suppose some people are wondering how you can get eighteen months for driving a car after you've had four beers and only twice that for murder,' said the sergeant.

As the inspector had promised, Otto Reichauer acquired on the day following a tail who never left him night or day. It was an obvious tail and the pusher must have thought that the Narcotics Section had taken to hiring incompetents. Oddly enough, the only time that the shadow was not present was when Reichauer was actually selling and, as the inspector had reckoned, he soon got rid of his stock in hand. The only thing to do now was either to cease business or go for more.

Reichauer could not go for more, however. The moment he left the news-stand, there was the police shadow at his heels. For three days, the pusher fought a battle within himself between greed and caution. In the end greed won.

'Willi,' he said. 'You want to make a buck this afternoon?'

Franck, who was masquerading under the name of Willi Hellmich, agreed, but not too eagerly. 'How much time will it take?' he asked. 'I have to go to a lecture this afternoon.'

'You'll get back in plenty of time,' said Reichauer. 'I just want you to pick up a parcel for me. It's in a baggage locker at the railway station. I'll give you the key and you go down and pick it up.'

'Okay,' said the sergeant. 'Where's the key?'

'I'll give it to you at two o'clock' said Reichauer.

Franck agreed, but he was dismayed. He had grasped immediately how the system worked and it was close to foolproof.

Reichauer would now make a telephone call. His contact would place the merchandize ordered in a parcel and put it in one of the coin-operated luggage lockers at the railway station. He would then come to the news-stand, buy a newspaper and hand Reichauer the key with the money. Reichauer would hand over the agreed price with the change and the transaction would be complete. All that Reichauer had to do was pick up the parcel.

There would be no point in arresting Reichauer or the contact either. Neither would have any narcotics on him and the contact would almost surely be a go-between and not a principal.

In any case, the sergeant's interest lay not in breaking up the drug ring. That was a problem for the Narcotics Section. What he wanted was evidence that Sahl and Hartmann had been involved in the drug traffic and might, therefore, have had motives for murdering each other more substantial than the sexual favours of teenage girls, however attractive.

It had been twenty minutes past eleven when the sergeant left the news-stand, and he went directly to the railway station. Sometime before two o'clock someone would be putting an inconspicuous parcel into one of the lockers and, although he could not hope to identify the parcel, he could identify Jürgen Sahl if it was he personally who made the drop.

Almost to his surprise, it was, but he had a long wait before the insurance salesman arrived at a quarter to two with a brown-paper parcel carried in a net bag. Sahl was cautious. He did not want the merchandise lying there in the railway station any longer than necessary.

Franck watched him put the net bag and parcel into one of the lockers and then ran outside to catch a cab to within a block of the news-stand. Taking up a station in an entrance, he waited to see the remainder of the transaction.

Although he had not expected that it would be Sahl himself who picked up the money and turned over the key, the young dealer was apparently a man who believed in keeping his overheads as low as possible and it was.

The transaction went off as smoothly as a boiled egg. Sahl drove up in his Mercedes, got out, bought a newspaper, looked briefly at the magazines and, getting back in his car, drove off. The key and money had changed hands, but even the sergeant who knew what was happening, had missed it.

At two o'clock, the sergeant appeared at the news-stand, picked up the key and went to fetch the brown-paper parcel. Handing it over to Reichauer, he was rewarded with two twenty-mark bills, a generous fee for picking up a parcel at the railway station.

Unfortunately, being on duty, he could not keep the money, but he did not mind. He now knew that Sahl was engaged in the drug traffic and all that remained was to determine whether Hartmann had been. That would not, of course, guarantee the solution to the case, but it would go a long way towards establishing a motive.

As Hartmann was dead and Sahl was certainly not going to provide any information on the subject, the only source he could hope for was Reichauer, but he doubted that the man knew very much about the business or who the people in the echelon above him were.

There was, however, no alternative at the moment and he pursued the advantage he had gained with the drug pusher when he had picked up the shipment from the railway station. Putting on a convincing act of being almost permanently under the influence of narcotics and simultaneously broke, he had little trouble in gaining Reichauer's confidence. Although the man was shrewd, he was not particularly intelligent and the sergeant looked far more like what he was pretending to be than what he was.

'I wish I could get on to some money,' whined the sergeant. 'I don't ever have any money. You know what there's lots of money in now?'

'Not the news-stand business,' muttered Reichauer, apparently apprehensive that Franck was working up to asking for a loan.

'Come off it, Otto!' said the sergeant. 'You don't make your money selling newspapers. Why don't you and me set up in business for ourselves? You finance the deal and I'll take a run down to Turkey and pick up enough to make us both rich. It's easy.'

Reichauer looked alarmed. They were sitting on piles of old newspapers in the crowded, dirty, little room behind the news-stand and drinking beer. Getting hurriedly to his feet, he stuck his dark, wrinkled, weasel's face out into the news-stand. There were no customers.

'Don't talk like that, Willi,' he said nervously, sitting back down. 'There's no room for independents in that business. You could get yourself killed.'

'You read too many of your own magazines, Otto,' said the sergeant. 'This is Freiburg, not Chicago. Who's going to kill anybody here? Al Capone? The Mafia? Come off it!'

He was deliberately needling Reichauer, trying to irritate him to the point where he could lose his caution and it worked.

'Awwww, you smart-ass college kids!' snarled Reichauer. 'What do you know? You ever hear of Wolfgang Hartmann?'

'Sure,' said the sergeant. 'It was in all the papers. Some little girl shot him because he was cozy with her and he was going to tell her husband. It didn't have anything to do with the hash trade.'

'That's what you think!' said Reichauer. 'Listen! If Hartmann hadn't got the same kind of smart ideas you're talking about, he'd be drinking beer in the Racing Club right now.'

'Really?' said the sergeant. 'You know for a fact that Hartmann was killed because he was mixed up in the narcotics business?'

'I know it for a fact,' said Reichauer.

'I hope you do,' said the sergeant, producing his official identification. 'Freiburg Criminal Police. You are under arrest. Please close your news-stand and accompany me to police headquarters. If you desire legal council, you will be given the opportunity to obtain the services of an attorney there.'

As the sergeant had intended, the shock was mind-wrenching. For several moments, Otto Reichauer sat petrified, his eyes bulging at the official police identification card and his mouth hanging open so that the saliva ran down his chin.

'A cop on hash!' he said finally in an awestruck voice. 'I'd never have believed it.'

Taken to police headquarters and turned over to an interrogation team, Reichauer, still in a state of shock, soon began to babble everything he knew concerning the Hartmann murder. Unfortunately, it was not much and it was based mainly on underworld gossip. Hartmann and Sahl had been the local wholesalers of hashish and some other drugs, but were not high in the organization and did not, consequently, make very big money. Hartmann had wanted to set up in business for himself and it was believed that Sahl had been given a contract to eliminate him. Instead of doing it himself or hiring a killer he had made use of his teenage wife, as he was aware that her age made her practically immune to prosecution. By those in the know, this was considered to be an act of great sagacity.

Inspector Weisacker was inclined to agree. 'He's taking advantage of our modern, progressive legal system,' he said. 'According to the theory, adolescents are supposed to have all of the rights and privileges of adults, but, curiously, none of the responsibilities. The absolute maximum sentence under the

Juvenile Code is ten years and nobody serves that. Sahl has committed a perfect murder and there's nothing we can do about it.'

'Unless Mrs Sahl decides to come clean,' said the sergeant. He had had a bath, a shave and a haircut and now looked so little like the starving drug addict of his student days that he did not think even Reichauer would be able to recognize him, an important matter if he was to remain in active criminal investigations.

'She won't,' said the inspector.

'She might,' said the sergeant.

She did.

Three days before Christmas of 1968, Sylvia Sahl, who had been in custody since March 17, asked to see the inspector and presented him with a statement which varied substantially from her original confession. It was couched in somewhat extravagant language and reflected, in the inspector's opinion, a too exclusive interest in the cheaper forms of literature and the less intellectually challenging television programmes. He was, however, glad to have it.

'My name is Sylvia Sahl,' ran the written version. 'I am the wife of Jürgen Sahl and the mother of our son Frank, now three years of age.

'On March 17, 1968, I shot to death in the Racing Club Bar Wolfgang Hartmann with whom I once had an intimate relationship. At that time, I stated that the motive for my act was that Wolfgang was attempting to blackmail me by threatening to expose our relationship to my husband.

'This was not true. Jürgen knew of my affair with Wolfgang even at the time when it was going on. Anyway, there was nothing to hide, as Jürgen and I were not yet married, although I was pregnant with Frank.

'Now the newspapers are calling me the Devil with the Angel's Face and the Cold-Blooded Murderess. In my heart I do not feel that I am a murderess, even though I know that I have the life of a fellow human being on my conscience.

'My only hope is that I can find a merciful judge who will send me home to my little boy. Once I am freed, I shall live only for him and we will go away to some place where we are not known, to make a new beginning and to become useful members of society.

'I accept that a cold-blooded murderess deserves no pity. Wolfgang's wife must hate me. His parents must hate me. But I was not acting of my own free will. I was a machine, a tool in the hands of another. It is only now after such a long time that I awake from this terrible nightmare and realize that I have killed, yes killed! But with a weapon pressed into my hand by my husband, Jürgen Sahl, whose will it was that pulled the trigger and not mine!

'I do not wish to harm my husband. I bear him no ill will, but I must confess the truth for the sake of my beloved child. What can be his future if his mother is sentenced to a harsh prison term? How can he face the world knowing that his mother, little more than a child herself, was unjustly condemned to bear the punishment for a crime by his father?'

'How indeed?' said the inspector. 'Or worse yet, how can he face the world knowing that both his parents were subjected to this inhuman punishment which, in his mother's case, might actually extend to as much as two years not counting pre-trial detention?'

Mrs Sahl did not reply to these rhetorical questions, as she was not present. Only the sergeant was and he did not see fit to reply either.

Jürgen Sahl did.

'She is a Devil with an Angel's face!' he cried, demonstrating that he had been following the progress of the case in the newspapers. 'She pretends to be naïve, but she is in reality sophisticated and fiendishly clever. When I think of the suffering and misfortune that she has brought upon me . . .! But no matter! I love her still and I shall always love her as I have from the moment I met her and she brought me under her cruel spell.'

'Cruel spell!' said the inspector. 'The child was thirteen years old at the time. He could have been prosecuted for contributing to the delinquency of a minor if we were not living in such a liberal, progressive age. On the other hand, I don't doubt he's right. It's a little hard to believe when she says it took from the middle of March to Christmas for her conscience to start bothering her. Why do all these people talk like cartoon characters?'

This was another private conversation between the inspector and the sergeant. Jürgen Sahl had been taken into custody, had denied all responsibility for the murder and had been indicted for inciting to homicide anyway. He was now sitting in a detention cell, although not the same one as his wife, while the investigators tried to find some evidence of his guilt other than the unsupported word of Mrs Sahl.

'They talk like cartoon characters because they are cartoon characters,' said the sergeant. 'They see so much of this sort of thing on television that they're not entirely real people living real

180

lives any more. Sahl thinks he's the slick, suave, young gangster, making big money with his brains and living it up in the night spots, driving a Mercedes . . . Mrs Sahl thinks she's the heroine, terribly pretty, terribly young, sexy, but nice, and with a heart of gold. Courageously, she fights to save her beloved child from the brutal police . . . In the end though, all will turn out well. Sylvia will be vindicated. Jürgen will develop a heart of gold too. The happy little family will be reunited . . .'

'. . . and make a fortune peddling dope to schoolchildren,' said the inspector. 'As for the brutal pig in charge of this investigation, he will be going into retirement and I can tell you that it's not a minute too soon.'

'Well, they're both indicted,' said the sergeant. 'More we cannot do. What do you think they'll get?'

'Sahl?' said the inspector. 'Nothing. There's no evidence. Mrs Sahl? Three years with eighteen months suspended and pre-trial detention taken off. She'll walk out of the court a free woman.'

He was perfectly right.

14

NEIGHBOURLY

In Belgium, the summer of 1979 was magnificent. From the sluggish current of the German Rhine to the grey waters of the English Channel, the green plains of Flanders lay baking beneath the rays of the golden sun. It was a cheerful summer, a happy summer, exactly the sort of summer in which to celebrate a birthday.

And, by a stroke of good fortune, the birthday of Natalie Dister fell precisely at the height of that marvellous summer, August 19, to be exact. She was looking forward to it very much. It would be an important birthday. Her fifth.

Her mother, twenty-three-year-old Jeannine Dister, was also looking forward to the birthday celebration, of course, although she had certain problems with which she had to cope, the most pressing being where she could find a place to move to.

The fact was, Jeannine was becoming very nervous about living in the old stone house in the tiny village of Gomze-Andoumont. It was cheap, which was the reason why she had moved there in the first place, but it was also spooky. The walls were too thick. The windows were too narrow. And the steep, cramped staircases were pitch dark even in the middle of the day. At night, there were strange rustlings, muted sounds barely heard, the creaking and groaning of a too old house adjusting its timbers as the warmth of the sun seeped slowly out of the stone.

Or so she told herself. Some things there were that were not so easily explained. Such as the broken pane of glass in the window of the room at the back of the house. It had apparently been broken some time during the night of August 4.

Less than a week later, on August 10, there had been another strange incident. The copper tubing bringing oil into the house from the tank outside had, somehow, been severed and a good deal of the oil had run out. Although she was not, of course, heating the house in August, she had smelled the strong fuel-oil odour the moment she got up in the morning. The break was a clean one and she thought that it looked as if it had been cut with something, but who would do such a thing and why?

The final straw had been, however, the strange shadow which had passed across the window of Natalie's bedroom the following night. Natalie and Jeannine had their bedrooms side by side on the second floor and there should have been no shadows flitting across the windows.

Natalie, who had still been awake, had screamed with fright and Jeannine, fearless as are all mothers, had run out of the house in her baby-doll nightdress and bare feet to face the danger, but all that she had found was a ladder leaning against the house-front in the moonlight. There was no one in sight.

The following day, Jeannine had gone to the Wise Woman. Although she was now called a Consultant on Psychic Phenomena, the time was not long past when she would have been called a witch and Jeannine still thought of her as one.

The witch had been terrifying. 'Flee!' she had cried. 'Go home. Pack your things and leave. The time is dreadfully near. I see blood! Much, much blood! Your house is filled with an evil spirit! Leave at once or someone will die!'

Most frightening of all, she had refused to accept money. 'You will need it more than I,' she had mumbled.

It was, of course, true. Jeannine did need money. Unemployment benefit in Belgium is not overly generous and she could expect no help from Jacques, her twenty-eight-year-old estranged husband. His unemployment benefit was even less than hers.

Estranged was, perhaps, not exactly the right word. She and Jacques were still on good terms. He often came to visit Natalie and sometimes he stayed the night. When he did, they shared the same bed. Theirs had been a modern marriage. She had barely turned eighteen when she gave birth to Natalie. And theirs was a modern separation. Neither could afford nor particularly wanted a divorce, but Jeannine and Natalie lived in Gomze-Andoumont and Jacques lived in the equally small village of Forêt-Trooz, three miles to the west. The marriage, which had been founded largely on mutual sexual attraction, had not developed into anything more permanent.

Returning to the house in the Rue d'Andoumont, Jeannine pondered briefly whether she should call Jacques and ask him to stay with her and Natalie in the house until she could find somewhere to move to. Although the Consultant on Psychic Phenomena had frightened her badly, there was no question of moving before the end of the month. She could not afford to sacrifice half a month's rent, and cheap housing, even in the villages, was not easy to find.

In the end, she decided not to call Jacques. He would have come, she knew, but he might misinterpret the request. She was afraid that he would think she was trying to trick him into resuming the marriage, and she did not want that.

Moreover, quite apart from the financial considerations, she was reluctant to move because she did not think that she would find such good neighbours again. There was only one house nearby, but she was on such good terms with the occupants that it gave her a feeling of security.

There was also something of a feeling of being in the same boat. Like herself, the neighbours lived on government allowances, in the case of nineteen-year-old Jeanne-Marie Severyns, unemployment benefit, and in the case of her forty-five-year-old mother, Marie-Antoinette, a disability pension.

Marie-Antoinette was badly crippled and could only get around with the aid of crutches. She also suffered from diabetes and she had had a difficult life. Married to an Italian who had deserted her ten years earlier and gone back to Italy, she had borne four children, but Jeanne-Marie was the only one still at home. The other three were in institutions for the mentally handicapped and would never leave them.

And finally, of course, there was the matter of the birthday party. Marie-Antoinette and Natalie were great chums and, as Marie-Antoinette's birthday was on August 15 and Natalie's on the nineteenth, they were planning a joint celebration on the seventeenth. Natalie would be heart-broken if anything went wrong with the joint birthday party plans.

Once the birthday party was over, however, serious efforts would have to be made to find another place to live. On the thirteenth, she would be going down to the administration centre to collect her unemployment money. She would start asking around then. Perhaps there would even be something right in Gomze-Andoumont and the friendship with the Severyns would not have to be terminated.

The morning of the thirteenth dawned clear and sunny with a promise of heat later in the day. Jeannine rose early, washed, dressed and put on the coffee pot. It had just begun to boil when Jeanne-Marie scratched on the door and entered. The two girls often had coffee together in the morning and this morning they would be going to the administration centre together to collect the government allowances for themselves and for Mrs Severyns who could not be expected to go in and collect it herself.

At precisely eight-fifteen, Jeannine and Jeanne-Marie left the house. As a rule, Jeannine took Natalie with her when she went to collect her unemployment benefit, but the little girl had played hard the preceding afternoon and was still sound asleep, her chubby fists tightly clenched and her round, little cheeks flushed with slumber. She was a beautiful child and Jeannine had to suppress an impulse to scoop her up in her arms and smother her with kisses. Instead, she tiptoed silently out of the room and left her to sleep. It was not far to the administration centre. She would be back in half an hour at the most.

Actually, it was slightly less than half an hour. The warnings of the Wise Woman had left her jumpy and nervous and she had no sooner left the house than she had regretted leaving Natalie alone. It would have been better to take her and let her make the sleep up with a longer nap in the afternoon.

Jeannine had, therefore, hurried home without even stopping to inquire about housing. She returned alone as Jeanne-Marie had remained in the village to make some purchases at the local shops.

Hurrying into the house she went directly to the kitchen where she made a cup of hot cocoa in the white mug with the bunnies painted on the side, filled the cereal bowl with dry cereal and fruit and set another place for Theodore, Natalie's teddy bear, who always took breakfast with her.

She then climbed the steep stairs to wake her daughter.

Natalie was lying on her back in her bed with her throat cut.

In an involuntary reaction of self-preservation, Jeannine's mind, unable to withstand the shock, fled reality. She did not lose consciousness, but a single thought repeated and repeated itself like an echo in her brain.

'It cannot be true. There is not so much blood in a baby.'

There was, it seemed, an immense quantity of blood. It covered the white sheets of the little bed. It lay in pools on the floor. It was splashed along the wall. There were even drops on the low ceiling.

Jeannine stood staring at it dully, her hands hanging at the sides and saliva dripping from her open mouth. Her involuntary nervous system had been disturbed by the shock and she was not breathing.

Suddenly, reality returned with a rush and with it the unendurable pain of comprehension of what she was seeing and what she dared not see if she were to retain her sanity.

And, stabbing through the agony and the horror of loss, came like lightening bolts the vain regrets. Why had she not listened to the advice of the Wise Woman? Why had she not fled this accursed house as if it were filled with the plague? Why had she not called Jacques? Why had she not taken Natalie with her to the village? Why had she ever let her out of her sight? Why? Why? Why? Oh God, why?

But only a single answer came back.

Too late.

'Natalie!' she screamed, the violence of the word literally tearing her vocal cords so that she would never again speak in the same voice as she had before, fell to the floor, writhed briefly like a worm impaled on a fisherman's hook and was granted the boon of unconsciousness.

In the house next door, Marie-Antoinette heard the scream and, struggling to her feet, seized her crutches and hobbled out of the house. She did not go in the direction of the house next door, but headed down the street in the direction of the nearest other neighbours. Whatever it was that had made Jeannine scream like that, it was nothing that a crippled woman could deal with.

Jeannine's cry had, however, been piercingly loud, the full-throated, terrifying scream of the human female passing beyond the limits of endurance and, long before Marie-Antoinette reached the nearest other house, the occupants were boiling out into the street and hastening to the rescue.

They soon found, of course, that there was nothing to rescue. Jeannine was unconscious and Natalie was dead, so horribly dead that the man who first arrived in the doorway of the bedroom turned around and literally pushed the women behind back down the stairs. The sight was one that no woman should be permitted to see.

It was not even a sight that a hardened highway patrol police officer should see. A car from the highway patrol was the nearest police vehicle and it arrived first at the scene of the murder, following a frantic telephone call to the police station in the nearby town of Spa.

They did not take long to get there, but they found most of the population of the village assembled in front of the house. Jeannine had been carried out and lay on the grass, still unconscious and surrounded by crying women, none of whom had seen the body, but who knew that the little girl had been horribly murdered. The men were gathered in tight, little knots, some glumly silent and others swearing savagely under their breath. Several were armed with clubs or tools of some kind and one man had gone off to return with a coil of rope. It was obvious what they had in mind if the murderer could be located.

The highway patrolmen went into the house and came out shortly with tears running down their cheeks. They were both fathers and, inured as they were to the sight of mangled bodies locked in the twisted steel of wrecked cars or strewn over the blood-smeared pavement, the innocence of the little victim and the unbelievable deliberate malice of the act cut through their emotional armour to the quick. Regulations required that they disarm and disperse any potential vigilante groups, but they made no move to do so and one of the officers later said that, had the murderer been present, he would have personally helped tie the noose around his neck.

The murderer was, however, not present or, if he was, no one knew it except he, and the highway patrolmen called police headquarters in Spa and reported that a vicious and unprecedented murder of a small child had taken place in Gomze-Andoumont and that it seemed to have taken place very recently. The murderer could be expected to show signs of blood on his hands and clothing.

Upon receiving this information, the co-ordinator in the police headquarters reacted instantly and massively, throwing every police vehicle at his disposal into a wide circle around the village and blocking all movement in and out of the area. Off-duty police officers and those stationed in other parts of the district were rushed to the scene and parties began combing the space within the circle of patrol cars and vans. Speed was of the greatest importance. If the murderer was trapped inside the police cordon, it was vital that he be apprehended before he had had time to wash away the traces of blood.

In the meantime, the Coroner's Office and the Department of Criminal Investigations had been alerted and senior investigations officer Jean-Jacques Courtois was hurrying to the scene accompanied by his assistant, Detective-Sergeant Louis Vilmain.

They arrived almost simultaneously with the Spa coroner, Dr Vincent Poulain, and the three men ascended together the stairs to the bedroom where the corpse of Natalie Dister lay beside the blood-soaked but faithful Theodore.

Inspector Courtois, a tall, thin man with a long, nervous sort of nose and a nearly bald head, took one look, turned on his heel and left the room.

The sergeant followed him. It was their case and they would handle it, but the investigation would be in no way advanced by their remaining to look upon the heart-breaking spectacle of the murdered child.

That was Dr Poulain's job and he did it, coming down stairs a short time later to report that the case was exactly what it looked. Someone had deliberately cut Natalie Dister's throat.

'It was just one slash with a very sharp knife or a razor,' said the doctor in a low, slightly husky voice. He was an elderly man, white haired and white moustached, and he kept taking off his gold-rimmed glasses and wiping them. 'I don't think . . . I hope she didn't suffer much. It was very quick . . . the cut goes all the way through to the spine . . . all the major blood vessels were severed . . . loss of blood supply to the brain . . . maybe . . . didn't wake up . . . no pain . . .'

His voice died away in unintelligible mumbling and he blew his nose violently in the handkerchief with which he had been wiping his glasses.

'Indications of motive?' said the inspector, compressing his lips into a thin line.

The doctor raised his head and looked at him in complete astonishment. 'Insanity, of course,' he said. 'What other possible motive could there be to cut a little girl's throat?'

'I mean, was she sexually molested?' said the inspector. 'I have to know what kind of a madman we're looking for.'

'No,' said the doctor. 'There are no indications of a sexual motive. Whoever it was, he just slashed her throat. There's no reason to believe that he even touched her.'

'There would have been blood on his hands and clothing, wouldn't there?' said the sergeant.

The doctor nodded. 'A great deal,' he said. 'Excuse me now. That's all I can tell you. I'm going to the morgue to prepare for the autopsy.'

He walked quickly across the yard to his car, got in and drove away.

'I don't envy him having to perform an autopsy on that baby,' said the sergeant. 'My God! This is a horrible case!'

'The worst I've ever seen or heard of,' said the inspector. 'We're going to spare nothing to track down this fellow, but we're going to have to work fast. For all we know, he may be cutting some other child's throat at this very minute. Raise headquarters and see if they have picked up any suspects inside the cordon.'

A good many persons, nearly eighty in all, had been intercepted inside the police circle of cars and seven were being held for further questioning. None were, however, more than potential witnesses and, eventually, all were released.

What remained was a mystery. By this time, it was known that the crime had been committed between eight-fifteen and eight forty-five or a little earlier, as Jeanne-Marie had been interrogated and had been very certain of the time when she and Jeannine had left for the administration centre and the time when Jeannine had left her to return home. The time when the police cordon went into place was also known and, even assuming that Natalie had been murdered the moment her mother had left the house, there still would not have been time enough for the murderer to clear the area before the police had sealed it off.

'Which means,' said the inspector, 'that it was no stranger. It was some one living right in Gomze-Andoumont. He cut the child's throat, went home, washed the blood off his hands and was drinking coffee and reading the newspaper while we were combing the district.'

'Well, we're checking medical records,' said the sergeant, 'but, so far, we haven't located anyone in the area with a background of such serious mental illness as that. One thing is certain, there've been no escapes from any of the top-security mental hospitals. No releases of any patients considered to be dangerous either.'

'Doesn't mean anything,' said the inspector. 'Half the murders in Europe are committed by psychopaths who were not considered dangerous. We simply have to continue with the interrogations. We know it's someone in the area. We'll keep interrogating until we find out who it is, even if it takes the next twenty years.'

'Pity we can't interrogate the mother,' said the sergeant. 'She might be able to suggest something.'

'The doctor says it will be months,' said the inspector, 'and maybe never. In any case, I doubt that there's much she could tell us that Miss Severyns hasn't already. She apparently confided in her a great deal.'

Jeanne-Marie Severyns had, of course, been questioned exhaustively, as had her mother. They were the closest neighbours and also the closest friends of Jeannine Dister.

Jeannine had told Jeanne-Marie about the strange happenings, the broken pane in the window, the severed fuel line and the shadow which had passed across Natalie's bedroom window, and only that morning on the way to the administration centre she had told her of the Wise Woman's warning and had said that she and Natalie would be moving as soon as she could find a new home.

On the basis of this statement, it seemed probable that the killer had been lurking about the house for some time prior to the murder, but with what intent it was impossible to say.

The murder itself was now thought to have been an impulsive act, not planned in advance, for the technicians from the police laboratory had found the murder weapon, a nearly new butcher's knife with a razor-sharp edge which Jeannine had bought a few weeks earlier. Although it had been put back into the drawer in the kitchen and apparently wiped, it was still stained with the child's blood.

The technicians had also discovered the means of entry into the house. Jeannine had, of course, locked the door when leaving, but a small window next to the front door had a faulty catch and, by pushing it open, the murderer had been able to reach through and release the spring lock on the door. It had, of course, snapped shut again when the murderer left the house.

'A strange combination of madness and cunning,' said the inspector. 'The murder itself was a totally irrational act, but the efforts to conceal the identity of the murderer were logical and effective. Everything he touched, he wiped, the door handle, the catch on the window, the handle of the butcher's knife. I don't understand it.'

One of the lab men told me they think it was a sex crime that went sour,' said the sergeant. 'Mrs Dister is an attractive, young woman and the murderer had been hanging around the house at night intending to rape her. When he failed to get in, he cut the fuel line and broke the window out of anger and frustration and then, when he finally located the faulty window catch and did get in, he found Mrs Dister not at home and took out his frustration on the child.'

'Well, it's a theory,' said the inspector doubtfully, 'but I find it hard to believe that with anybody that crazy, it would be his first offence. Yet we know that there's not a soul in the area with a record of anything like this.'

'And no reports by anyone else of any prowlers or unusual incidents,' said the sergeant. 'It was just Mrs Dister. The Severyns live right next door and the girl is even younger and more attractive than Mrs Dister, but nobody bothered them.'

'The mother and the daughter both confirm that?' said the inspector.

'The daughter, yes,' said the sergeant. 'The mother's statements aren't too reliable. She's sick and, to tell the truth, I don't think she's too bright. She had three other children and they're all in mental institutions. She's pretty broken up over the child's death too, of course. She seems to have looked on her like a grandchild.'

'What do you mean, her statements aren't reliable?' said the inspector. 'Does she talk gibberish or what?'

'No, not gibberish,' said the sergeant. 'It's just that they change all the time. She never makes the same statement twice. Sometimes, she doesn't seem to realize the child is dead.'

A silence fell over the office and the inspector sat staring thoughtfully at his assistant for some very considerable time.

'One of the basics of investigation work,' he said finally, 'is that a witness who contradicts his or her own statement has to be interrogated until the discrepancy is explained. If it is not explained, the witness becomes a suspect.'

'The woman's mentally handicapped,' said the sergeant, 'and she's crippled. What could she possible have to do with . . . ?'

'She looked upon the child as a grandchild, you say,' said the inspector. 'And she knew that the mother was going to move and take her away.'

'But she didn't,' said the sergeant. 'Mrs Dister only told Jeanne-Marie that morning on their way to the administration centre. Mrs Severyns didn't know then and she probably doesn't know now. Besides, it's ridiculous!'

'No doubt,' said the inspector dryly, 'although when I was a sergeant, I was not quite so blunt in my criticism of my chief's theories, which may account for the fact that I am inspector now.'

'Sorry,' mumbled the sergeant, 'but you must admit . . .'

'I'm prepared to admit anything, if it will help solve this case,' said the inspector. 'Even the most improbable things. Call Liège and see if they can lend us a psychologist for a day or two. You're probably right and this is ridiculous, but I want better opinion on it than yours or mine.'

Liège is a large city nearly on the German border and only about twenty miles to the north of Gomze-Andoumont. It has a large police department and the Department of Criminal Investigations includes a section for forensic medicine. The psychologist came down that same day.

Having listened to an account of the circumstances of the murder and a tape recording of Mrs Marie-Antoinette Severyns' previous statements, he went out to the house in Gomze-Andoumont and took a statement himself.

The following day, he came back down from Liège and took another statement from the crippled woman. The only response that he made to Inspector Courtois' questions was that he was not yet ready to make a report.

On the third day, he came down again and, this time, spoke to Jeanne-Marie. He then came to the inspector's office and said that he was ready with his report.

His first statement was a bombshell.

'I think Mrs Severyns is the murderess,' he said calmly. 'She is capable of it. She is very severely handicapped mentally. And she had a motive.'

'A motive!' exploded the inspector. 'What motive? What possible motive?'

'She believes that her daughter is involved in a homosexual relationship with Mrs Dister,' said the psychologist. 'From my interview with the daughter, I am inclined to think that she is not. Mrs Severyns obviously believes it, however, and she repeatedly used expressions like "taking her away from me" and "coming between us". She is psychopathically jealous and, in my opinion, she should have been sent for psychiatric treatment long ago.'

'But she's also physically handicapped!' exclaimed the sergeant. 'She can't walk without crutches. She isn't able to climb stairs. How could she have . . . ?'

'I have no idea,' said the psychologist. 'You wanted a medical opinion. You have one. The rest is up to you.'

Whereupon, he returned to Liège, leaving the inspector and the sergeant in a highly puzzled state. They did not doubt that the psychologist's opinion on the case was correct, but for the moment, they did not know what they were to do about it. There was little hope of getting an indictment for murder against a diabetic woman so crippled that she could not climb stairs when the murder had taken place on the second floor.

'We're worse off than we were before,' said the sergeant. 'It was bad enough not knowing the identity of the murderer, but knowing it and not being able to do anything about it is sickening. That woman has to be put away somewhere before she harms someone else.'

'We could probably get her committed on the basis of a psychological observation,' said the inspector, 'but for how long? In any case, the daughter would have to cooperate and, unless we told her the truth, she probably wouldn't. Even then, she might not. We'll have to think about this. Maybe by tomorrow morning . . .'

But it was actually three days before an idea came to the inspector.

'The fact is,' he told the sergeant, 'we don't actually know that

Mrs Severyns is guilty, but, if she is, then she must not be as crippled as she is supposed to be. If, on the other hand, she really is too crippled to climb stairs, then she has to be innocent, for we know that the murderer did climb the stairs to the child's bedroom. What we must determine is, just how crippled is Marie-Antoinette Severyns?'

'A medical examination?' said the sergeant.

'I think not,' said the inspector. 'Something like that can be faked well enough to deceive even a doctor. Don't forget that the woman is on a full disability pension. She would have had to undergo a thorough physical examination at the time she applied for it. She knows what to do to convince a doctor that she is crippled.'

'Well, what then?' asked the sergeant. 'Have you thought of some kind of a trick?'

The inspector had.

On the following day, the sergeant, accompanied by two detectives, went to Gomze-Andoumont and took Marie-Antoinette into custody. Bringing her back to police headquarters, he seated her in the inspector's office, took away her crutches and handbag and left the room.

The inspector was fierce. 'You, Mrs Severyns,' he shouted, 'are the murderess of Natalie Dister! There is no use in trying to deny it! The proof of your guilt is in black and white in this folder! Here! Let me read to you . . .'

At this point, the sergeant opened the door of the office, stuck his head inside and announced, 'Emergency conference in the commissioner's office, chief. We're both wanted immediately.'

The inspector laid the file he had been waving at Mrs Severyns down on the desk. 'You wait right here, Mrs Severyns,' he said. 'We won't be gone over half an hour.'

He got up from his desk and walked out through the office door, closing it behind him and leaving Marie-Antoinette Severyns alone in the office.

Three minutes later, he flung open the door again and rushed into the room, followed by the sergeant.

As they had been able to determine by looking through the keyhole, Marie-Antoinette Severyns was standing beside the desk holding in her hand the file which contained merely information reports that had been collected on the crime. The chair where she had been seated was on the other side of the room, fifteen feet away.

'For a helpless cripple, you walk rather well, Mrs Severyns,' said the inspector.

'Will I lose my pension?' asked Mrs Severyns anxiously.

'Possibly,' said the inspector. 'But you have no cause to worry. You will be provided for. Now, will you answer a few questions for me?'

Marie-Antoinette would. Having been caught walking without her crutches, she apparently felt that she had nothing to lose and she made a curiously off-hand confession to the murder of Natalie Dister. She had not, she said, wanted to harm the child, but her mother was luring Jeanne-Marie away from her with dirty things and she thought that if she killed Natalie, Jeannine would move away.

She was right, Jeannine Dister never returned to the house in the Rue d' Andoumont, but, on the other hand, neither did Marie-Antoinette.

Placed under psychiatric observation, she was quickly found to be so seriously underdeveloped mentally that she could not be held responsible for her actions. As this was a hereditary defect and no improvement in her condition could be expected, she was committed to an institution for the mentally handicapped where she will remain for the rest of her life.

15

INSTANT DIVORCE

The night of January 9, 1982, was a Saturday and on that evening the Red Lion tavern in the town of Wels, Austria, was about as full of customers as it ever got. The actual number was not large because Wels is not a very big town and, like most European communities, it has a great many taverns and bars. On the other hand, the Red Lion tavern is not so very big either and, therefore, the customers who were there filled it comfortably.

Not a few of the customers had come to listen to forty-two-year-old Theodor Baumert relate his fascinating anecdotes about his many years spent in the French Foreign Legion. A handsome, tall and athletically built man, Baumert, if he could be believed, was a survivor of practically every military engagement in North Africa in the past twenty years and a survivor of even more encounters with the North African ladies.

It was universally agreed that his stories were far better than what was being offered by the state-controlled Austrian television. Whether they were true or not did not matter. Nobody believed what was being offered on television either.

Seated at his side was Baumert's bride of five months, the handsome and startlingly well-built, thirty-seven-year-old Ilona. A suitable consort for the French Foreign Legionnaire come home at last from the wars, she had had, in her own way, almost as adventurous a life as he and without ever even leaving Wels.

The fact was Ilona was generally acknowledged to be the hottest sex kitten that Wels had ever produced and there were few males and not all that many females in the Red Lion that evening who could not have attested to it personally.

Ilona was not, however, given to relating anecdotes of her personal close encounters other than to a few of her closest friends, and it had to be admitted that at the times when she was married, she had been unwaveringly faithful to the spouse of the moment.

The moment was, perhaps, too critical a term. Most of Ilona's

195

marriages had lasted for at least two or three years, and in none of the cases had she instigated the divorce proceedings. There remained, moreover, a certain amount of bitterness. All three of the ex-husbands were still living in Wels.

Theodor Baumert had just finished a particularly stimulating account of a lost weekend spent in a North African brothel when a slender, dark-haired woman with enormous, sultry, black eyes appeared as if out of nowhere and snuggled into the seat beside him. To the applause of the other persons seated at the table, she remarked in a matter-of-fact voice that Baumert was talking about amateurs. If he was really interested in learning about sex in North Africa, she could give him a few tips.

Whether the woman knew anything about sex or not, she certainly knew about North Africa because she was a North African from Tunis. Her name was Fatima Gigovic, she was twenty-eight years old, married to a Tunisian construction worker, and a waitress at the Red Lion, but now off-duty as she worked mornings.

Fatima's husband was not present in the Red Lion. A male, North African guest-worker in Austria, he would have found himself sitting conspicuously alone at a table far back in the corner, and he might have had some trouble in getting served. The Red Lion did not cater to foreign guest-workers. There were taverns where they could mix with their own kind in other, and perhaps slightly less desirable, sections of the town.

Fatima was, however, regarded as a woman rather than a North African because she obviously was one, and women, even North African ones, are generally deemed capable of providing more valuable services than construction work. According to the gossip, Fatima was not overly reluctant to provide such services. She was also very pretty.

This being the case, and Theodor and Ilona Baumert enjoying the reputation of being modern, open-minded individuals, no one was very surprised when the Baumerts and Fatima Gigovic left the Red Lion together at approximately ten o'clock. Although they had not said so, the general assumption was that they were going to the Baumert's apartment at 55c Heimstättenring.

If no one in the Red Lion was very surprised at what appeared to be a Saturday night threesome forming up, Inspector Anton Schreiber, head of the small Wels Department of Criminal Investigations was very surprised to be pulled out of a sound sleep at a few minutes after midnight by an urgent telephone call from the station.

There had, said the excited desk sergeant on duty, been a murder. Some North African woman had stabbed Theodor Baumert to death.

The report reflected the fact that Theodor Baumert was far better known in Wels than was Fatima Gigovic. Ilona Baumert, of course, knew who she was, but she had been hysterical when she telephoned the station and she had merely used a racist term for the Tunisian waitress without mentioning her name.

Wels is not the sort of place where senior investigations officers are often pulled out of bed in the middle of the night, and the inspector, initially confused and not as certain as to who Theodor Baumert was as the officer on duty appeared to be, demanded confirmation.

North Africans, he pointed out, frequently stabbed each other, but they rarely stabbed their Austrian hosts. Stabbing an Austrian could get them deported back to North Africa, and not only were jobs scarce there, but they paid a fraction of what could be earned in Europe.

The officer on duty said that, so far, all he had was a telephone call from Ilona Baumert, but that a patrol car was on the way and he would connect the inspector direct as soon as they reported back. It being the late shift on a Saturday night, he was, of course, a very young officer and he was beginning to feel a little uneasy. It occurred to him now that he should have waited until he had confirmation or otherwise from the patrol car before pulling the head of the Criminal Investigations Department out of bed. If Ilona Baumert was simply drunk and Theodor was not murdered after all, his impetuosity would not do his career very much good.

Baumert was, however, dead and the patrol-car officers so reported to the inspector over the car's radio-telephone. He was lying in the middle of the living-room floor with the handle of what looked like an ornamental dagger sticking up out of his chest, and a very large quantity of blood had run from his mouth and nose. There were no signs of breathing or pulse and, from the location of the dagger, the officers thought that it had probably gone straight through the heart.

The inspector told them to remain where they were until relieved and to take into custody anyone present. He then instructed the desk sergeant, who was still waiting on the line, to call an ambulance. He did not doubt the patrolmen's judgement that Baumert was dead, but regulations called for an ambulance to be sent in any case. It was better to have the ambulance make a dry run than to pass up an opportunity of saving a life.

The desk sergeant said that he had already done so, which was not entirely true, but he made it so by immediately telephoning the ambulance service. In the meantime, the inspector had hung up the telephone and departed for the scene.

The desk sergeant, certain now that he was sitting in the middle of a major case and anxious to be as efficient as possible, turned out the inspector's assistant, Detective-Sergeant Peter Moosberger, and the Wels coroner, Dr Karl Josef. He informed both that a homicide had taken place and that Inspector Schreiber had already left for the scene.

At the apartment building located at 55c Heimstättenring, the inspector found Ilona Baumert crying hysterically in the kitchen of the apartment and one of the patrolmen from the patrol car guarding the corpse in the living room. The second patrolman was sitting in the car so that the station would be able to contact them over the radio-telephone if necessary.

As the inspector had had further to travel, the ambulance arrived only a minute or two after him and the medical officer who had come with it made a quick but thorough examination of the corpse.

The only thing that he could say was that it was just that, a corpse. Like the patrol-car officers, he thought that the dagger had probably passed directly through Baumert's heart and that death had been almost instantaneous.

The ambulance then returned to the hospital. There was nothing that they could do for Baumert and the body could not be moved until it had been seen and examined by the Wels coroner.

In the meantime, the inspector went to the patrol car, raised the officer on duty at headquarters on the radio-telephone and told him to turn out a squad from the police laboratory. The technicians were to pick up their equipment and report immediately to Heimstättenring 55c. As he understood it, Mrs Baumert had been a witness to the crime, so there should be no difficulty with the case, but the court would want whatever material evidence there was and the laboratory people should come and secure it.

He had just finished and was going back into the building when Sergeant Moosberger and Coroner Josef arrived separately but simultaneously. While the coroner went to examine the body and the sergeant followed him to provide any help that might be needed, the inspector returned to the kitchen where, with the aid of a small, portable tape recorder, he took Ilona Baumert's statement.

Although he did not know Ilona personally, he knew who she was and something of her reputation, so he was neither startled or shocked when she said that she and her husband had brought Fatima Gigovic home with them for a quiet three-way sex party. Theodor had been nostalgically attracted to North Africans because they reminded him of his days with the French Foreign Legion and she personally had found the dark-haired, dark-eyed Tunisian exotic and rather stimulating.

They had arrived home at a little after ten o'clock and, all three being in a state of aroused anticipation, had immediately stripped down and indulged in what might be called a preliminary bout in the living room.

This had ended a little after eleven or, at least, it had ended for Theodor who, being a male, did not have the sexual staying power of his companions.

While Ilona and Fatima continued to amuse themselves and each other on the living-room carpet, he had gone to the kitchen and had returned with a loaf of bread, a mug of beer and some cheese. He had sat down at the table in the living room and, using an ornamental Finnish dagger which normally hung on the wall as decoration, had begun cutting up the bread and cheese for a little snack.

At this point Ilona, who had drunk a good deal of beer that evening and whose bladder was nearly bursting, had excused herself and gone off to the toilet. She had been there rather longer than she anticipated and she had heard Theodor and Fatima speaking together. It had seemed, for a moment, that their voices were raised loudly and then she had heard nothing more.

When she had come out of the toilet and had returned to the living room, she had found Theodor lying as he was lying now with the handle of the dagger sticking up out of his chest and no sign of Fatima.

She had tried to help him, but then realizing that he was dead, had called the police.

How long, the inspector wanted to know, had she been in the toilet?

Ilona could not say with certainty. She had been drinking that evening and she was a little giddy from her sexual exertions. It could have been five minutes; it could have been fifteen. She might even have dosed off for a minute or two.

What about Fatima when she had left the room? asked the

inspector. Was she fully clothed?

Ilona shook her head. Fatima, she said, had been totally naked with the exception of a pair of long, white stockings which belonged to Ilona, but which she and Theodor had asked Fatima to put on to provide added stimulation.

The inspector wanted to know if the stockings were still there, and Ilona said that she did not know, but that she would go and look as soon as Theodor had been taken away. She did not want to go into the living room as long as his body was still lying there. After all, she said they had not even been married a full five months.

The inspector could understand and respect her feelings. In any case, the white stockings were not particularly important. What was important was to locate Fatima Gigovic before she cleared out of Wels and, if given the opportunity, out of Austria altogether. It was imperative that she be brought promptly to justice or, otherwise, North African guest-workers might get the idea that they could kill Austrians with impunity.

He, therefore, took down all details concerning the woman that Mrs Baumert was able to provide him and, going down to the police car again, telephoned them into the station with instructions that the search for the murderess begin at once.

Any further information needed would be easily come by. The woman's home address and nearly everything there was to know about her would be on record at the local foreigners' registration office. It would, however, be necessary to turn someone out of bed to come down and open up the office.

At the scene, the inspector went briskly about the task of establishing the physical evidence which would make Fatima Gigovic's conviction a certainty, the most important item being the dagger still sticking in Baumert's chest. As there was no blood on the handle, he had high hopes that the laboratory technicians would be able to recover identifiable fingerprints from it.

As a matter of fact, they were able to and, to be on the safe side and avoid unpleasant surprises later, the inspector instructed them to take Ilona's fingerprints for comparison. This was done. The fingerprints on the handle of the dagger were not those of Ilona Baumert.

Nor were they those of Theodor Baumert. Unlikely as it might seem, it was always possible that Baumert had committed suicide or that the murderess might, at least, maintain that he had. The inspector wanted a tight case. Otherwise, all of the potential clues found in the apartment by the laboratory technicians tended to confirm Mrs Baumert's story of a three-way sexual encounter, traces of semen and rather more substantial traces of female sexual secretions being recovered from the living-room carpet, the spread thrown over the sofa and one of the armchairs.

The investigations at the scene having been thus concluded, the body of Theodor Baumert was transferred to the police morgue where Dr Josef carried out the preliminary stages of the autopsy that night. His most significant findings were that Baumert had engaged in sexual intercourse within an hour prior to his death and that the Finnish dagger had passed directly through his heart, killing him almost instantly.

The dagger had been drawn out of the body, it was sent to the police laboratory where it was found that the prints on the hilt were of the full hand of a person who had presumably known something about using a knife, for it had not been gripped with the thumb pointed away from the blade, as a normal, inexperienced person would do, but with the thumb towards it in the manner of a trained knife fighter.

Despite the intensive search which had begun immediately after the inspector learned the identity of the supposed murderess, no trace of Fatima Gigovic could be found. However, her fingerprints were on record with the foreigners' registration office and the Identification Department was able to report that they corresponded to those found on the handle of the knife.

The husband of the fugitive Tunisian was brought to police headquarters and questioned intensively as to possible places where his wife might have gone, but said that he knew very little about her affairs.

He had married her in Austria and not in Tunisia and she was badly infected by European ideas of independence and women's liberation, so that she was scarcely of any use to him at all.

He wanted to know if he would be automatically divorced if she were caught and sent to jail for a long period of time.

The inspector was not convinced by this apparent sincerity, but, although the interrogation was intensified a great deal, nothing else could be got out of Gigovic. In the end, it had to be assumed that he was either very resistant or telling the truth, and he was allowed to return home.

In the meantime, the police switchboard had been deluged with the usual crank calls which attend murder cases, particularly when spectacular and well-known personalities are involved. Nearly all of them were anonymous and at least half of the callers said that they knew for a certainty that Ilona Baumert had murdered her husband. Many added that it was because she had been plotting with one of her previous husbands to get Baumert out of the way so that they could remarry. Among these, the choice fell heavily with husband number two, twenty-six-year-old Boris Leonov, a Yugoslav who had married Ilona because being married to an Austrian gave him the right to remain permanently in Austria.

Ilona had met him during a vacation at Attersee Lake a few miles to the south-west of Wels not long after divorcing her first husband and, for her, it had been true love.

Almost everyone in Wels knew the details and almost everyone knew and had known at that time that it was not true love for the Yugoslav. A computer specialist, he had been earning far more money in Austria than he could have hoped to have earned in communist Yugoslavia and he was anxious to remain. He had spent money freely on the divorced woman, but once they were married and he had his permission to remain in Austria, he had turned his attention to others. Boris, it seemed, was attracted to very young women, preferably under the age of eighteen and, for him, Ilona was already an old woman.

There had been frightful scenes which scandalized the entire community and, eventually, there had been a divorce.

Rendered cautious by this experience, Ilona had remained single, if not celibate, for three years before marrying husband number three, forty-two-year-old Georg Fuchshuber, who, as she told her best friend Ann Riedinger, was a delight in bed, but not much good at making money.

A tailor and not a particularly good one, Fuchshuber had not had the income to support Ilona in the style to which she was accustomed, at least occasionally, but which she always demanded.

The fact was that Ilona, who had been born Ilona Toth, had begun life under very modest circumstances and, although her sex drive was such that she had managed to make herself notorious by the time that she was seventeen, her desire for love was equalled if not surpassed by her desire for money.

She had, it seemed, never been able to combine the two. Her first husband, Sebastian Cerweg, whom she married when he was thirty-three and she was twenty-six, owned a filling station, had money and was satisfactory in bed until he got married. Unfortunately, he was a very hard worker and this left him so tired that he tended to fall asleep immediately most nights. The marriage lasted for three years.

She had become sick and tired of the smell of petrol and motor oil, she told Ann Riedinger. Life in a filling station was not what she was looking for.

It was possible that her expectations had been raised too high by the succession of lovers that she had had prior to her marriage. Among the more notable was an exceedingly rich industrialist from Linz who had put her up in a luxury apartment and had treated her like a pet kitten. As a husband, he had everything. He was rich and he was as sexually active as a mink in May. Unfortunately, he was also married and he had no intention of getting a divorce. When he became tired of Ilona's youthful charms, he simply bade her farewell, pressed a modest sum into her hand and put her out of the apartment. Two days later another girl was occupying it.

Ilona had been heart-broken but she had been consoled and comforted by a prominent fashion designer who also put her up in an apartment and sent her on shopping trips to Vienna in his chauffeur-driven Mercedes.

He was not quite as wealthy as the industrialist and he was a great deal less active sexually, but Ilona still felt that this was, at last, true love.

Alas! The designer had lasted for an even shorter time than the industrialist. His was a mercurial nature and he bored rather quickly.

There had followed the series of four marriages, none of which had worked out, with the exception of the last. Everyone agreed that Theodor and Ilona were made for each other. He had not been wealthy, but he had been comfortably off and, as Ilona had told Ann Riedinger, he was a holy terror in bed, having garnered experience in a thousand brothels in the Near East and North Africa. If there was anything in the way of sex in which he was not expert, it was because it was either dangerous or physically impossible.

It had not been necessary to take either Theodor's or Ilona's word for this. Theodor had also been married once before and was divorced, but, before marrying Ilona, he had run through a series of short-term affairs in his home town that had left the local maidens gasping for breath.

Nonetheless, if Theodor was still extremely active in affairs of the heart and on lower levels as well, his primary interest, as he told everyone in the Red Lion who would listen to him, was stability. He was tired of knocking about the world, of sleeping with this one and that one; what he wanted was a home and a wife in it.

He had found that in Ilona. She was now thirty-seven years of age, rapidly approaching the fatal fortieth anniversary, and she was not quite the sex bomb that she had been. She had never been truly beautiful. Her features were too strong for that, but her cheeks had been plump and round and she had been cute. Now, the juvenile plumpness had disappeared and the strong bone structure was coming out.

The body too, which, unlike the face, had been truly magnificent, was not quite the same. The thighs were a little heavier. The hips were a little rounder. The waist was not quite so small. Despite exercises, the breasts had begun to sag.

Looking at herself in the mirror, Ilona was forced to face the facts. She was past it. It was time to find a good one, if not the ideal one, and settle down. After all, security and stability had always been among her primary concerns.

Theodor had been an outstanding compromise. He was not rich, but he had money. He was, by her standards, a bit long in the tooth, but he was still a sexual whirlwind. All in all, it was as much or more than she could have expected.

And now, it had all been taken away by that wretched North African who had murdered Theodor without even any reason for doing so.

Because there was the problem. Neither Ilona nor Fatima's husband nor Inspector Schreiber could think of the slightest trace of a motive for the murder of Theodor Baumert.

It was not that there had been a dispute over money.

Fatima was a nice girl. She did not charge for her services. There was ample testimony to that.

It was not that Baumert had made an indecent suggestion to her. She would have been delighted. Besides, according to all accounts, there was nothing that she would have regarded as indecent.

Why then had she destroyed her own existence by making it impossible for her to remain in Austria, a country which she had repeatedly said she hoped never to leave?

Could it have been an accident? Could Baumert have, in some way, fallen on the knife so clumsily as to literally impale himself? And could Fatima have seized the handle sticking out of his chest in an instinctive gesture to pull it out? Would she have lost her head, realizing that her prints were on the knife, and fled from the apartment?

These were all questions which gradually began to arise in Inspector Schreiber's mind as the days passed and he was still unable to find Fatima. In an otherwise perfect case, the total lack of any plausible motive was troubling.

And there was something else. Like all telephone calls to an Austrian police station, the crank calls concerning the Theodor Baumert murder were taped. Listening to the tapes, it became obvious that some of the callers had called more than once. The champion among these, however, was a female voice which had called no less than seven times. The message had always been the same. Ilona Baumert had murdered her husband because he refused to give her a divorce. Fatima Gigovic was innocent.

Needless to say, the calls were anonymous and of too short duration to trace. People read crime stories in Austria as much as in any other place, and most people know that a telephone call can be traced if you stay on the line too long.

The thing which intrigued the inspector about this persistent caller was, however, that he seemed to detect a slight foreign intonation to the voice.

Fatima Gigovic had been many years in Austria and she spoke fluent German with the accent common to the Wels district, but, even so, there was still a faint echo of the gutteral North African Arabic in her pronunciation.

In short, the inspector thought that the persistent caller was Fatima Gigovic.

The question was, of course, where was she calling from, but, almost equally important in the inspector's mind, was the question of why she was calling at all.

Was it possible that she was really innocent and that the theory of the accidental nature of the wound was correct? But, if it had been accidental, why did she not say so? Why did she continue to accuse Ilona Baumert?

As far as the inspector could see, the accusations made no sense. Ilona and Theodor had only been married for a short time and, if they were still both playing the field, then that was only normal in a modern, liberal couple.

But had they both been playing the field? The inspector decided to look into that a little more carefully and, somewhat to his surprise, he found that the extramarital activity had been almost entirely on the side of Baumert. Ilona had taken part in threesomes and moresomes, but she had not had any liaisons in which Theodor did not take part. Considering her reputation, this seemed strange.

The inspector got out the tape recording of Ilona's original statement and played it back. Now, it seemed to him oddly pat.

Baumert had been cutting up bread and cheese with the knife. That was true. The bread and cheese and the half-drunk mug of beer had been found on the living room table.

She had gone to the toilet and, under the influence of alcohol, had perhaps dozed off for a few minutes. And during these few minutes, Fatima, for no reason, had stabbed Theodor to death, had dressed and had fled the building. Looked at objectively, the statement now seemed very remarkable indeed.

The inspector was not a man to fail to act on something that he found suspicious and he immediately ordered the sergeant to bring the widow Baumert to police headquarters for further interrogation. By the time that she arrived there, he had decided on a tactic that he had often used, particularly with female suspects, the sudden-shock treatment.

Seating Ilona Baumert in the chair in front of his desk and switching on the tape recorder, he announced brusquely that the police laboratory technicians had succeeded in removing the upper layer of fingerprints on the handle of the knife which had killed Theodor Baumert, and the fingerprints underneath them were hers. How, he wanted to know, could she explain that?

As it often did, the shock treatment worked perfectly. Ilona Baumert gasped as if someone had thrown a glassful of iced water into her face, turned pale, half rose from the chair and then said weakly that she had not done it.

For the inspector, who had heard a great many such denials, it was nearly as good as a confession. Although he had found it difficult to believe before, he was now convinced that Ilona Baumert had murdered her husband.

Ilona had begun to cry and he waited patiently until she had finished, passing her over a box of Kleenex from the desk drawer.

The crying did not go on for very long and then Ilona Baumert raised her head and looking the inspector straight in the eye said that she had done it because he refused to give her a divorce.

'I wasn't getting any younger,' she said, 'and he was running around with every teenager he could get his hands on. It wasn't my idea of a marriage and I'd already told him that I wanted a divorce. All my other husbands were reasonable but not him. He wanted it both ways. He wanted security and a home and at the same time he wanted his freedom to do whatever he wanted to.

'Fatima was just the last straw. They had just got through making love on the carpet and I asked him again for a divorce. He was cutting up his bread and cheese with a knife and he said he wouldn't think of it.

206

'I didn't actually mean to, but I just grabbed the knife and stabbed him. Then, I was scared to death and I yelled at Fatima to pull it out. She took hold of the handle and I said, "All right now, it's your fingerprints on it."

'She turned pale, got herself dressed and left the house without another word. I waited until she was gone before I called the police.'

Ilona Baumert was brought to trial on October 11, 1982, and pleaded guilty to unintended homicide. She was, she said, sorry.

The jury apparently believed her, for they granted her certain extenuating circumstances and she was sentenced to a modest eight years' imprisonment.

Two days after the indictment was announced in the newspapers, Fatima Gigovic reappeared and resumed her duties at the Red Lion. The inspector never found out where she was hiding during the time she was being sought for murder, but he has reason to believe that it was somewhere right in Wels.

16

GIRLISH PRANKS

When thirty-four-year-old Henriette Malnou, proprietress of the Matelot Bar in the French port of Dieppe, saw the splintered door jamb where the tongue of the lock had torn through the wood, she immediately realized that something bad had happened.

'Colette?' she called, but less loudly than she had called the name before while ringing the doorbell.

It had only been when she placed her hand against the door that it had swung open and she had seen the broken lock. Her voice was lower now because she was apprehensive of who or what might be inside the room.

The sight which met her eyes, however, as she pushed the door open wider and stepped hesitantly in, was far beyond anything that she could have feared.

Forty-five-year-old Colette Vain, a small woman who sometimes helped out in the Matelot Bar, lay spreadeagled on her bed. She was wearing a nightdress which hung in shreds about her neck and shoulders, but her body was obscenely naked.

It was not that the body itself was obscene, but rather what had been done to it. The huge letter Z which had been slashed into the breasts had filled with dark, dried blood and stood out startlingly black against the white flesh.

Below it, a veritable chessboard cut into the woman's belly extended from the pubic hair to the navel. It too was black with dried blood.

Nor was this all. From between the thin, wide-spread thighs the bottom of a Rémy Martin cognac bottle, forced for nearly its entire length into the woman's body, protruded stiffly.

Her head tipped and her wide-open eyes staring at the ceiling, the dead woman's face was a mask of agony and terror beneath the short, light-brown hair, now stiff with blood.

Henriette Malnou staggered backwards out into the second-floor hall of the apartment building at number two Rue Menard, fell to her knees on the verge of fainting, recovered herself and ran down the stairs to the street.

At that moment, she had no very clear idea of where she was going. Her flight was a purely instinctive reaction of recoil from an unbearable sight. Like many of the people in the neighbourhood, she had been attached to Colette Vain.

'Obviously, a sex criminal of the worst sort,' said Inspector Gerard Dubois, chief of the small Department of Criminal Investigations of the Dieppe police.

The department was small because Dieppe, located on the Atlantic coast between Le Havre and Calais, has a population of little more than thirty-five thousand and a correspondingly low crime rate.

'Probably incapable of achieving sexual satisfaction any other way,' said Dr Sebastian Breton, the Dieppe coroner, who was examining the corpse on the bed. 'I can't see any traces of semen on the body or the bed sheets. There may be some in the vagina once I remove the bottle.'

He was a comparatively young man, square-faced and stocky with short, black, stiff hair and horn-rimmed spectacles, and he was obviously finding the examination distasteful. It was the first such crime that he had had to deal with since taking office.

Detective-Sergeant Pierre Ligier, the inspector's young, thin-faced and rather worried-looking assistant, put his head in the door and said, 'They're on the way.'

He was referring to the entire staff of the police laboratory whom the inspector had ordered turned out the moment he had seen the room. It was such a shambles that he felt quite certain that some clues to the identity of the murderer would be found there.

It was not the ideal time to be starting a major homicide case. The date was January 2, 1979, and nearly everyone, police included, was still recovering from the end-of-the-year celebrations.

It was, of course, the very heart of the central European winter and the storms and gales were blowing in, in almost unbroken succession, off the Atlantic, to dump sleet, snow, hail and freezing rain over the little city. Although it was nearly eleven o'clock in the forenoon, it was still so dark outside that the lights were turned on in many buildings.

While the doctor continued with his examination of the body, the inspector prowled thoughtfully up and down, looking at the smashed porcelain, the badly dented, enamel wash-basin lying on the floor and the other indications of a savage struggle, but touching nothing. He was hoping that there would be fingerprints on some of the objects and that those fingerprints would be in the police files. It was unlikely this would be the first offence for a sex deviant so inclined to violence.

First offence or not, he had obviously never been apprehended for, although the number of fingerprints made by someone who was, presumably, the murderer were recoved from the enamel wash-basin, they did not match anything in the police files. In addition, they had been made by a remarkably small hand, almost as small as that of a child.

'Very puzzling,' said the inspector, stuffing tobacco into his stubby, blackened pipe with his thumb. A quiet, thoughtful sort of man with sandy, curly hair and a firm jaw, the pipe was seldom out of his mouth. 'Is Paris certain?'

'They say negative,' said the sergeant. 'It's all handled by computer at the Central Identification Section now. I doubt that there's any error.'

A man with faith in modern technology, he had come into the inspector's office with a reply to the request telexed earlier to the Paris police.

The local police files had already been checked without result, something which did not surprise the inspector as he did not believe that the murderer could be a local man. In a town with thirty-five thousand inhabitants, anyone as disturbed as this man would obviously be known to the police and, probably, everyone else in the community.

'Well, then we'll have to identify him ourselves,' said the inspector, puffing on the pipe. 'We'll see what Dr Breton says when he's finished with the autopsy. In the meantime, you can have the Records Section pull out the files of known sex offenders, just on the off-chance. We don't know that the prints on the wash-basin are the murderer's.'

It was nearly five o'clock in the afternoon of the same day and, so far, all that the inspector had was the negative reports on the fingerprints. The body was now at the police morgue where Dr Breton was performing the autopsy. As he had a good deal to do, it was not likely that the autopsy report would be ready before the following morning.

At the apartment building in the Rue Menard, the entire staff of the police laboratory was still going over the scene of the crime and teams of the detectives were interrogating the occupants of the building. So far, there had been no reports of anything particularly significant.

210

Nor were there to be any yet that night. At eleven o'clock, the technicians from the laboratory returned to police headquarters, but were unable to make a report. They had assembled an enormous amount of material and it would have to be analyzed and evaluated before any conclusions could be drawn. The chief of the laboratory did not think that that would be much before late afternoon of the following day.

The teams of detectives who had been interrogating the occupants of the building had come in with the laboratory technicians, and they reported that everyone living in the building had now been questioned and all had stated that they knew nothing about the murder and had noticed nothing suspicious over the past few days. It was still not known precisely when the murder had taken place.

'It's not the sort of building in which anyone would say if they did notice anything,' said one of the detectives. 'It's a slum tenement. Almost all of the occupants are on public assistance or they're making a living in an unorthodox and probably illegal manner. Lots of North Africans. In fact, it's hard to tell who's living there and who isn't. Some of them don't rent apartments in the building, but they sleep there most of the time and probably don't have any other address. It's the sort of place where there are people coming and going seven nights a week.'

The inspector nodded. He had been born and raised in Dieppe and he knew what kind of a building the apartment house in the Rue Menard was. It was not the only one in the town. The French economy was catastrophic and there were great numbers of poor and unemployed people.

The sergeant had gone to collect background material on the victim and the inspector did not think that he would report in again that night. So he went home himself.

The following day, there was more information available on the case, but much of it was confusing.

The sergeant had assembled a reasonably complete background on the victim, mainly from Henriette Malnou, the woman who had discovered the body.

According to her, Colette Vain had been mentally handicapped, but had had a lovable personality and had been popular throughout the neighbourhood. From early childhood she had suffered from the delusion that she was male and had, consequently, dressed like one and had even shaved every day although she had no more beard than any other woman. She had often startled persons who did not know her by using men's public-toilet facilities, although it was not clear exactly how she managed this.

Classed as a mental deficient by the social welfare office, she had received a small pension from the government which had, together with odd jobs, such as helping out in the Matelot Bar, been enough to meet her rather simple needs.

As she believed herself to be a man, Colette had had for the past two years what she regarded as a homosexual relationship with a lover scarcely less strange than herself. A dwarf who stood not quite four feet eight inches tall, his name was Gustave Léger and he was fifty-five years old.

Although neither Léger nor Colette was married and there was no obstacle to their living together to save rent, Léger had maintained his own one-room apartment on the other side of the town and had been visited once a week on Fridays by his girlfriend or, as she believed, boyfriend.

The sergeant had interrogated Léger who said that they made love on these occasions and that, sexually, Colette was completely normal and no different from any other woman.

Dr Breton was convinced that the murderer would have a record of sexual offences. He had completed the autopsy and had established that Colette Vain had died at between four and five o'clock in the morning of December 31, as a result of a fractured skull. Whatever it was that had fractured her skull, it had been broad, smooth and flat and he suspected that it was either the enamelled wash-basin or the tile floor itself.

Sickeningly, the letter Z had been cut into her breasts, the chessboard had been gouged into the skin of her belly and the cognac bottle had been forced deep into her vagina, so deep as to rupture the walls and penetrate into the intestinal cavity, while she was still alive and, it was feared, conscious.

The doctor's final conclusion was startling.

'There were at least two of them,' he said, reporting verbally to the inspector while the autopsy report was still being typed up. 'Somebody was holding her while she was being tortured. There are clear bruises on her arms where he gripped her with his hands.'

'Well, then he was different from any sex criminal that I ever heard of,' said the inspector. 'Sex psychopaths are almost always loners. I never heard of two of them working as a team.'

'Neither have I,' said the doctor. 'However, there's no question about it. There were at least two of them. There's no way that one man, however strong, could have held the woman and tortured

212

her at the same time, particularly not the rape with the bottle.'

'Then, it can't be a sex crime,' said the inspector, frowning and poking with his forefinger in the bowl of the pipe which had gone out. 'The murderers must have faked a sex crime to throw us off.'

'No,' said the doctor. 'It was a real sex crime. I don't believe that it was fake.'

'It seems to me, that you're contradicting yourself,' said the inspector. 'In one breath, you say that sex criminals working as a team are unknown and, in the next breath, you say that this was a team which committed a sex crime.'

'I didn't say that they were unknown,' said the doctor. 'There have been a great many sex crimes committed by teams, but not teams of two men. It's a man and woman team who stimulate themselves sexually with such acts. Sadists, in short.'

'You suggest then, that this was a man-and-woman team?' said the inspector.

'That or a group,' said the doctor. 'It was more than one person and it was a compulsive sex crime. The only other thing that occurs to me is some kind of drug that drives people completely out of their minds.'

'That's a possibility, at least,' said the inspector. 'Science progresses all the time. Why not a drug that makes a sadistic sex criminal out of you?'

Actually, the theories made very little difference, for the police had no more leads on the identity of a couple of opposite sex than on a couple of the same sex. In fact, they had no leads at all.

However, after having given the matter a great deal of thought, the inspector came up with a few conclusions.

'To begin with,' he told the sergeant. 'I think that we may safely assume that the murderers had some reason to be in the building and on either the second or a higher floor. Out of all the apartments and rooms in the building, there was no reason why they should particularly pick on the one occupied by Colette Vain.'

'Unless they knew her,' said the sergeant. 'We still don't know the motive. Dr Breton says it was sex, but was it?'

'Any other motive is almost unthinkable,' said the inspector. 'We know that the victim was a gentle, simple and very popular person. She had no enemies and she was probably incapable of making any. It wasn't money. She had none and the total value of everything in the apartment wasn't five hundred francs. If it wasn't sex, what was it?'

'All right, it was sex,' said the sergeant, 'but I still say that the murderers knew who she was. What's more, I think that she must have known that she was in danger. Otherwise, why didn't she open the door? Why did the murderers have to smash the lock?'

'Well, I suppose that she would have been afraid to open the door at that hour of the morning.' said the inspector. 'But you do have a point about their smashing the door in. It's hard to believe that they would have smashed down the door of just any apartment without knowing who was inside. It could just as well have been some half-mad strongman with a knife two feet long. I think you're right.'

'They must have known who lived in that apartment.'

'Which brings us back to what you were saying.' said the sergeant. 'The murderers were people who had some reason to be in the building. They weren't strangers. They knew the building well enough to know who lived in that apartment and I suppose they picked on her simply because she was small and helpless. There couldn't have been any other reason that I can think of.'

'Well, let's hope we're right about this,' said the inspector, 'because that could provide us with the only lead that we're apparently going to have. The lab hasn't found anything to serve as an indication to the identity of the murderers. The autopsy only established that there were two or more of them. I think what we have to do now is concentrate on persons living in the building and persons frequenting the building but not living there. What about the occupants? Are there any likely couples among them? All I saw was the report that said nothing significant had turned up.'

'That's the report I saw too,' said the sergeant. 'I'll talk to the boys who are out there and then I'll go out and take a look myself. They didn't know at the time that they were questioning the tenants that we were looking for a couple.'

Once again, the result of the sergeant's investigations were negative. The only couple actually living in the house were in their late seventies and very feeble. Some of the other apartments were occupied by what amounted practically to communes and it was impossible to determine whether any of the members were joined in couples or not. Like most such groups, they were made up of unstable collections of the unemployed and unemployable who seldom remained in one place or maintained a personal relationship for any very extended period of time.

One of the biggest communes was not exactly a commune but more a family, as the core was made up of forty-one-year-old Aimée Leroux and a large and constantly varying number of her children, some of whom were already adults and all of whom came and went as they saw fit. Although Mrs Leroux, who had never been legally married, was not certain about the precise number, there seemed to be over a dozen of them, some of whom used the surnames of their supposed fathers and some the name of Leroux.

Mrs Leroux, who was listed as the sole tenant of the apartment, lived comfortably from her children as the French government, anxious to stimulate population growth, pays generous allowances for all children after the second, whether legitimate or otherwise.

The Leroux apartment lay partly over the one occupied by Colette Vain and was a busy place with varied social functions going on nearly every night. Aimée Leroux was a woman with a gregarious and carefree nature and her children had obviously taken after her.

Although the other tenants of the building had proved to be disappointing from the point of view of the investigation, the Leroux apartment on the third floor gradually began to take on something of the aspect of a gold-mine. The number of persons running in and out of it at all hours of the day and night was incredible and, as the sergeant would soon learn, there had been couples among them, although not always in the conventional sense.

Most conspicuous of these couples was a pair of forty-year-old Algerians, both of whom were named Mohammed although they were not related. They were, however, inseparable and were known as Big Head Mohammed and Little Head Mohammed, nicknames based on their physical characteristics.

Although the Mohammeds were generally believed to be partners in a homosexual marriage, something which would have made them unlikely suspects in the murder of Colette Vain, the sergeant was inclined to believe that they were at least bisexual, for they were keeping in their apartment a plump, pretty, five-foot-tall girl named Patricia Nalais.

Twenty-year-old Patricia, it seemed, did the housework and the cooking and, reportedly, provided sexual services to the two Mohammeds, whether alternatively or simultaneously could not be ascertained.

In her spare time, Patricia had worked up a rather profitable sex service for sailors on the cargo vessels anchored in the port. This was not an original idea as most of the European ports have girls who come out to the ships to comfort and entertain sailors who, for one reason or another, cannot or will not come ashore.

Patricia was, however, unusually successful, due, no doubt, to the fact that she was very pretty.

Half French and half North African, she used the maiden name of her mother, who had not had time to find out her father's surname before his departure.

For a time, one or the other of the Mohammeds and Patricia Nalais headed the inspector's list of suspects. The Mohammeds were petty criminals, drug pushers and procurers and, apparently, far from normal in some respects. Patricia had also had a chequered career for one so young, having been placed in a series of foster homes starting from the age of three. She had been kicked out of school for attacking one of the other pupils with a knife and had finally set up house with a fifty-year-old Turkish construction worker at the tender age of fourteen.

The Turk had beaten her like a carpet and she had responded by planting her seven-inch switchblade, which never left her person even in the most intimate moments, between his ribs.

The Turk had survived, but had refused to prefer charges as he was not anxious to explain how he came to be living with a fourteen-year-old girl. Patricia had bounced around to a few dozen other lovers and had eventually ended up with the Mohammeds and the sea-going sex business. Like the Mohammeds, she had been one of the regulars at the parties in the Leroux apartment.

The drawback to Patricia and one of the Mohammeds as suspects in the murder of Colette Vain was simply that the Mohammeds were inseparable and the indications were that there had been only two murderers involved. With Patricia, it would have made three.

The lead of Patricia and the two Mohammeds was, however, not completely worthless, for it led to the identification of yet another unusual personage who had frequented the Leroux apartment and with whom Patricia had been on intimate terms.

Gisèle Poulain had, it seemed, encountered Patricia Nalais some time during the summer of 1978 and the two girls had found each other so compatible that they had been practically inseparable since.

Physically, they were far more different than the two Mohammeds. Gisèle, although quite as pretty as Patricia, stood just short of six feet tall and had the muscles of an ice-hockey goalkeeper. Her instincts were similar and she was one of the most feared and respected bar-room brawlers in the city. Unlike the diminutive Patricia, she did not carry a knife nor have any need

216

of one. Her fists and feet were fully adequate.

In their backgrounds and way of life, however, the girls resembled each other more closely. Gisèle too had been kicked out of school for mangling her fellow pupils, had had countless lovers and had settled down with a male companion at an early age, namely sixteen.

There had been less difference in the ages than with Patricia and the Turk. Alain Layet, a commercial fisherman, was now twenty-four, one year older than Gisèle. A fearless bar-room fighter in his own right, he had found in Gisèle not only a wife and companion, but also a sparring partner. Their bouts had been epic and were spoken of with awe in the parts of the city where they were known.

Bruising as it was, they had apparently found it a meaningful relationship and on August 30, 1975, they had gone to the length of getting married, although Gisèle continued to use her maiden name.

During 1977 there had been at least a brief truce in their running battle, for in December of that year Gisèle became the mother of a little son who was christened Jérome.

Although both parents agreed that he was, without doubt, Alain's son, he apparently interfered with the boxing matches and was promptly turned over to Gisèle's mother for raising.

It was probably just as well, for Gisèle was not a woman to sit home nursing a baby and Alain was often absent in jail. A reasonably competent fisherman, he was a remarkably clumsy thief and was constantly being marched off to the local prison for shorter and longer terms.

Unpleasant as this was, he could, however, comfort himself with the thought that his family was provided for. By a mutually agreed upon arrangement, when Alain went off to jail, his best friend and fellow thief, twenty-five-year-old Joël Malieux moved in with Gisèle. Although not the puncher that Alain was, he kept the spouse in fighting trim and, being a more cautious thief, went to jail only occasionally and never while Alain was there.

It was, perhaps, an unorthodox arrangement, but, with young people everywhere in the 1970s, there were efforts to break free of old, stifling life-styles and find new ways of establishing significant personal relationships. This one, at least, worked.

For Inspector Dubois, it worked too well and he quickly came to regard Gisèle and Joël Malieux as his prime suspects. Alain, who had been in jail at the time of the crime, was eliminated, but his wife and his substitute were both persons with long records of acts of violence and both were known to have frequented the parties in Aimée Leroux's apartment on the floor above that of the victim.

According to the inspector's theory, on the night of the murder Gisèle and Malieux had attended one such party which had lasted until early morning. On their way out, they had happened to pass the door of Colette Vain's apartment and, being in all probability falling-down drunk, had achieved the amusing idea of giving the mentally handicapped little woman a fright. The sadistic violence of their natures being, however, aroused by the presence of a helpless and terrified victim, they had simply gone too far.

Both were arrested and brought to police headquarters for questioning where, to the inspector's dismay, Joël Malieux promptly produced an absolutely unshakable alibi for the evening of the crime. As a professional, he kept track of his whereabouts.

Gisèle could produce no such alibi and, when a waiter in an all-night café was found who testified that she had come into the cafe only shortly after the estimated time of the murder and asked to wash her bloody hands, saying that she had been in a fight, she broke down and confessed.

The waiter's testimony also implicated someone else. A short, plump, pretty girl with long, black hair had been with Gisèle and her hands had been as bloody as hers.

Patricia Nalais was arrested and added her confession to that of Gisèle Poulain. The two chums had been together at Aimée Leroux's and, on leaving to go home, had passed the door of Colette Vain's apartment. For no reason that either of them could offer, Gisèle had kicked the door in and they had robbed the terrified woman of six francs, all the money which she had in her possession at the moment.

Neither murderess was able to explain why they had killed Colette or why they had tortured her sexually. In response to questions on these subjects, they simply replied that they did not know.

At their trial on October 7, 1980, they made no effort to defend themselves, and merely repeated what they had told the police. As a result, they were sentenced to twenty years' imprisonment each.

17

GIRLFRIEND

On the last day of his life thirty-eight-year-old Wolfgang Ihns rose at four-thirty in the morning and made briskly off to the huge central produce market in the city of Hamburg, West Germany.

The date was March 13 1973, and a Tuesday, which meant that greengrocer Ihns would need to have his vegetables and fruit ready for the early-morning customers when he opened at seven o'clock.

Whether Ihns would still have got up early and gone to the market if he had known that he was to be murdered that day is a question impossible to answer, but it seems not unlikely. A prosaic, hard-working man who had eliminated competition in his neighbourhood simply by being better, the grocery store was his life and he might not have been able to think of a more interesting way to spend the last half-day of it.

Perhaps things would have been different if the Ihns had had a son who might be expected to take over the family business one day, but they had had only the one daughter, now five years old, and Marion, a stunningly beautiful, voluptuous woman, was thirty-five years old and showed little inclination to produce any more offspring. There was enough work as it was, what with keeping the apartment on the third floor of the building next door clean, cooking, taking care of the child and, of course, helping out in the grocery store in the afternoon.

Wolfgang took care of the shop alone in the morning, so that Marion could get her housework done, but, after lunch, she was expected to take over, either alone or with Wolfgang if business was heavy.

As for Wolfgang, he would be fresh and ready to continue until seven that evening when the store closed. Although he had been up since four-thirty in the morning, he took a nap in the basement beneath the store from after lunch until opening time at two-o'clock.

It was all he needed, but he very definitely needed that and, having found that his little daughter's sometimes boisterous play disturbed his sleep, he had set up an old iron cot in one corner of the cellar and took his naps there.

On that Tuesday in early spring, when snow and ice still lay in the streets of Hamburg, and the bitter wind lashing the estuary of the Elbe with showers of sleet and hail picked up from the grey, savage billows of the North Sea whined and snarled around the sturdy buildings of Germany's largest port, Wolfgang Ihns, a man of ordered habits, ate his lunch and descended to the basement to take his nap. He never awoke from it.

At two o'clock, Marion Ihns went down to wake him. Usually, he awoke by himself, but, if he were very tired, he might sleep on past opening time and this would upset him very much. He was exceedingly conscientious about his opening hours.

There was no access to the store from the apartment building and it was necessary for Marion to go outside and enter through the front door, which she would have to unlock as Wolfgang would have locked it from the inside before descending to the cellar.

To her consternation, she found the door unlocked!

This was something utterly unprecedented. Wolfgang Ihns was not a man to forget to lock the door to this store, nor was he likely to open it before the prescribed hour of two.

Marion immediately began called out his name, her voice growing louder and louder as no reply was received. Persons in the neighbouring shop, an electrical goods store which had just opened up for the afternoon, heard her and wondered.

While she had been calling out her husband's name, Marion Ihns had been crossing the store to the door and the stairway leading to the basement. As she later told the police, it had occurred to her that Wolfgang had, perhaps, already opened the shop for business and had then remembered something that he had to bring up from the basement. The store's stocks were kept down there.

Even calling from the head of the stairs, however, there was still no reply from Wolfgang and Marion began descending the steps. Later, she would not be able to remember whether she had had to turn on the light or whether it had already been on. She did remember that she had stopped calling.

It was a normal reaction. A human going into a place which he or she finds frightening or dangerous has a tendency to keep quiet. It is better that whatever there is there that is frightening or dangerous is not alerted. And Marion Ihns had always found those sprawling, old cellars stretching down deep into the earth beneath Hamburg frightening, even if not actually dangerous.

Now, however, it seemed that they were dangerous too for, by the light of the unshaded electric bulbs hanging from the low ceiling, she saw her husband lying on his cot on his back, the position in which he always took his nap, but his right hand, hanging over the edge of the bed was bright scarlet and from the tips of the fingers a thin stream of the same colour was adding to an already large pool on the cement floor.

Marion screamed once, not the name of her husband or any word, but the inarticulate scream of a badly frightened woman, turned and stumbled up the stairs, out of the front door of the store and into the shop next door, where she gasped out that her husband was injured in the basement and would somebody call a doctor.

The startled, but clear-thinking shopkeeper did better. He called an ambulance.

It was, of course, the correct thing to do, but it unfortunately turned out to be in vain. Wolfgang Ihns was dead and the only thing that the houseman who had come with the ambulance could do was to confirm this fact and inform Marion Ihns that, whatever her husband had died from, it was not a natural death and that she should notify the police immediately.

Instead, Mrs Ihns became hysterical so the houseman called the police himself over the ambulance's radio-telephone, and would have taken Mrs Ihns off to the hospital had she not regained enough control of herself to inform him that her five-year-old-daughter was alone in the apartment. He, therefore, helped her up to the apartment, gave her a massive injection of tranquillizers and left her. There was nothing more that he could do.

Although in the early seventies, life in the big cities had not yet become quite as exciting as it later would, there was still enough violent crime in Hamburg for a homicide squad to be on duty twenty-four hours a day and, the houseman having said that it looked to him like murder, it was the duty homicide squad which came.

Initially, this consisted of only three men, Inspector Wilhelm Krause, Detective-Sergeant Peter Hartmann and Dr Walter Reichauer who was an expert in forensic medicine attached to the Hamburg Department of Criminal Investigations. Their first task was to determine whether there actually had been a homicide. Not all homicide reports turn out to be one.

This one was and the doctor, a serious-looking young man who wore horn-rimmed glasses and a conservative business suit, said so within a minute of beginning his examination of the corpse.

'Fatal fracture of the left temple,' he said. 'It appears to have been only a single blow administered with a heavy hammer or, perhaps, the butt of an axe or hatchet. Secondly, a single, deep stab wound made with a large knife or dagger in the right side of the chest. Probably penetrated the heart or severed some of the major blood vessels around it. Also a fatal wound.'

'In that order?' said Inspector Krause. He was a tall, athletically built man in his late forties with a thoughtful, handsome face and long sideburns reaching down below his ears.

'Probably,' said the doctor. 'There are no indications that he tried to defend himself or even suspected what was coming, so it seems probable that the murderer came upon him when he was asleep, hit him on the head with the hammer or whatever it was and then stabbed him through the heart to make certain that he was dead.'

'The wife says that he took a nap down here every day,' said Sergeant Hartmann, who had just come down from speaking with the widow of the victim.

'Strange,' said the inspector.

'I suppose he was tired,' said the sergeant. 'I myself often feel a little heavy after lunch.'

The observation was justified. A blond, innocent-faced, young man, the sergeant weighed well over two hundred pounds, although he was a head shorter than the inspector.

'No, I mean the murder,' said the inspector. 'This man was apparently deliberately assassinated in what amounts to a professional manner. But who assassinates a greengrocer?'

'The husbands of wives with whom the greengrocer is too friendly?' suggested the sergeant. 'We've been having a lot of New Morality murders here lately. Maybe this is one.'

'Well, it's possible,' said the inspector. 'What does the wife look like?'

'Wow!' said the sergeant, making the obligatory movements for such appreciative descriptions with his hands. 'A bit like a zombie at the moment, but she says the ambulanceman pumped her full of tranquillizers.'

'She made no suggestion as to who might have wanted to harm her husband though?' said the inspector a little stiffly. His assistant belonged to the Now generation and he belonged to the Then, so that he did not always appreciate his manner of speaking. He was, however, a good assistant, clever, well-trained and incredibly tenacious.

'No one in the world, she said,' said the sergeant. 'She said it two or three times. Which was a little funny because I hadn't asked her yet. Then she said she thought it was robbery. Said the city was full of young punks on drugs who'd kill you for ten pfennigs if they were broke and needed a fix.'

'Perfectly true,' said the inspector, 'but I have seen few addicts with enough co-ordination or wits to carry out such a neat homicide. Did you check the till in the shop?'

'I'll go check it now,' said the sergeant and did.

The cash drawer was full of money, the receipts from the morning's business and, as Ihns had kept careful track of his transactions for tax purposes, it was not difficult to determine that not a pfennig was missing.

Neither was anything else. Later that evening when Marion Ihns had recovered from the tranquillizers, she came down and went through store and basement with the sergeant. As far as she could determine, nothing had been taken.

'Which leaves us with more of a mystery than I care for,' said the inspector. 'Mysteries are fine in detective stories, but, in criminal-investigations work, they tie up too many personnel and by the time things get straightened out, new mysteries have come up.'

'A thankless business,' agreed the sergeant. 'If the case gets solved, we're merely doing our job. If it doesn't, we're a bunch of clowns and you can forget about the next promotion. Nothing in the autopsy, I take it?'

It was the morning following the day of the murder of Wolfgang Ihns and the sergeant, who had worked late the night before, had just come into the office which he shared with the inspector.

The inspector shook his head. 'I didn't expect there to be,' he said. 'Fairly close fix on the time of death. A quarter to two, plus or minus five minutes.'

'The lab people said they were finding fingerprints last night,' said the sergeant.

'Scarcely strange in a grocery store,' said the inspector. 'They report a hundred and seventy-two latent prints in the store and in the basement, not counting those of Ihns or his wife, but none of them are placed so as to show a connection to the murder. Some are apparently from persons with police records, but that's not strange either. Crooks have to buy groceries like the rest of us.'

'Otherwise, nothing. The door to the shop wasn't forced. It was opened with a key or it was already open when the murderer arrived.'

'Mrs Ihns said that was out of the question,' said the sergeant, 'and I believe her. Ihns wouldn't be so careless as to go down to the basement for his nap leaving the cash drawer full of money and the door unlocked.'

'You wouldn't think so,' said the inspector. 'Well, we'll get started on the background material now. Better do Ihns first. I can't give you enough men to do both him and his wife simultaneously right now. Usual thing. Deadly enemies. Anybody who made threats. Romantic involvements.'

'It'll be that if anything,' said the sergeant. 'What was your impression of Mrs Ihns?'

'Wow,' said the inspector solemnly, causing the sergeant to do a double-take.

The investigation into the background of Wolfgang Ihns did not produce any very satisfactory results, but it did have the advantage of being short.

'There's nothing to investigate,' reported the sergeant. 'This bird was the perfect greengrocer. He didn't do anything else. No girlfriends. No wife swapping. No sex clubs. Nothing. While the rest of us were being liberated to wallow in sex orgies, he was up to his ears in lettuce and Brussels sprouts. The only time he could have seen a girlfriend was when she came in to buy her groceries. Running a retail business like that single-handed is no joke.'

'I suppose not,' said the inspector, 'but profitable, I dare say. Mrs Ihns will come into a rather nice inheritance.'

'There, you're barking up the wrong tree,' said the sergeant. 'They were making a good living from the store, but the total estate is going to run under ten thousand marks. Most of the stock is perishable and not worth much and the goodwill died with Ihns. Mrs Ihns is already looking for a job.'

'Stranger and stranger,' said the inspector. 'Well, perhaps she will be able to find a suitable second husband. Pull your people off investigating Ihns and put them to investigating his widow. Who knows? Perhaps she had that improved-model second husband lined up before the first one got so conveniently killed.'

'With her looks, she could have lined up half a dozen,' said the sergeant who was very taken with Marion Ihns, 'including me.'

'Be thankful you weren't included,' said the inspector, 'because I think that's where we're going to find our murderer. It was not someone who wanted Ihns' money. He wanted Ihns' wife.'

But, once again, the inspector turned out to be wrong. Marion Ihns had not had a lover, and had no lover now even after her husband was dead and there was no reason why she should not have one.

'A disappointingly virtuous woman,' said the sergeant. 'We've checked very carefully and I'm prepared to swear that she had not had the slightest contact with any male apart from her husband. The only friends she has are women. I hate to say it, but I'm afraid that, despite her looks, she's frigid.'

'Well, she didn't murder Ihns herself,' said the inspector. 'The people in the shop next door saw her come out of the apartment building and go into the store at exactly two o'clock. They know the time because they were just opening up themselves for the afternoon.

'Ihns was killed at a quarter to two, plus or minus five minutes so that would mean that Mrs Ihns would have had to get into the store without being seen by anybody, go down to the basement, murder her husband, dispose of the murder weapons, get back to her apartment and then come out again and go to the store all in twenty minutes. It's simply not possible.'

'Hardly possible for anyone at all,' said the sergeant. 'According to Mrs Ihns, her husband finished his lunch at around one o'clock. He didn't lock the store until one-thirty. He stayed upstairs another fifteen minutes or so and then went down for his nap. Taking the shortest estimate of the time of death, he'd barely have had time to fall asleep before he was murdered.'

'Which could mean that the murderer was already waiting down there for him,' said the inspector. 'The place is big enough. There would be plenty of spots to hide in.'

'And that, in turn, would mean that he got into the basement some time before seven o'clock when Ihns opened for business,' said the sergeant. 'From then until lunch time, Ihns was in the store and he would have seen anybody going to the basement. Unless, of course, he managed to get in during the half-hour or forty-five minutes Ihns was upstairs having lunch.'

'Probably early in the morning or even the night before,' said the inspector. 'I'm thinking of the banana skin.'

The banana peel was something which the technicians from the police laboratory had recovered from the basement, but no one knew whether it represented a clue or not. It had been found lying on the floor of an alcove near the back of the basement and a laboratory analysis had shown that it had been stripped from its banana within six hours prior to Ihns' death.

The question was, who had peeled and, presumably, eaten the banana?

It had not been Wolfgang Ihns. An examination of the stomach contents at the time of the autopsy showed no trace of a banana having been eaten within the preceding twelve hours and, in any case, Ihns had not been a man to throw banana peel on the floor of his own basement. In fact, he had been almost fanatically tidy and, with the exception of the banana peel, the floor of the entire basement had been swept clean.

It had not been possible to determine whether the banana came from Ihns' stock or not. It was the same type of banana as he sold, but these same bananas were also sold all over Hamburg. It could have been one of Ihns' bananas, but it did not have to be.

The most obvious explanation for this mysterious banana peel was that it represented a light lunch made by the killer while waiting for his victim to arrive and take his nap, but some of the detection specialists were inclined to question this. They did not think that a man waiting to commit a murder would be relaxed enough to develop an appetite.

'Unless he was a professional,' said the inspector. 'Then, it would just be all in the day's work. And the more I learn in this case, the more I'm convinced that it was a professional. The murder was too efficient, too cold-blooded. Somebody wanted Ihns out of the way and he or she hired a professional to kill him.'

'There doesn't seem to be any other possibility,' agreed the sergeant, 'but the trouble is, nobody wanted him out of the way. He had no enemies. Nobody benefited from his death financially or otherwise. There's not the slightest evidence that he ever had any sexual relationship with any woman other than his wife and there's no evidence that she ever had a flirtation with any other man. I think it was an insane ape.'

'Insane ape?' said the inspector, staring at him in astonishment.

'The banana skin,' said the sergeant. 'It was driven insane over the price of bananas.'

The inspector sighed. 'How are things with Mrs Ihns now?' he said. 'Have you been keeping track of her?'

'According to your instructions,' said the sergeant. 'Well, she's living in Schenefeld with a Danish girl named Judy Andersen. Old friend of hers although she's ten years younger. She moved out of the apartment immediately after the murder and she's been looking for work. Hasn't found anything so far. The only thing she has any experience in is working in the grocery store.'

'Seeing any men?' said the inspector hopefully.

'She apparently doesn't even know any,' said the sergeant. 'We've had a watch on her twenty-four hours a day and she doesn't even leave the apartment except to buy groceries and apply for jobs.'

'And this Judy Andersen?' said the inspector. 'Does she have any male visitors? Is she working or is she at home all the time?'

'No male visitors,' said the sergeant. 'There hasn't been a man enter the apartment since Mrs Ihns moved in and we put a watch on it. Andersen is a crane-operator. Makes good money. Better than police detectives.'

'Probably works harder for it,' said the inspector. 'Big girl, I take it?'

'Around five feet,' said the sergeant. 'Slender, blonde, cute. Probably has muscles, but you don't see them. Maybe she murdered Ihns so that Mrs Ihns would move in and do the cooking.'

'Slightly better than your insane ape theory,' said the inspector. 'Have you tapped Miss Andersen's phone?'

'No,' said the sergeant. 'Should I? You don't really consider her to be a suspect, do you?'

'I consider her to be a possible go-between,' said the inspector. 'Statistically, Mrs Ihns stands the highest chance of being responsible for the murder of her husband. Everything that we've learned so far tends to indicate that she was the only person who knew him well enough to want to murder him. If it wasn't Mrs Ihns then we have to suppose that it was a total madman who had no motive at all, but carefully planned and carried out the murder of a person he scarcely knew. It's not impossible, but, if it's true, we'd never solve the case.'

The sergeant was inclined to think that they would never solve the case anyway. A very considerable amount of time had now passed since the murder of Wolfgang Ihns and nothing more had been learned than had been known on the day following. He thought it wiser, however, not to point this out and went quietly away to carry out his instructions concerning the telephone tap.

To his amazement, it produced results within a few days of being installed, but no one would ever have known about them had the technicians who installed it not thought to connect the tap to a tape recorder which made an automatic recording of all calls placed and received.

The reason that the call would have been without value to the investigation had it not been taped was that it was in Danish, a language which the officer monitoring the tap did not speak. It

227

was only when the tape was run off at police headquarters in the presence of a Danish interpreter that the importance of the call was realized.

It was a long-distance call from Copenhagen in Denmark from what sounded like a boy or a young man with a high voice who identified himself simply as Denny and who, from his manner of speaking, knew Judy Andersen, who took the call, very well.

The conversation had not been long and had definitely not been social. Denny asked when he was going to get the rest of the money. Judy replied that he would have to be patient, the will had not yet been probated. The minute it was, he would be paid. Denny said he hoped so, but rather doubtfully as if he were not at all confident and hung up.

'Well, this could be completely innocent or it could be our big breakthrough,' said the inspector. 'The first thing to do is to find out if Miss Andersen is expecting an inheritance.'

The sergeant investigated exhaustively. She was not.

'Very good,' said the inspector, rubbing his hands. 'The next thing we do is place an official request with the Copenhagen police to trace a long-distance call to Miss Judy Andersen in the Hamburg suburb of Schenefeld on the date and at the time in question. Following that, we shall all join in prayer.'

'For what?' said the sergeant. 'That he's licensed as a hit-man in Denmark?'

'That would be asking too much,' said the inspector. 'Particularly as the Danes do not license professional killers to my knowledge. What we shall pray for is that he made the call from his own phone and not somewhere it is impossible to trace.'

Whether these prayers were actually offered by the Hamburg Homicide Squad, they were, at least, answered, for twenty-four-year-old Denny Svend Pedersen had, indeed, made the call from his own telephone and, it being long distance to another country, the telephone office had a record of the call. It took the Copenhagen police less than two hours to identify him.

'Well, here's the run-down on our suspect,' said the sergeant, coming into the inspector's office with a sheaf of telex sheets in his hand. 'He may be the murderer, but he sure isn't Mrs Ihns' boyfriend. The guy's a prostitute.'

'You mean he has female clients?' said the inspector, stretching out his arm for the telex sheets. 'I believe the correct term is "gigolo".'

'The Copenhagen police say, "prostitute",' said the sergeant. 'And he doesn't have female clients. He has male ones.'

'I see,' said the inspector. 'Well, his voice did sound rather high in the tape recording. Any police record?'

'Only for prostitution,' said the sergeant. 'And some petty theft. Apparently his first excursion into the big-time.'

'Very neat job for a first attempt,' said the inspector. 'He may not be our boy after all.'

'Boy?' said the sergeant.

Boy or not, Denny Svend Pedersen was the murderer of Wolfgang Ihns, a man whom he did not know and whom he had never seen before the afternoon when he smashed in his temple with the butt of a hatchet and drove a kitchen knife through his heart.

It really was, it seemed, Denny's first venture into the big-time and he did not hold up well under interrogation. A youth so handsome as to merit the description of pretty, he was neither tough nor a strong character, and he quickly broke down and confessed to the crime.

He had been approached, he said, by Judy Andersen who had asked him if he wanted to make a little money.

He had replied that he did and Judy had said that there was a very evil man in Hamburg that had to be put out of the way. He could come down from Denmark and do it without anybody suspecting him because this man did not know anybody in Denmark.

This had struck Pedersen as reasonable and he had agreed. Judy had not mentioned any names and had merely given him an address in Hamburg. He was to go there at exactly six-thirty in the morning of March 13 and ring the bell. A pretty, dark-haired woman would come out and tell him what to do. Once he had finished the job, he was to leave immediately for Denmark.

Things had gone off smoothly. He had come down to Hamburg on the night train and had gone to the address given him. There he had been met by the pretty, dark-haired woman whom he would later identify as Marion Ihns.

She had not told him her name and he had not known her relationship to the victim or his name either until he read of the murder in the newspapers.

Marion Ihns had led him down into the cellar of the building next door and had given him a bucket containing a knife and a hatchet. She had shown him the cot where her husband would take his nap and had said that he would come down at between one and one-thirty in the afternoon. He was to remain hidden in the basement until then and, as soon as he was certain that Ihns was asleep, he was to kill him by knocking him unconscious with the hatchet and driving the knife through his heart. There was to be no mistake. He had to make certain that the man was dead.

Denny was able to repeat these instructions almost verbatim, as he had been very impressed by them. They had seemed to him totally out of character with the woman's appearance.

Denny had pointed out that he had had no breakfast, that it was now six-thirty in the morning and that he would not be able to get anything to eat until after two. He had said that he was already hungry.

Marion Ihns had given him a banana and two apples from the store, automatically picking out bruised and over-ripe ones. She was, after all, a greengrocer's wife.

Denny had eaten the apples core and all, but, finding the banana peel unpalatable, had thrown it on the floor.

After what had struck him as a very long wait, Ihns had come down, had stretched out on the couch and begun to snore almost immediately.

Denny had emerged from his hiding place and had carried out his instructions.

Marion had said to put the knife and the hatchet back into the bucket when he was finished and bring it up to the store on his way out. The door would be locked, but the keys would be in his victim's right-hand jacket pocket. He was to leave them hanging on the inside of the door.

Denny had done exactly as he had been told and had gone back to Copenhagen to wait for the balance of the payment. Judy had already paid him a part upon their reaching agreement. In what was almost certainly one of the most remarkable lapses of memory in the history of crime, he was unable to remember what the amount agreed upon had been.

As a matter of fact, Denny's entire attitude towards the murder was one of careless nonchalance. He had not, he said, felt badly about killing Ihns. After all, he had not known him and, in any case, Judy had assured him that he was a very bad man. He knew what bad men were. He had run into enough himself and that was the reason he had wanted to make a little extra money. There was no future in prostitution. When you got a little older nobody wanted you. He had been hoping to get together enough money to open a little café or maybe a bar.

This remarkable confession contained everything that the inspector needed to complete his case except for one thing. Why had Judy Andersen and Marion Ihns hired Pedersen to murder Marion's husband?

Although he was fairly certain of the answer, he took the trouble to ask his colleagues in Copenhagen to ask Denny if he could suggest any motive.

In this, as in everything else, Denny proved cooperative. He assumed, he said, that Judy and Marion had wanted to get rid of Wolfgang so that they could get married.

Denny Svend Pedersen's frankness and cooperative attitude towards the police gained him great sympathy with his judges and, in the following year on May 10, 1974, perhaps taking into account his youth and innocence, they sentenced him to the modest term of sixteen years' imprisonment, a not overly cruel punishment for the cold-blooded murder of a man he had never met for an amount which he could not remember.

This effectively terminated the investigation into the murder of Wolfgang Ihns. Denny Svend Pedersen had murdered him, had confessed to the crime, would be convicted before a court, sentenced and begin serving his sentence in prison.

In Hamburg, however, the inspector's problems were not over. Pedersen might have swung the hatchet and held the knife, but it was Judy Andersen and Marion Ihns who were responsible for his doing so. They were the real murderesses.

The question was, what was the inspector going to do about it?

It was not that he would have any difficulty in laying hands on the culprits. They were, as a matter of fact, in the detention cells four floors below his feet and they had been there ever since the news of Denny Pedersen's confession to the murder of Wolfgang Ihns had appeared in the Hamburg newspapers.

Things at that time had not worked out quite the way that the inspector had hoped they would, although he had gone to a great deal of trouble to carry out a spectacular arrest.

The building in which Judy Andersen's apartment was located was, of course, already under surveillance and the telephone was still tapped. On the morning when the news appeared in the newspapers, the sergeant and a squad had been waiting in the room in a neighbouring building where the telephone tap had been set up.

The inspector thought that when the woman learned that Pedersen had confessed, they would attempt to flee and, as neither of them owned a car, they would probably call a taxi to take them to the railway station or the airport, depending upon how far and how fast they planned to go.

In this respect, he was quite right. Less than half an hour after the paper with the headline story on the confession had been delivered, the tap picked up an outgoing call from the apartment. Judy Andersen was ordering a taxi.

She did not say where she wanted to go, but this made no difference as the inspector had a different destination in mind in any case.

The taxi was intercepted and a detective took over the wheel, drove to the apartment house and honked the horn.

After a moment, Judy Anderson and Marion Ihns came out. Judy was carrying two suitcases. Marion had one suitcase and was carrying her little daughter on her other arm. They seemed in a hurry.

Climbing into the cab, Judy told the driver to take them to the main railway station and, indeed, the cab set off in that direction, but on the way, it abruptly made two quick turns and swung into the compound of the central police headquarters.

The cab was followed in by the unmarked police car which had been behind it all the way from Schenefeld. The sergeant stepped out, opened the cab door and informed the passengers they were being placed under arrest in connection with the murder of Wolfgang Ihns and that anything they said would be taken down and might be used against them. He then asked if they wished to make a statement.

Judy Andersen said that her only statement was that she wanted to see a lawyer and, after a moment's hesitation, Marion Ihns said the same thing. She also said that, if she was going to be held for any length of time, she would like to telephone a relative to come and take away her daughter.

The request for the attorneys and the relative to care for the little girl were, of course, immediately granted, but it was by now obvious to the inspector that his plan was not going to work out the way he had anticipated. He had hoped that the shock of the sudden, unexpected arrest would throw the girls into a panic and result in an admission of some sort which could then be used as a lever to pry open the entire case.

'Weaker sex!' snorted the inspector. 'You could string those two up by their thumbs and they'd laugh at you!'

This was, of course, an exaggeration, but the police had resorted to practically everything else without extracting the slightest admission of guilt from the suspects.

Judy Andersen said that she knew Denny Pedersen casually. He frequented some of the same bars as she did in Copenhagen. She denied that she had ever hired him to murder anybody and asked where a crane-operator was supposed to get the money to engage hired killers.

This was an embarrassing question for the police. Denny had never been able to recall the amount agreed upon for the murder of Wolfgang Ihns, nor the amount that had been paid in advance. There was no way, therefore, of knowing whether it had been thousands of marks or hundreds. A court would, however, be little inclined to believe that even an amateur killer such as Denny Pedersen could be hired cheaply.

The situation was no more favourable with Marion Ihns. She stated that she had never heard the name of Denny Svend Pedersen, which was, perhaps, true, nor had she known that such a person existed until she had read that he was her husband's murderer in the newspaper.

Asked why she and Judy Andersen had left so hurriedly after the news of the confession appeared, she said that it was to avoid the reporters who would, she had no doubt, be swarming over them like maggots on a dead horse.

Questioned in her turn, Judy said the same thing, although she did not use the same expression for reporters.

'And the devil of it is, it's logical,' said the inspector. 'If we hadn't intercepted them, the reporters would have been crawling into bed with them for interviews before the story ever hit the street. In their position, that's what practically anyone would do. Clear out.'

'Unless, of course, you wanted to make a fortune selling your story to the press,' said the sergeant. 'The ladies do not strike me as so shy or so unwilling to turn a mark either.'

'How it strikes you, doesn't matter,' said the inspector. 'You're right, of course, but what does matter is what a defence attorney will make out of it. Under the law, the accused have to be given the benefit of the doubt. What would you do if you were one of the jurors?'

'Acquit them,' said the sergeant. 'We haven't proved the case beyond a shadow of a doubt. Pedersen will be tried in Denmark and he's in jail in Denmark. It's his unsupported word against theirs that they hired him, and he can't even say for how much. Besides, the motive is impossible to prove. The minute that the prosecution opens its mouth to say lesbian relationship, the defence is going to obtain a sustained objection on the grounds that the relationship is not proven.'

It certainly was not. Both Judy Andersen and Marion Ihns swore emphatically and consistently that the only relationship between them was that of two women friends who had known each other for a long time. Judy had often visited Marion when her husband was still alive and it was only to be expected that she would invite her to come and live in her apartment after her husband had been murdered and she was in financially reduced circumstances.

The result of all this was a sort of stalemate. The inspector had enough evidence to hold the suspects for extended questioning and, probably, even enough to obtain a formal indictment, but this latter he did not want to do. Judy and Marion would then be bound over for trial, they would be required to make no further statements to the police and, under the present situation, he estimated their chances of an acquittal at around eighty per cent.

'We've got to break this united front they're putting up,' said the inspector. 'They're both in the same boat, of course, and they've made up a simple story in advance. Deny everything and stick to it like iron. The cops won't be able to prove a thing.'

'And they won't either,' said the sergeant. 'You'll never break those two down. You just don't understand what true love is.'

'Oh yes I do,' said the inspector, 'and that's just what I'm going to break them down with.'

Although not personally a lesbian, the inspector knew something about the sisterhood as the result of having been in police work for a long time, and one of the things he knew was that lesbians were frequently more jealous of their companions than were heterosexuals. The fact that a legal recognition of the relationship was in most countries not possible left the lesbian with greater feelings of insecurity.

Seeking to take advantage of this weakness, the inspector put into operation a plan which in a former age would have been called, and which actually was called by present-day women's liberation organizations, dastardly.

The inspector, however, maintained that it was fair. 'The women say they are nothing but good friends,' he said. 'If that is true, then my scheme will have no effect other than to help prove their innocence. If, on the other hand . . .'

Actually, the plan was rather simple. Judy Andersen and Marion Ihns were being held in different sections of the detention cells and, theoretically, they had no means of communicating with each other. However, as the inspector was aware, there are few prisons in the world where the security is so tight that no communication between the prisoners takes place.

The detention cells of the Hamburg police were certainly not top security and the inspector planned to make them even less secure.

The policewomen assigned as guards in the parts of the detention cells occupied by Judy Andersen and Marion Ihns were replaced by others younger, prettier and, on orders from the inspector, more sympathetic to their own sex. It was not long before a supposedly illicit correspondence between the suspects began.

The inspector was careful to see that neither woman had any reason to suspect that the notes were being read by the police. When a guard received a note, it was taken into a room, photographed and, minutes later, it was in the hands of the woman to whom it was addressed.

Despite this caution, results were meagre. There was a great deal at stake and Judy and Marion remained cautious. The notes contained nothing other than the warm expressions of sympathy between two good woman friends and complaints over the injustice of the accusations against them. Although some words and expressions were used continually and it seemed probable that these were code words which had a special meaning for the women, there was no way of knowing what that meaning was and certainly none of proving it. Had these first notes been offered in evidence before a court, they would have contributed greatly towards an acquittal.

'Very well,' said the inspector. 'Let us increase the pressure a little.'

He began by clapping one of his own colleagues into the detention cells. An elderly and far from handsome policewoman within a year of retirement, she joined Marion Ihns in her cell. Although a normally good-natured woman, she followed the inspector's instructions and made herself as unpleasant as possible.

At the same time, Judy Andersen received a far more attractive cell-mate in the form of thirty-three-year-old Inge Schultz, a sultry, black-haired lesbian, who was not a policewoman but who was very anxious to cooperate with the police as she was due to be tried on a number of minor charges and she thought, quite rightly, that her cooperation would have an effect on the length of her sentence.

'Now,' said the inspector, 'whenever Mrs Ihns is brought up for questioning, see that she passes by the cell occupied by Miss Andersen and Miss Schultz. I may be wrong, but I suspect this will make her correspondence more interesting.'

He was right. Marion held out for a week and then, on July 10, she wrote a short, desperate note which was, of curse, duly photographed by the scheming inspector.

It read: 'I have done everything for you. Please, please, do not see Inge any more. I have sacrificed everything for your sake. Don't think of my parakeet. Think of my love. Write to me. I will kill myself if you desert me. I cannot stand it any more . . .'

'Good,' said the inspector. 'I can hardly stand it any more myself. Just good friends, eh? We'll see now whether it is true love or simply nasty sex.'

'What does she mean by her parakeet?' asked the sergeant. 'She doesn't own a parakeet.'

He was a little out of sorts. Marion Ihns appealed to him very strongly, just as she appealed to a great many other men and women, and, although he had agreed that she was probably guilty of the murder, he had secretly been hoping that she would turn out to be an innocent tool in the hands of the blonde, Danish crane-operator.

'It's undoubtedly a code word,' said the inspector, 'and I would judge that it refers to some part of Mrs Ihns' anatomy. Which part, I shall leave to your imagination. Now, get busy and arrange for some rumours of the scandalous conduct of Miss Andersen and Miss Schultz to be spread around in the detention cells.'

'Hardly any need,' said the sergeant glumly. 'They really are scandalous. Schultz apparently wants to cut her sentence to a minimum.'

The rumours were spread and definitely came to the ears of Marion Ihns, but she did not believe them. Judy had written her an answer to her desperate note in which she swore that her relations with her cell-mate were not only platonic, but almost coldly formal. She was much more careful of her wording than Marion had been.

Reassured and convinced now that the notes were getting through without interception by the police, Marion responded with an even more frank letter.

'My only, beloved treasure,' she wrote. 'I love you so. We must be wise and strong. I only hope that we can see each other again soon. The first few weeks I thought I would go mad. Now I realize how much I love you. When we get out of here, we will start again from the beginning. I kiss your picture. It was so hard for me to get.'

'Not as hard as you think,' said the inspector, who had arranged it. 'Well, the literary quality is poor, but it conveys a certain sense of sincerity which I find quite moving. I am inclined

236

to think that it is true love after all.'

'Not by the Dane,' said the sergeant sourly. 'She and Schultz are practically celebrating a honeymoon in the detention cells.'

'Leave the jealousy to the girls, Peter,' said the inspector. 'You and I, enthusiastic participants in the New Morality, know that such things are old-fashioned and not in the least chic.'

He was in an almost unbearably good humour. His scheme was working perfectly and he already had enough to make a conviction of both suspects highly probable. All that he was waiting for now was a direct reference to the murder and a week later, he got it.

'Are they asking you a lot of questions?' wrote Marion Ihns. 'Be careful you don't say too much. I am sick. I've got myself infected. I can't understand it. I've already had three injections. Tell me, I haven't made you sick too, have I? Or did he do it with you too? Be honest and tell the police. Then they won't be surprised that you wanted to do away with him. When will I be able to hold you in my arms again? I love you and my thoughts are constantly with you. Burn this letter after you read it. Don't forget, our love can never die. It will only get stronger and stronger. Do you have a picture of me? Kisses, kisses, kisses. Yours eternally, Marion.''

'Pitiful,' said the inspector. 'Mrs Ihns apparently does sincerely love Miss Andersen. She is obviously very unhappy and I am afraid we are going to have to make her more unhappy still. See to it that she learns beyond a shadow of a doubt exactly what the faithless Miss Andersen and her cell-mate are doing.'

'I find the letter confusing,' said the sergeant. 'She apparently thinks she got the infection from her husband, but the autopsy found no venereal infection on the body. Where could she have got it?'

Mrs Marion Ihns who, by now, had been in police custody for over four months, had been found to be suffering from gonorrhoea and was being given treatment. Judy Andersen was not infected.

'Hard to say,' said the inspector, 'but it does indicate two things. One, she was having relations with her husband up until shortly before she had him murdered, and, two, she had some kind of sexual contact with somebody other than Ihns or Miss Andersen.'

The operation was now practically complete. Marion Ihns had made an unmistakable reference to Judy Andersen's responsibility for the murder of Wolfgang Ihns and the inspector did not think it would take much more to extract a full confession from her, although she might deny her own part in the matter.

As a matter of fact, she did not. Learning that all of her fears concerning her friend's unfaithfulness with Inge Schultz were, if anything, short of the reality, she demanded to see the inspector and dictated a bitterly savage confession in which she did everything in her power to assure the conviction of the untrue lover even at her own expense.

Generally speaking, there was nothing in the confession concerning the murder which the inspector did not already know, but there was one supplementary piece of information which proved slightly startling.

Judy Andersen, said Marion Ihns, was her husband. They had been married in Denmark approximately eight months before the murder of Wolfgang Ihns.

It was true. Denmark, like some of the other Scandinavian countries, was an almost hysterical adherent to the new principles of sexual liberation and posed no objections, legal or otherwise, to marriages between members of the same sex.

Mrs Ihns' confession now being on tape, Miss Andersen was brought up from the detention cells and allowed to listen to it. Having done so, she confirmed that it was essentially true, but stated that the entire idea and responsibility for the murder were her wife's. She, Judy, had acted only as a go-between in procuring the services of Denny Svend Pedersen. She did not exactly describe herself as a hen-pecked husband, but she gave the investigators clearly to understand that she had been very much under the influence of Mrs Andersen and/or Ihns.

True love had not triumphed and, like so many lovers who murder a spouse standing in the way of their happiness, Judy Andersen and Marion Ihns came to trial in an atmosphere of hate, resentment and knowledge of betrayal by the loved one. Their judges were unable to find any extenuating circumstances in their actions and, on October 2, 1974, equitably sentenced both of them to life imprisonment.

18

RAPE!

Being located in the southern hemisphere, the little town of Hopefield, South Africa, is normally little troubled by cold weather in late autumn, but, on the night of October 12, 1979, the solitary figure hurrying along the lonely lane on the outskirts of the village was shivering.

Temperature had nothing to do with this, however. The quaking flesh and goose-pimples were caused by fear, the fear of what might be lurking in the deep pools of darkness beneath the trees bordering the path.

It was in precisely such isolated spots that the Welluh rapist, over the past two years, had struck so many times before and could be expected to carry out the same vile acts again.

Still, all had gone well up to now and the cottage which spelled home and safety was not far off. Already, the lights from the living room could be seen shining cheerily through the trees. Inside, the family would be gathered tensely around the window, striving to pierce the darkness with their eyes. They knew only too well the dangers that skulked there in the shadows, but there was no alternative to this late home-coming. With such a large family and only one member working, the overtime at the printing plant was essential to the budget.

In the dark lane outside, terror was gradually beginning to subside and be replaced by relief. There were only another three hundred yards to cover, one more turn and then straight to the front door. On the black velvet of the night sky, the diamond necklaces of the stars, displayed but not for sale, shone reassuringly. Safe at last!

The hard, round muzzle of the revolver pressed suddenly against the spine just above waist level was like an injection of iced water into the veins.

With an involuntary gasp, the victim halted in mid-stride, knees buckling with the realization that that which had been dreaded so long had now, finally, arrived. The light from the cottage window, so near, but now so desperately far away, swirled and merged with the exploding constellations of the sky as the horror-struck mind teetered on the verge of a swoon. The rapturous feeling of relief and security was replaced by resignation.

There was no hope. In all the long and shameful series of rapes which had terrorized the town, no victim had ever escaped from the lust-maddened clutches of the Welluh Rapist until the ultimate horror had run its course.

In the darkness, the voice of the rapist was low, calm, assured, but filled with hideous undertones of barely restrained, mad desire.

'Hands behind your back,' it ordered. 'One false move and I pull the trigger.'

The victim complied apathetically. The only possible course now was to get it over with as quickly as possible and do nothing that might incite the rapist to yet worse acts. If there was no resistance, it would not be painful, or so they said. No one had been, as yet, physically injured. As for the emotional damage . . .

Handcuffs snapped briskly over the victim's wrists extended behind the back and a strip of cloth was bound quickly over the eyes. In the darkness, the blindfold was hardly necessary, but it was a part of the pattern, a practised routine which had, so far, functioned perfectly every time.

Helpless and vulnerable, the victim stood waiting, head bowed in shame and breast heaving with mingled humiliation and indignation. Would the violation take place right there in the middle of the path and practically in sight of the cottage?

It seemed not, for the rapist now urged the victim with little nudges of the revolver across the strip of grass next to the path and into the trees. There was to be no chance of a passer-by disrupting the proceedings.

Beyond the trees, the victim was pushed to the ground and the chaste, pleated skirt was raised, leisurely and sensually, to be tucked neatly in around the waist. The breasts remained covered. The Welluh Rapist never showed interest in anything above the waist.

The skirt was followed by the modest, white, nylon panties which were drawn voluptuously down over the rounded hips, slipped over the feet and removed entirely. Exposed from half stockings to waist, the nude body gleamed palely in the darkness beneath the trees, its whiteness broken only by the black triangle of the pubic hair.

The cringing victim smothered a little gasp as the tongue of the belt buckle clicked across the holes of the belt, followed immediately by the tiny, shrill scream of the zipper of the fly. Underclothing whispered across bare skin and there was the sound of heavy breathing.

For an instant, there was the hushed, expectant tension which invades the atmosphere before a thunderstorm and then the feeling of hands, greedy, groping, caressing, oh-so-terribly-skilled hands, seeking out relentlessly the most sensitive and secret places, playing on the erogenous zones like some great master of the organ drawing the utmost from his ravished instrument.

For this it was, above all, which made the Welluh Rapist so feared and so different from all other rapists. Of all the nearly thirty victims known, not one had been able to avoid arousal to the point of orgasm while the rape was yet in progress!

Nor would this be an exception on this night of October 12, 1979. As penetration took slowly and gently place and the rhythmic movements of the rapist gradually increased their tempo, the victim gave vent through clenched teeth to a deep, gasping moan, but it was not a cry of pain or even of protest.

It was the sound of ecstasy.

After it was over, the criminal, lust now sated for the moment, was matter-of-fact. The handcuffs were removed, but not the blindfold. The usual warning was issued, now almost recited because of the many times that it had been repeated. Not a move until five hundred had been counted. Then, remove blindfold. Then, dress. Report to the police if so desired, in which case, extend greetings from the Welluh Rapist.

Like most of the other victims, Lee Engelbrecht followed instructions. The worst had already taken place. There was no point in risking a revolver bullet to gain another few minutes before calling the police. The rapist would not be captured anyway.

Lee counted to five hundred. Removed the blindfold. Dressed. Went wearily home.

For those victims who were married or engaged, this was nearly the worst part. The disbelieving friend or spouse. The false sympathy. The snide remarks. 'Well, was it as good as they say? Did you enjoy it? Oh, don't lie to me. Look at your face. Of course, you enjoyed it. All the others did, didn't they?' And so on, far, far into the night. The sole comfort, if comfort it was, was the fact that the victim now no longer needed to fear going out after dark. The Welluh Rapist never attacked the same victim twice.

'The Welluh Rapist struck again last night,' said the sergeant, coming into the inspector's office in the small Hopefield Department of Criminal Investigations the following morning.

'A stupid name for a rapist,' said the inspector irritably. He was a heavy man of medium height, roughly pyramidal in shape and with a gradual transition from shoulders to head in place of a neck. 'Simply because the victims sometimes begin their statements to the police with, "Well . . . uh . . ." The whole business is stupid from beginning to end.'

'The victims always begin their statements that way,' said the sergeant. 'I've kept track.'

As a matter of fact, he had not. A blond, shock-headed, young man with the mildly startled expression and slightly protruding front teeth of a buck rabbit, he did not always take his work quite as seriously as the inspector sometimes wished he would.

The inspector sighed. Life for him had not been easy since the advent of the Welluh Rapist. Before that, it had been pleasant. Hopefield had never had a great deal of crime to investigate in the past.

'Well, at least the offence was reported,' said the inspector. 'The victim was married, I presume?'

The sergeant nodded, giggling. 'Think there'd have been a report filed otherwise?' he said.

'Don't be facetious,' said the inspector sternly. 'What about the report? Was there anything useful in it?'

'No more than the others,' said the sergeant. 'The name is Lee Engelbrecht. Twenty-nine years old. Worked late on overtime last night. Got nailed three hundred yards from home. No description. No clues. Just the piece of cloth used for the blindfold.'

'We now have nineteen of those,' said the inspector. 'Lab says they're torn from an old sheet. They estimate that there'll have to be sixty-one more victims before the sheet is used up.'

'That's if it's a single sheet,' said the sergeant. 'It'll be twice as many if it's double. Anyway, the estimate is useless because nobody knows how many actual rapes there have been. They certainly don't all get reported.'

'It will be a marvel if ten per cent are,' said the inspector. 'They're just like any other rape cases. The victims are embarrassed. They don't like talking about it to some sceptical police officer and even less in front of a court. A lot of them must feel that there's been no harm done so why get involved?'

'We could have them make their statements to a policewoman,' said the sergeant, sniggering offensively. 'I'll bet they'd pour their little hearts out then!'

The inspector closed his eyes. 'Why it should be impossible to attract a better grade of officer into criminal investigations today, I will never know,' he said. 'Be serious. Don't you realize that this lunatic is running around out there with a heavy-calibre revolver in what must be a state of great excitement. One of these days, something is going to go wrong. A victim will try to resist . . .'

'Haw! Haw! Haw!' roared the sergeant. 'Resist? Not bloody likely!'

'All right,' said the inspector, choking back what in a lesser man might have been a guffaw. 'Maybe they won't, but that doesn't make it any less a crime or any less dangerous, even if some of them do bring it on themselves.'

'Hanging around in lonely places!' gasped the sergeant, nearly strangling with laughter. 'Flaunting their soft, white bodies . . . Oh God! I can't stand it!'

'You won't have to stand it much longer,' said the inspector. 'At least, not in a professional capacity. Neither of us will. You know what kind of a press we're getting. How long do you think the commissioner's going to put up with this before he puts somebody else in this office and you and me out in the factory district?'

Obviously, there was no answer to this question and the sergeant did not attempt one. He did, however, stop laughing.

The inspector was right. For the criminal police of Hopefield, the Welluh Rapist was no laughing matter.

In a community the size of the Hopefield, the number of potential suspects was sharply limited and yet it was almost certain that the Welluh Rapist was a local person. No one else would have been able to move so easily and inconspicuously around the town. No one else would have had such an intimate knowledge of every obscure path and alley.

Nonetheless, despite more than twenty known attacks over the past two years, the police had yet to take into custody a single suspect.

Some people in the town, but especially the women, were beginning to say that the Welluh Rapist was not being caught because the police did not want to catch someone who was paying them off and not necessarily with money. It was even whispered that the rapist was a member of the police force. Who else would know how to use handcuffs and a heavy revolver?

Although no one knew it outside the police, the thought had occurred to the inspector long before it had to anyone else and he had investigated his own colleagues discreetly, but so thoroughly that there had been complaints to the heads of other departments.

The investigation had convinced the inspector that whoever the rapist was, no one on active duty with the police was involved. The number of possible suspects was extremely limited and it had been possible to establish the whereabouts of every one of them for the time when the very first known offence had taken place.

Looking back on this first case made the inspector shudder for he had failed to believe the authenticity of the complaint and had actually come within an ace of throwing the victim into the detention cells.

It had been the morning of June 11, 1977, when Leslie van Sidow had been sent up to his office because the duty officer in the charge room below had not wanted to accept the First Information Report on the case without the approval of higher authority. The inspector had said to go ahead and fill out the report and then send the complainant up and he would listen to the story.

Blond, attractive and just turned twenty-two years of age, Leslie had had what struck the inspector as a remarkably improbable story to tell and an insultingly ridiculous request to make.

The story was not long or complicated. Like many others, Leslie was in the habit of stopping by a family-type tavern for a drink or two after work. Food being available, the drinks sometimes progressed on into dinner and this had been the case on the preceding evening.

Shortly after ten o'clock, Leslie had left the tavern alone and had headed for home, taking the usual short-cut through Stooropjt Alley, a narrow, little frequented and none too well lit street.

Approximately half-way through, Leslie had felt the cold muzzle of the revolver make sudden and unexpected contact with the spine and an authoritative voice had offered a choice of, 'Hands behind your back or I'll blow your kidneys out through your stomach!'

There had been little choice about complying with this suggestion and what would later become familiar routine took place for the first time. Leslie was handcuffed, blindfolded and urged at gunpoint into a car.

There followed a short drive to the edge of town where the rapist displayed such an intimate knowledge of the more sensitive parts of the human anatomy that Leslie climaxed once before the rape took place and once more during the course of it.

Following the rape, the handcuffs had been removed but not the blindfold, and the trembling, emotionally drained victim had been pushed out of the car which drove rapidly off, all lights extinguished. From the sound of the motor, Leslie, who knew something about such matters, thought that it was a four-cylinder, an older model and not very well maintained.

Apart from this information concerning the car, there was only a physical description of the rapist, who was slightly built, under five feet four inches tall and had long hair. From the voice and certain other indications, Leslie took the age to have been under twenty-five.

'And?' said the inspector, drawing down the lower lid of his right eye with his right index finger in a universal gesture of outraged scepticism. 'What do you expect the police to do?'

'Identify the culprit,' said Leslie. 'I want to know who it was.'

'You intend to prefer charges?' said the inspector.

'Are you kidding?' said Leslie. 'I want to do it again. I'm even prepared to consider marriage.'

It was at this point that the inspector had lost all control of himself and had begun shouting about, '. . . making idiots of the police . . . filing facetious charges . . . lewd utterances . . . moppery . . .' and pounding on the button on his desk to summon the sergeant and have Leslie tossed into the detention cells for a few months or, better, years.

The sergeant had appeared, but no one was thrown into the detention cells, partly because he was laughing too hard and partly because, as Leslie calmly pointed out, the charge was not only legitimate, but official. Rape at gunpoint was a crime and, whatever the victim's motives in attempting to identify the rapist, the police were duty-bound to investigate and, if possible, take into custody the offender. Whether charges were then filed would be up to the discretion of the victim.

The inspector had, therefore, ordered an investigation. Considering the circumstances, it seemed more than probable that the rapist had known very well the identity of the victim and it was not improbable that the victim too had a very good idea of the identity of the assailant, but merely wanted to use the police to force a more permanent relationship.

Unfortunately, it quickly turned out that this was not true. The rapist might have known the identity of the victim, but the reverse was certainly not the case. What the inspector had thought would be an open-and-shut case turned out to be insoluble.

And what everyone in the police and all Hopefield had

regarded as an isolated incident turned out to be the first offence in the longest series of unsolved crimes which the Hopefield police had ever known.

Within days of the rape of Leslie van Sidow, a second rape under practically identical circumstances had taken place, to be immediately followed by another and another and another . . .

'With a sex drive like that, nobody in Hopefield is safe,' said the inspector despairingly. 'Even the police . . .'

'We're all behind you, sir,' said the sergeant in a choked voice. 'Whatever sacrifice . . .'

'Very droll, sergeant,' said the inspector, 'but it may actually come to that. This is a small community. The number of potential victims is limited. What happens when the material runs out? No victim has ever been attacked twice.'

'There are bigger cities,' said the sergeant. 'Cape Town is not far away. Why not all Africa?' His voice took on a dreaming quality. 'And, after Africa, the Middle East . . . Europe . . . Australia . . . Hopefield may go down in history as . . .'

'. . . the place where an inspector of detectives was acquitted on a charge of dismembering an assistant for making some of the most stupid comments ever heard in connection with a serious criminal case,' interrupted the inspector. 'Now, get out there and do something! Put every man we have on the case. Maybe we could put out some suitably dressed officers as decoys. I'd be willing myself . . .'

'You're twenty years older than the oldest known victim,' said the sergeant unkindly. 'The Welluh Rapist likes them young and slender. Now, I am . . .'

'. . . going to end up with flat feet,' concluded the inspector. 'Those are long, hard beats out there in the factory district and you have a lot further to go to pension than I have.'

As usual, this reference to his future prospects in the police effectively terminated the sergeant's buffoonery and replaced it with a downcast attitude of deepest gloom.

'There's got to be a slip sooner or later,' he said uneasily, as if he did not really believe it himself. 'Nobody's perfect. It can't go on for ever.'

But it could go on for two and a half years and that was like forever to the harrassed and embarrassed police who were now the laughing stock of Hopefield and most of South Africa.

However, the sergeant was basically right and nothing is eternal. Even the longest series of sex crimes must come, sooner or later, to an end and the end for the Welluh Rapist came on

June 12, 1980, which was a fine, autumn day in the southern hemisphere and, therefore, a good day to be looking out of windows.

Thirty-one-year-old John Brentwood did look out of a window and what should he see but his neighbour, twenty-three-year-old Carey Arndt, handcuffed, blindfolded and in the process of being stripped for action by the dreaded Welluh Rapist.

The scene of the crime was a good six hundred yards distant and it was doubtful if he could arrive in time to prevent the worst, but the courageous Brentwood shouted to his wife to call the police and set off at a dead run.

It was only the famed slow approach of the Welluh Rapist which saved the final victim from becoming a victim. Although a fraction of a second and an inch away, penetration had not yet taken place when Brentwood came storming up and the rapist was forced to flee, leaving for the first time not only the blindfold but the handcuffs on the victim.

Despite this handicap, Carey Arndt succeeded in knocking the rescuer to the ground and had kicked him nearly unconscious when the police arrived and intervened.

The Welluh Rapist had made the first, fatal slip, but that did not mean that the case was solved. The near-victim had been blindfolded and Brentwood had not been close enough to catch a glimpse of the criminal's face. He was, in any case, not inclined to talk about his heroic deed and was sent home to have his minor cuts and bruises treated by his wife.

Carey Arndt was taken to police headquarters where the handcuffs were removed and immediately rushed to the inspector's office while the terrible news flashed like wildfire through the building.

What had so long been secretly feared was proved true. The handcuffs were police handcuffs. The Welluh Rapist was one of Hopefield's own officers!

In the meantime, unknown to the shocked members of the force, a drama was being played out in the inspector's office.

Ignoring the sulky near-victim, he had fixed his eyes upon the handcuffs and he roared out in a great voice, 'Fred! Fred Boulton!'

'Inspector Boulton has been dead for better than seven years now,' said the sergeant gently. He assumed that his superior's mind had finally snapped under the strain. 'He could not possibly . . . and, in any case . . .'

'I know Fred is dead,' said the inspector impatiently. 'I was one of his pall bearers. I'm talking about the cuffs. They're his. He customized them himself. Didn't like the regulation issue. The gun must be his old service revolver.'

The sergeant turned pale. 'But, my God!' he protested. 'That would make the Welluh Rapist Inspector Boulton's widow! She would have been given his gun and handcuffs.'

'Not his widow, you fool!' bawled the inspector. 'She's a respectable woman in her late fifties. His daughter, you idiot! His daughter!'

And, of course, it was the daughter, pretty, twenty-three-year-old Deborah Boulton, and, being a girl with a healthy regard for the forces of the law, she promptly confessed upon being taken into custody by a bemused sergeant and brought to the office of her father's old friend and colleague.

Miss Boulton, who was the librarian at the local library, said that she was sorry for what she had done, but that it was the fault of the son of the man who owned the garage next door.

The young man had, it seemed, persuaded her to enter into a sexual relationship at a relatively tender age and she had taken such a liking to the activity that her demands had quickly outstripped the young man's physical capacities.

Not a man to leave a lady in the lurch, he had called upon his friends for help, but, although he had many friends, they proved barely equal to the job.

Strangers had been enlisted in the cause and, eventually, Deborah had become so famous that news of her exploits came back to her mother's ears.

Mrs Boulton, a dignified woman of strict moral and religious principles, had come within a hair of joining her husband through sheer shock, and Deborah, a filial if slightly over-sexed daughter, had sworn by all that was holy never to do it again.

She had kept her word too, but, with her sex drive, the effort had been almost unendurable. The logical solution of marriage to some one with an equally strong interest in the matter was excluded for, in order to marry someone, she would have to have at least one date with him prior to the wedding and she did not think that she could last through the date without practically assaulting her proposed bridegroom. Worse yet, if he showed no interest in marriage or if the ceremony was to be delayed, she feared that she would fall straight back into her old habits and thus bring her beloved mother to an early grave.

The solution, if such it was, had come to her one day while she was going through some of her late father's effects. She had come upon his service revolver and handcuffs, both of which she knew how to use, and had begun to day-dream about being a police-woman and taking into custody some handsome, extremely healthy young man.

The dream had quickly evaporated. She was a librarian, not a policewoman. But then the idea had lingered and she had begun to think, 'Why not?'

This was, after all, the era of equal rights for women, wasn't it? Women had the same needs as men, didn't they? And wasn't the world full of men going around raping women by the thousands, millions even maybe?

The Welluh Rapist was born.

Unlike many sex criminals, Deborah Boulton had kept careful account of the number of her victims and she confessed to exactly thirty rapes of men carried out at gunpoint, although the revolver had actually been empty.

She was formally indicted on all thirty counts and ordered bound over for trial, but released without bail as an attempt at flight was considered unlikely.

The trial took place on May 27, 1981, and was extremely well attended. It did not last long. Although three of the victims were called upon to testify, they all began with, 'Well . . . uh . . .' and then gave up.

Deborah Boulton was convicted on the basis of her own confession in thirty instances of rape with use of a deadly weapon and sentenced to thirty terms of imprisonment of one year, all sentences to run concurrently and suspended. She left the court to the cheers of a group from one of the women's liberation organizations and the applause and hilarity of the rest of the spectators.

While awaiting trial, she received enormous numbers of proposals of marriage from all over the world and was, when last heard of, sifting through the mass of candidates.

BESTSELLING TRUE CRIME FROM ARROW

☐	The Shankill Butchers	Martin Dillon	£4.99
☐	Carnal Crimes	John Dunning	£3.99
☐	Cryptic Crimes	John Dunning	£3.99
☐	Deadly Deviates	John Dunning	£3.99
☐	Madly Murderous	John Dunning	£3.99
☐	Mindless Murders	John Dunning	£3.99
☐	Murderous Women	John Dunning	£3.99
☐	Mystical Murders	John Dunning	£3.99
☐	Strange Deaths	John Dunning	£3.99
☐	Truly Murderous	John Dunning	£3.99
☐	Murders Of The Black Museum	Gordon Honeycombe	£4.99
☐	Born Fighter	Reg Kray	£4.99
☐	Forensic Clues To Murder	Brian Marriner	£4.99
☐	Serial Killers	Joel Norris	£4.99

ARROW BOOKS, BOOKSERVICE BY POST, PO BOX 29, DOUGLAS, ISLE OF MAN, BRITISH ISLES

NAME————————————————————————

ADDRESS—————————————————————

——————————————————————————

——————————————————————————

Please enclose a cheque or postal order made out to Arrow Books Ltd. for the amount due and allow the following for postage and packing.

U.K. CUSTOMERS: Please allow 30p per book to a maximum of £3.00

B.F.P.O. & EIRE: Please allow 30p per book to a maximum of £3.00

OVERSEAS CUSTOMERS: Please allow 35p per book.

Whilst every effort is made to keep prices low it is sometimes necessary to increase cover prices at short notice. Arrow Books reserve the right to show new retail prices on covers which may differ from those previously advertised in the text or elsewhere.

BIOGRAPHY AND AUTOBIOGRAPHY

☐ Confessions of an Irish Rebel	Brendan Behan	£4.99
☐ Against the Tide (Diaries 1973–1976)	Tony Benn	£8.99
☐ Conflicts of Interest (Diaries 1977–1980)	Tony Benn	£9.99
☐ Office Without Power (Diaries 1968–1972)	Tony Benn	£8.99
☐ Out of the Wilderness (Diaries 1963–1967)	Tony Benn	£8.99
☐ Michael Collins	Tim Pat Coogan	£6.99
☐ Daughter of the Dales	Hannah Hauxwell	£4.50
☐ Seasons of My Life	Hannah Hauxwell	£4.50
☐ Lifewish	Jill Ireland	£4.50
☐ Lifeline	Jill Ireland	£4.50
☐ Ridding the Devils	Frank Palmos	£4.99
☐ The Marilyn Scandal	Sandra Shevey	£4.99
☐ Woodbrook	David Thomson	£6.99

ARROW BOOKS, BOOKSERVICE BY POST, PO BOX 29, DOUGLAS, ISLE OF MAN, BRITISH ISLES

NAME————————————————————————

ADDRESS—————————————————————————

————————————————————————————

————————————————————————————

Please enclose a cheque or postal order made out to Arrow Books Ltd. for the amount due and allow the following for postage and packing.

U.K. CUSTOMERS: Please allow 30p per book to a maximum of £3.00

B.F.P.O. & EIRE: Please allow 30p per book to a maximum of £3.00

OVERSEAS CUSTOMERS: Please allow 35p per book.

Whilst every effort is made to keep prices low it is sometimes necessary to increase cover prices at short notice. Arrow Books reserve the right to show new retail prices on covers which may differ from those previously advertised in the text or elsewhere.